# Outsourcing and Service Work
## in the New Economy

# Outsourcing and Service Work in the New Economy: The Case of Call Centres in Mexico City

By

## José-Luis Álvarez-Galván

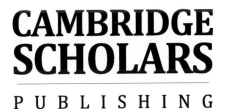

Outsourcing and Service Work in the New Economy:
The Case of Call Centres in Mexico City,
by José-Luis Álvarez-Galván

This book first published 2012

Cambridge Scholars Publishing

12 Back Chapman Street, Newcastle upon Tyne, NE6 2XX, UK

British Library Cataloguing in Publication Data
A catalogue record for this book is available from the British Library

ISBN (10): 1-4438-3738-5, ISBN (13): 978-1-4438-3738-5

*To Olivia*

*To my parents*

# TABLE OF CONTENTS

# LIST OF FIGURES AND TABLES

# ACKNOWLEDGEMENTS

This book is based on my doctoral dissertation. Its defence, in the Department of Sociology at the London School of Economics and Political Science (LSE), took place in September 2010. Both the research and the book were possible thanks to the financial support provided by the National Council for Science and Technology (CONACYT) of Mexico. I received complementary funding through several LSE Research Studentship Awards and the Morris Finer Memorial Studentship Award.

I want to thank the LSE for hosting my doctoral studies. Pat McGovern deserves special thanks not just as the lead supervisor of this research, but for giving me the opportunity to teach his seminars of Sociology of Work, a fruitful and stimulating experience. Judy Wacjman, as my second supervisor, provided me with valuable comments on substantial parts of this research.

Other members of the Department of Sociology at the LSE who kindly agreed to comment on parts of this document at different stages were Don Slater, Claire Alexander and Dick Hobbs. Also, Richard Hyman and Ian Greer gave me useful comments at different moments. Special thanks to Ginny Doellgast who read the whole manuscript and provided me with detailed comments and support in critical moments. More generally, I want to thank all the people that gave me the opportunity of discussing my ideas with them at different forums: the Society for the Advancement of Socio-Economics, the Work, Employment and Society conference, the American Sociological Association meeting and the International Sociological Association conference. Last but not least, I am grateful to Stephen Deery and Tim Strangleman, the examiners of my doctoral dissertation, for their time in reading the manuscript and their valuable comments. I would also like to thank Goodenough College and its staff for a wonderful place to live in at the heart of London during my doctoral studies.

My mother María Luisa (†), my father José Luis and my sister Frida have been an endless source of love and encouragement for me. Katinka, Rafi and Ivar have become a second family for me, turning Madrid into a second home full of Spanish-Swedish care. I was lucky to share with Olivia the process of giving birth to our PhD theses and, very importantly, to receive her support and advice. I am only her husband, but she is for me my most admired colleague in the study of the Social Sciences.

Although I revised this manuscript during non-working hours while working in Paris, France, as a consultant for the Organisation for Economic Co-operation and Development (OECD) there is no relation between the topics discussed here and my work in the organisation. Also, the points of view expressed here do not necessarily reflect those of the organisation.

Finally, I would like to thank all the participants in this research, the workers and managers that I interviewed. To all of them I want to express my gratitude for answering my questions and for sharing their experiences with me. It goes without saying that, any mistakes are my sole responsibility.

# INTRODUCTION

## Justification: outsourcing, flexibility and service work

This book analyses the outsourcing of front-line service work in the new economy. Its aim is to examine how workers' experiences and employment conditions are affected by the interactions between subcontractors and client firms.

In recent years, outsourcing has gained popularity as a mechanism to deal more effectively with the uncertainty of increasingly challenging business environments. According to mainstream business scholars and social scientists, intense competition, variations in demand and technical change have forced organisations to substitute hierarchical arrangements by market mediated transactions (Piore and Sabel 1984; Harrison and Kelley 1993; Harrison 1994; Porter 1998; DiMaggio 2001). In the case of labour, outsourcing is often 'praised' for achieving significant cost reductions thanks to a more efficient allocation of resources and specialisation (Watanabe 1971; Lacity and Hirschheim 1993). Nonetheless, the practice of outsourcing also raises important concerns. Outsourcing might blur organisational boundaries, fragmenting employers' authority and affecting coordination between organisations (Marchington et al. 2005; Walsh and Deery 2006). In other words, outsourcing embodies challenges and difficulties that, in practice, increase transaction costs and potentially affect workers' experiences and employment conditions.

In order to analyse these challenges, I have chosen the outsourcing of front-line service work in Mexican call centres as a case of study; a decision inspired by some of the most relevant theoretical and empirical aspects identified by the literature on outsourcing and service work in contemporary societies.

For the first time in the history of capitalism, service industries have overtaken agriculture as the largest source of employment in the global economy. According to the International Labour Organisation (ILO), in 2006 the proportion of people employed in service industries reached 40% while the proportion of those employed in agricultural industries decreased from 39.7 to 38.7%. Finally, the proportion of people employed in manufacturing industries was only 21.3% (ILO 2007:2). Therefore, service workers play a prominent role in the economic structure of many developed and developing societies today.

Within this context, the call centre industry is considered a 'flagship' activity of the new economy, growing rapidly and facing intense international and local competition (Frenkel 1999; Taylor and Bain 1999; Deery and Kinnie 2002; Korczynski 2002; Deery and Kinnie 2004; Moss et al. 2008). Also, call centre services represent a paradigmatic case of labour-intensive processes that are closely monitored and controlled by information technologies (Taylor and Bain 1999; Taylor et al. 2002; Baldry et al. 2007). The labour force in call centres is rich in social diversity and skills; there is a large proportion of female employees and call centres' recruitment strategies tend to target college-educated workers (Taylor and Bain 2005). Last but not least, call centres operate as a kind of 'node' in the service economy where many other industries converge to subcontract customer services (Batt and Moynihan 2002; Korczynski 2002; Glucksmann 2004; Batt et al. 2007; Kinnie et al. 2008).

The Mexican case is relevant as it provides a weak institutional setting where labour protection is low and business competition is largely unregulated in practice. Until now, most of the exploration of the experience of work and employment conditions in the new economy has been focused on the case of rich developed countries, creating the impression –not intentionally, I guess– that other regions of the world do not necessarily provide a relevant context for these analyses. However, Mexico is a good example of an emergent economy with attractive local conditions for the expansion of labour-intensive industries of the so-called new economy.

This investigation is based on extensive information collected through 65 in-depth interviews with call centre workers and managers concerning their work experiences in four outsourcing companies in Mexico City from the end of 2006 to the first months of 2007. Also, 18 additional interviews were undertaken with union representatives, officials of the Mexican Ministry of Labour, academics, consultants, industry representatives and other relevant informants.

The findings presented in this book identify those elements that can be more affected by, or associated with, the interactions between subcontractors and client firms: job designs; customer segmentation; the use of contracts for services; the supervision approach; union avoidance; the use of internal labour markets to secure management loyalty; and the reinforcement of social divisions in the workplace. Of course, these practices and elements are not exclusively designed or created to deal with the problems and tensions generated by the relationship between client firms and subcontractors, but they play a fundamental role in solving the conflicts between organisations in the administration of the workforce. Importantly, these findings suggest that a number of practices that were common in the old economy are still relevant in the organisation of work in the twenty-first century.

## The structure of this book

This book is divided into two major sections. The first part, consisting of the first two chapters, sets the theoretical framework, and the methodological and empirical context of this research. The second part, the four empirical chapters, embodies the analytical core of this investigation. The book closes with a concluding chapter that revisits the initial questions, evaluates the general findings and reflects about future investigation.

The first chapter presents and discusses the three major themes informing this investigation: outsourcing, employment relations and service work. As mentioned, the aim of this research is to analyse subcontracted front-line service work in the new economy, investigating how subcontractors respond to the challenges of coordination and negotiation with the client firm and how these processes affect workers' experiences and employment conditions. Flexible inter-firm arrangements, such as outsourcing, are generally understood as strategies to face a more competitive and changing environment. Therefore, this research starts with an exploration of outsourcing, its definition and purpose. The basic idea behind outsourcing is that it allows a more efficient and rapid allocation of resources (Watanabe 1971; Lacity and Hirschheim 1993). This argument is popular in the business and economics literature where labour is simply understood as any other commodity (Samuelson and Nordhaus 2001). In this respect, the transaction costs logic predicts that hierarchical arrangements must be replaced by market transactions if the latter is less costly for the organisation (Williamson 1979; 1981).

However, this economics-based approach to outsourcing has been criticised on several fronts. For sociologists, the complex nature of work imposes important challenges for market transactions; in other words, labour should not be considered as any other commodity and its allocation and control inside organisations or markets must take into account more complex mechanisms (Granovetter 1992; Grint 1998; Fernandez et al. 2000; Castilla 2005; Granovetter 2005).

The complex nature of work as a social activity takes us to the second aspect explored in the literature review undertaken in chapter one:

employment relations. In order to understand the difficulties faced by outsourcing arrangements it is essential to consider the complexities of employment relations in a historical perspective. It is important to have in mind that outsourcing, and the flexible firm model in general, presupposes the flexibility of employment relations and, very importantly, a reconsideration of workers' motives, from solidarity to individualism, from life-time contracts to high mobility (Atkinson 1984; Handy 1989; Pink 2001; Donnelly 2009; Reed 2009).

The first chapter closes with considerations about how the nature and characteristics of service work might affect the relationship between outsourcing and employment relations. Specifically, this research suggests that the customer-oriented interface adds substantial complexity to the problems of coordination and negotiation between subcontractors and client firms in call centres; something that has been certainly identified by other authors but not analysed as a central research question (Batt 2000; Batt and Moynihan 2002; Moss et al. 2008).

After setting the conceptual and theoretical ground, the second chapter presents the research design, methodology and context of this investigation. Bearing in mind that this research is based on an institutional setting that might not be familiar to most readers, I wanted to offer certain detail in its description and analysis. In general terms, the Mexican case is relevant not just because there has been little attention to this national experience but also because the Mexican case offers the possibility of looking at how inter-firm relationships and employment relations interact in an environment of strong liberalisation policies and weak institutional support for workers (Bensusán and Rendón 2000; Dussel Peters 2000; Stiglitz 2003; de Buen Lozano 2005; Ruiz Duran 2005a; De la Garza and Salas Páez 2006).

After dealing with the characteristics of the Mexican context, the second chapter explores the advantages of undertaking a case study to address the research questions of this investigation. After this, the chapter presents the organisations selected and explains why they were considered important for the research questions presented here. For each organisation, the 'account' was considered the unit of analysis. 'Account' is the name given to the outsourcing contract between call centres and their commercial clients. In all the accounts and organisations chosen for this research, I conducted in-depth interviews with workers and managers, and gathered information about the experience of work and employment conditions in subcontracted workplaces through non-participant observation. I also interviewed a group of people outside these companies in order to get a general perspective of the context in which these workers' experiences and employment relations take place. These participants included union representatives, academics, consultants, industry representatives and government officials.

Chapter three opens the second and core analytical part of this book. This chapter presents and discusses the main challenges in administering a subcontracted workforce. The first challenge is the problem of distrust and opportunistic behaviour from participants (Williamson 1979; 1981; Lorenz 1988; Simon 1991; Stiglitz 1991; López 1998; Lorenz 1999). This is evident during the setting up of the different accounts and the recruitment and selection processes undertaken by subcontractors. Often the organisations involved in outsourcing have divergent interests (Simon 1991; Sako and Helper 1998; Korczynski 2002). On the one hand, the primary interest of the client firm is not just to reduce costs but also to provide a maximum level of service quality to satisfy customers; the incentive is towards more quality for less money. On the other hand, subcontractors are more concerned about increasing the revenue from their accounts without necessarily increasing the investment needed to monitor and supervise workers in order to secure high levels of service quality. In other words, they want to be paid more for less.

These tensions and divergences are also translated to the selection and training procedures where workers appear to be confused by contrasting types of demands from different *employers* but in the same job (Korczynski 2002). As mentioned, call centres seem to be more concerned with the number of calls processed, while clients are concerned with their quality. These tensions become even more complicated when the dimension of the customer–worker is added into the equation. At this point workers' identity and commitment is subjected to pressures from at least four fronts: subcontractors, client firms, customers (Cooke et al. 2005) and other workers. In addition, downsized workers might play an essential role in strengthening the communication and coordination between client firms and subcontractors. In this chapter, the findings of this research suggest that downsized workers might embody a valuable source of expertise and tacit knowledge for subcontractors, training and supervising new workers and even providing advice to supervisors and coordinators about specific services and procedures. Nonetheless, downsized workers seem to suffer high levels of anxiety and frustration, in addition to experiencing tensions with other workers in the subcontracted workplace.

At the middle of this apparently chaotic situation it makes sense to ask to what extent outsourcing arrangements could be truly efficient, when the transaction costs seem to be, in fact, so high, and cooperation among organisations seems to be scarce. From the point of view of organisations, flexible and precarious employment relations might be of critical importance since they could be of considerable help in counterbalancing the negative effects of inefficiencies in the operation and administration of the workforce.

The fourth chapter deals with the technical division of labour or job design as a strategy to organise the workforce in a multi-employer environment and in turns facilitate cooperation and negotiation between subcontractors and client firms. As mentioned, the main tension in service-oriented outsourcing is the confrontation between standardisation initiatives of call centres (in order to reduce costs) and the demand for the customisation of the service from client firms (to retain customers) (Korczynski 2002; Moss et al. 2008). Also, as a response to these tensions, service-oriented organisations with multiple clients tend to develop strong divisions based on the revenue reported by each client (Batt 2000; Batt and Moynihan 2002).

In this respect, it is expected that there will be a direct relationship between the level of customisation in services and the revenue generated by clients: services for low income markets tend to be standardised while services for high income markets are more likely to be tailored to the individual needs of clients (Batt 2000; Batt and Moynihan 2002). However, not all the differentiation of work experiences and employment relations is expressed in vertical divisions related to revenue generation.

The evidence collected in this research reveals that there are substantial differences within the same job designs, that is, differences at the horizontal level. To explain this unexpected finding, I rely on the role of supervisors and client firm representatives as elements of mediation between the labour force and the organisations involved. Findings of this research indicate that supervisors and client firm representatives actively negotiate shifts, absence permissions, medical leaves, holidays, extra-payment and account's rotation directly with workers, something that seems to be in line with findings reported about British subcontracted service workers (Deery et al. 2010). In other words, the interplay between subcontractors, client firms and workers is again of critical importance in explaining employment conditions and work experiences in outsourcing.

Therefore, different employment conditions within the same job design or job category are potential sources of tensions and problems between subcontractors and client firms because employees do not believe that there is a difference in the skills required for them that justifies the varying conditions. Hence, it seems that there are considerable incentives to carry out horizontal mobility in large service organisations with multiple clients when these differences emerge. However, information collected in this research shows that there is relatively low mobility of workers between different accounts. How is it possible to explain this counter-intuitive phenomenon?

Chapter five addresses this question highlighting the importance of social divisions inside the workplace as a mechanism for controlling and disciplining workers. In this regard, it is important to remark that workers cannot be seen as a homogeneous group, with a solid collective identity and interests. In call centres, as in many other service-oriented organisations, recruitment practices are largely based on employees' referrals (Fernandez et al. 2000; Castilla 2005). Therefore workers themselves end up as key decision makers about who joins the organisation or not at entry level positions (Maguire 1986; 1988). In doing so, external social divisions are reproduced inside the workplace and, very importantly, this seems to reduce the transaction costs of recruitment. Overall, there are two relevant consequences of this practice: one external and the other internal.

On the one hand, it is argued that much of the success of front-line service work depends on the creation of a 'customer enchantment' (Korczynski 2002), the creation of pre-configured interactions between customers and employees. This is achieved not just through the use of scripts or job designs but also through the reproduction of external social stereotypes that can be perceived in the tone of voice, volume or pronunciation type. For example, it is expected that female workers are more likely to be chosen for sales work and men for technical support services, just because this gender selection corresponds to Mexican stereotypes of service work. On the other hand, it seems that there is an internal and powerful consequence of the use of social networks for recruitment. As mentioned, it might be difficult to control the labour force when employment conditions diverged between accounts that, in practice, require similar skills. Nonetheless, social divisions (in the form of family, friendship or community links) appear to control and discipline workers as well as to operate as a glass wall to limit employees' attempts to move. The effect of these social barriers is reinforced by human resources practices such as internal competitions where teams are based on individual accounts.

Interestingly, despite the strict control exerted by organisations and peer pressure derived from social divisions, it seems that workers still have an important degree of autonomy in front-line service work (Leidner 1993). Findings of this research indicate that workers use this autonomy in order to cope with the pressures and stress of their work. To illustrate this point, chapter five also presents some cases where employees use their autonomy and discretion in order to cope with the demands of customers, supervisors, client firms and other workers.

To conclude with the mechanisms for coping and resisting the stress of front-line service work, chapter five analyses the experience of unions in the call centre industry in Mexico. It seems that job designs and the use of social networks in recruitment have been effective means for fragmenting workers' collective actions and responses to managerial practices. The only union in the industry is located within an organisation that does not have a large diversity of commercial clients but only provides services to organisations of the same corporate holding.

The first three empirical chapters (from three to five) focus on how the strategies of subcontractors, in dealing with the problems of negotiation and cooperation with client firms, have effects on the experience of work and employment conditions of non-managerial workers. The sixth and final empirical chapter of this book is about the experience of managers and their role in the operation of the subcontracted firm and its expansion. In most of the literature about the experience of work in the new economy, managerial careers are also the target of the labour flexibility logic (Handy 1989). Moreover, managers themselves are supposed to enjoy the opportunities of being more mobile and having less firm-specific skills to satisfy their more individualistic and goal-oriented professional motivations (Reich 1991; Reed 2009). In this regard, managers are observed as agents who circulate 'freely' across the diffusing boundaries of organisations.

However, the findings of this research suggest that managers tend to be attached to organisations and remain the target of several retention mechanisms such as internal labour markets, training opportunities, attractive pensions, private medical care and paid holidays. There is no question that managers' experiences contrast with non-managerial employees in call centres. In this sense, it is possible to see how the boundaries of the firms are re-established in managerial circles whose loyalty and commitment in the long run seem to be crucial for the expansion of the organisation. In the four companies studied here, almost all the managers interviewed have climbed the whole organisational ladder. Very importantly, most of them share a common background from other organisations, revealing the importance of social capital for progression in managerial careers. However, it is possible to perceive that there is a difference between the experiences of managers depending on their gender. Apart from the area of human resources, men are still the dominating group in managerial circles and, notably, female managers seem to progress in their careers using more meritocratic mechanisms than their male counterparts.

Finally, the concluding section of this book revisits the initial research questions, provides a general evaluation of the findings and reflects on the topics for further research.

# CHAPTER ONE

# OUTSOURCING AND SERVICE WORK
# IN THE NEW ECONOMY

## 1.1.  Outsourcing and the blurring boundaries
of the modern firm

### 1.1.1. The flexible firm

It is argued that intense competition, technological change and
variations in demand have forced organisations to substitute hierarchical
arrangements for market mediated transactions in order to respond faster
and more efficiently to the challenges imposed by this environment
(Atkinson 1984; Piore and Sabel 1984; Harrison and Kelley 1993; Harrison
1994; DiMaggio 2001). Perhaps, the most elaborated link between new
and more flexible organisational forms on the one hand and employment
relations on the other, corresponds to the flexible firm model formulated
by Atkinson (1984). In his model, Atkinson suggests that the segmentation
of the labour force inside the firm would allow organisations to deal more
effectively with intense competition and quick changes in demand.
Crucially, in Atkinson's model this labour market segmentation also
corresponds to two different types of labour flexibility: numerical and
functional (Atkinson 1984; Pollert 1988; 1991; Kalleberg 2001).

On the one hand, 'functional flexibility' is the enhancing of employees'
ability to perform a variety of jobs and participate in decision-making; in
doing so workers can collaborate with faster and more efficient responses
to volatile conditions in the market. This functional flexibility tends to be
applied to workers in primary labour markets. On the other hand,
'numerical flexibility' refers to the strategies used to reduce costs by
limiting workers' involvement in the organisation. Benefits for workers
(expressed by the employment relationship) are reduced to a minimum,
removing those components that are likely to gain loyalty and
commitment from them, such as career ladders, life-time employment

contracts, or benefits. In other words, this numerical flexibility applies to workers in secondary labour markets.

It is clear that Atkinson's flexible firm model was designed not just to provide the organisation with more flexibility but also to protect workers with firm-specific skills working in the core activities of the company (Cappelli 2000; Cappelli and Neumark 2004). The protection mechanism would consist in providing workers on the periphery (or secondary labour markets) with non-standard forms of employment in order to facilitate the adjustment in the size of the workforce (Atkinson 1984; Handy 1989; Cappelli and Neumark 2004). This approach certainly suggests a dual labour market structure where workers whose skills are more firm-specific tend to be allocated to primary labour markets and receive better employment conditions. On the other hand, workers holding less firm-specific skills are more likely to be allocated to secondary labour markets. Therefore, according to this logic, those activities considered peripheral are more likely to be subcontracted and workers in these activities to be subjected to non-standard employment conditions.

### 1.1.2. Outsourcing

Outsourcing is understood here as an arrangement where a client firm establishes a relationship with a subcontractor for the purchase of a final product, component, part or service under the specifications of the client firm (Holmes 1986; Lacity and Hirschheim 1993; Child 2005; Marchington et al. 2005).

The logic of outsourcing is inspired by centuries of economic thought such as Adam Smith's famous example (1776) about the technical advantages of the division of labour in the pin factory: production is more efficient when the whole process is divided into tiny pieces of specialised processes. In this respect, it seems that contracting out could be a useful mechanism in the division of labour. The economics-based literature (Watanabe 1971; Holmes 1986; Lorenz 1988; Harrison and Kelley 1993) frequently argues that labour might be subcontracted for three basic reasons:

- Capacity: when additional workforce is needed to complement existing capacity.
- Specialisation: when the client firm requires the use of specialised labour that is not available 'in-house'.
- Cost-cutting: when the client firm subcontracts a segment of the production that might be produced more cheaply by a third party.

It seems that organisations use outsourcing when they have not got enough capital or labour for their production needs (to speak about only two basic production factors). An example of this can be seen in the tourist industry, which experiences fluctuating demand throughout the year. During the high-demand seasons, such as summer and Christmas, hotels and other tourist-related businesses tend to rely largely on temporary and part-time workers. Demand for the rest of the year can normally be covered by using a permanent workforce. On the other hand, an organisation might opt to outsource for reasons of specialisation. Let's stay with examples in the tourist industry. Like any other businesses, hotels require adequate accounting controls and financial supervision. Large hotels with complex financial operations normally subcontract or outsource their accounting affairs to external firms; accounting is not hotels' 'core' business but it is critical for them to have good accountants if they are to be successful businesses.

Finally, organisations may use outsourcing for purely cost-reduction reasons. In this case, the organisation probably has the internal resources to face cyclical changes in demand or the knowledge to deal with an apparently peripheral activity, but it outsources the activity because there is a 'third-party' which is able to do the same activity more cheaply. A final example could be the catering services in hotels. Restaurants are perhaps not the actual core of hotels' business, but there is no doubt that catering services have a big impact on customers' satisfaction. Some hotels, although they know how to manage their catering services and have catering facilities and staff 'in-house', simply decide to subcontract the service to a cheaper external supplier.

There is also a fourth justification for the use of outsourcing that is not commonly identified in most of the literature: imitation. During the interviews, specialists from the Mexican Institute of Tele-services (IMT, *Instituto Mexicano de Teleservicios*) told me that many small and medium sized companies frequently want to adopt outsourcing solutions in call centres. When IMT consultants explain to these clients that a business diagnostic must be carried out in order to evaluate whether call centre outsourcing is really needed, the common reply is: "There is no question about it. We already know that we need one. Big companies do it and we must follow their example if we want to remain competitive". (Interview with an IMT consultant). Interestingly, one CEO in the call centres interviewed said that there is nothing new about the existence of outsourcing, that it is used in the business world from time to time and is not exclusive to present times: "It has been here for a long time; I used to say to my clients that Christopher Columbus started outsourcing!"

A key assumption of the model of the flexible firm is that flexible organisations need a network of flexible inter-firm relationships to operate (Porter 1998; DiMaggio 2001) because this network of inter-firm arrangements is used to allocate activities considered peripheral. In this regard, almost by definition, it is impossible to have a flexible firm without a set of connections to other organisations to carry out activities that, otherwise, would have to be undertaken inside the organisation. As a consequence, the giant and vertically integrated corporation that dominated the world during the post-war period (Whyte 1956; Chandler 1977; Lazonick 1991) would be replaced by a network of smaller firms using a relatively small, flexible and horizontal workforce nowadays, in which outsourcing might play a key role as a mechanism for building connections between organisations[1] (Piore and Sabel 1984).

In this respect, it is evident that most of the discussions on outsourcing are rooted in historical analyses about the nature of the firm (Coase 1937) and debates about hierarchies versus markets (Williamson 1979; 1981; Simon 1991; DiMaggio 2001). In this regard, the transaction cost concept coined by Coase (1937) and later reformulated by Williamson (1981) are crucial in understanding the rationale of outsourcing for many companies. Williamson pointed to the split of costs in two different categories: production and transactions (Williamson 1979; 1981)[2]. The second category is the costs associated with the coordination, monitoring, controlling and managing of transactions. Thus, when firms have to make decisions about which activities to 'internalise' and which others to 'purchase' in the market, managers must consider transaction costs (Williamson 1979; Lacity and Hirschheim 1993). A transaction cost approach would predict that those activities involving the transaction of specific and strategic assets for the firm tend to be internalised or, if using the market, to be ruled by contracts that guarantee mutual cooperation for the compliance of the specifications agreed. On the contrary, if this type of operation relies

---

[1] The rise of the network concept has triggered intense debates about the extent to which networks are completely new (Castells 1996) or whether they are just another intermediate stage in the continuum between markets and organisations (Stinchcombe 1990; DiMaggio 2001). Also, it is argued that networks do not represent any kind of historical discontinuity or radical chance because both organisations and markets tend to operate alongside combinations of cooperation, bureaucratic rules and price mechanisms (Barley and Kunda 2004; Marchington et al. 2005).

[2] Williamson (in the 1970s and early 1980s) was puzzled by the growth of large bureaucracies, which produced many operations internally (Williamson 1979; Lacity and Hirschheim 1993).

on the market, companies require higher levels of supervision and control over the exchange and this might potentially increase transaction costs (Coase 1937; Williamson 1979; 1981; Lacity and Hirschheim 1993).

When looking at all these considerations about labour segmentation, transaction costs and core-periphery models, it seems that a clear rationale emerges: peripheral activities and their workers are more likely to be subcontracted simply because they do not represent firm-specific assets and contracting them out is cheaper than undertaking their work inside the organisation. In other words, outsourcing is essentially related to transaction costs. However, other social scientists claim that the orthodox business logic of outsourcing oversimplifies the behaviour of participants (Perrow 1986; Granovetter and Swedberg 1992); underestimates power disparities and the asymmetry of information in economic relationships (Perrow 1986); and ignores the existence of intermediate organisational forms like market contracts that could operate like hierarchical arrangements (Stinchcombe 1990) or even the existence of new forms of coordination between organisations such as relational contracting (DiMaggio 2001).

In this regard, a critical approach towards outsourcing and numerical flexibility could be taken, suggesting that it allows for the redistribution of risks and uncertainties in production, distribution and trading activities (de Buen Lozano 2005; De la Garza 2005; Marchington et al. 2005) and this 'redistribution' of tasks and risks is marked by power inequalities. Consequently, in outsourcing, powerful companies tend to 'allocate' to 'weaker' partners those activities that are more vulnerable to unpredictable changes in demand, union militancy and technological obsolescence (Holmes 1986; Lacity and Hirschheim 1993; Child 2005; Marchington et al. 2005). Paradoxically, this power inequality creates a lack of trust and communication that obstructs the achievement of maximum efficiency and ultimately provides customers with products and services of less quality. This situation was noted earlier as one of the main disadvantages of considering only the cost-cutting advantages of numerical labour flexibility in the short run. Therefore, the whole argument that outsourcing is unequivocally efficient can be challenged.

The economic sociology critique of the conventional neoclassical and institutional economics framework on outsourcing seems to be particularly useful when dealing with the outsourcing of labour. According to this analysis, labour outsourcing implies 'distinctions' of control, supervision, trust, reward, stimulus and even physical allocation between permanent employees and subcontracted workers (Baron and Kreps 1999). These distinctions may elicit situations of trust and cooperation but also of distrust and exploitation, depending on power and information inequalities among participants (Lorenz 1988; 1992; 1999). In modern subcontracted firms it is common to see people working for different clients but 'within' the same organisation. Therefore, employment relations in labour outsourcing in a place with multiple clients can potentially result in important frictions and challenges for workers, clients and managers.

Despite these controversies, one cannot overlook the importance and popularity of outsourcing in present times. When thinking about outsourcing, it is almost irresistible to evoke Karl Marx's and Friedrich Engels's famous opening of the Communist Manifesto (1948): "A spectrum is haunting Europe, the spectre of communism", but the spectre of outsourcing goes well beyond Europe and has become a continuous challenge for the labour movement around the world. Wherever one looks, outsourcing has become a type of magical solution for almost every single one of today's challenges in the world of business.

In this research, the most important point in the relationship between outsourcing and labour is that it implies the reformulation of the traditional employment contract (Harrison and Kelley 1993; Marchington et al. 2005), that is, labour outsourcing implies the removal of the 'rigidities' of the employment relationship in order to reduce the costs associated with labour mobility[3] (Watanabe 1971; Harrison 1994). These economic rigidities consist of the set of responsibilities and obligations for employers and employees alike, which increase the costs of labour allocation in the market and within organisations (Samuelson and Nordhaus 2001). According to the flexible firm paradigm, this more flexible allocation of labour inside organisations and across the market would guarantee optimum efficiency and higher productivity levels (Porter 1998).

The dominance of the flexible firm model has been always a matter of dispute (Pollert 1988; 1988; 1991) but the explosive emergence of a business and management rhetoric inspired by flexibility principles is difficult to ignore (Sennett 1998; Stiglitz 2003; McMichael 2004; Sennett 2009). Nowadays, outsourcing is one of the most common forms of inter-firm relationship and work and employment relations play an essential role in this strategy.

---

[3] This does not mean that outsourcing is the only type of inter-firm relationship that is strongly associated with flexible employment formats.

## 1.2.    New employment relationships and employment in inter-organisational settings

### 1.2.1. The emergence of the classic employment relationship

For Hodgson, "a necessary feature of capitalism is the widespread use of the employment relationship, involving employer control over the manner and pattern of work" because "without the sale of labour power to an employer there can be no capitalism" (Hodgson 1998:161). In most western societies, this employment relationship is usually formalised in a written contract that specifies the rights and obligations of the two parties (Kay 1995); in other words, this contract specifies in which terms and conditions workers exchange their labour power for a salary (Marx and Engels 1978). Therefore, it is widely accepted that any study about work under capitalism must consider the employment relationship as an essential point of reference (Hyman 1987; Brown 1988; Hodgson 1998). In the end, the employment relationship is more than a simple contract ruling an economic transaction between two individuals; the employment relationship is also an expression of the power and social position that these agents embrace within the society in which this relationship is embedded (Hyman 1987: Brown 1988). In summary, the employment relationship reflects the impact of the social structure on work as a social and economic activity (Granovetter 2005).

It is argued that what is nowadays known as the traditional employment relationship came to dominate labour markets and organisations for most of the twentieth century (Cappelli 2000). This type of employment relationship includes: a) full-time schedules; b) open-ended contracts; c) career opportunities; d) seniority-based pay systems; e) on-the-job training; and f) benefits such as medical care, paid vacations and retirement pensions. Also, it is argued that this type of employment relationship was designed to encourage workers' loyalty and commitment, that is, to extract more and better labour effort from the employment relationship (Cappelli 1999; Cappelli 2000). To do so, in this type of arrangement the employer 'internalised' the major risks of dealing with external turbulence such as market fluctuations that might harm the revenues of organisations. Not incidentally, this traditional employment relationship prevailed in strategic industries (such as automobile, metalworking and public services).

Which factors explain the emergence of this type of employment relationship? Why did employers want to secure loyalty and commitment from workers? Most of the literature identifies three basic reasons to answer these questions: a) the political power of workers during the economic downturn of the inter-war period; b) transformations in the governance structure of firms (the emergence of the big corporation) (Chandler 1977; Lazonick 1991); and c) the technical change that produced mass production and therefore the need for mass consumption markets (Cappelli 1999; Cappelli 2000).

At macro social and political level, the first half of the twentieth century witnessed how the labour movement reached a peak with the beginning of a communist regime in Russia (1917) provoking consternation in more industrialised societies (such as Britain, France, Germany or the United States). The Russian society, a developing one at that time, was supposedly less exposed to the kind of industrial class conflict introduced by Marx as a precondition for the arrival of communism (Marx and Engels 1948). In addition, the economic downturn provoked by the Great Depression (starting about 1929 in most countries) put additional pressure on workers' lives, encouraging more labour militancy through unions and other social organisations.

Finally, technological and organisational innovations – such as the influence of scientific management designed by Taylor and the moving assembly line of Ford – made the supply of mass products possible. In order to take advantage of this situation, long-lasting and secure relationships with workers (with a relatively stable level of salaries and benefits) were needed to create a massive demand for this mass production.

All these elements together – the external reference of the Soviet regime, the effects of the economic crisis, the escalating labour militancy, and the need for stable markets – brought about the emergence of a more 'benign' social pact with workers, more generally known as the Welfare State. Among other things, the Welfare State brought about a new form of employment-relationship, one that secured life-time employment for workers in exchange for equal life-time loyalty and commitment with the organisation. Moreover, unions were 'invited', at least in certain cases, to play a central role in this collective strategy, as it was in the U.S. with the Wagner Act (1935) during the presidency of Franklin D. Roosevelt. However, not all workers in all countries and industries received the benefits of this pact (Silver 2003; McMichael 2004). In general, workers in industrialised societies and those working in manufacturing and public sector jobs were more likely to be included. In summary, and from a critical point of view, this employment relationship with a paternalistic flavour was designed as the most effective way to secure the loyalty and commitment of workers under the threat of communism and the need to support the expansion of mass production industries through the creation of huge and stable consumption societies (Lazonick 1991).

Whatever the exact reasons for establishing this social pact, there is little question that this type of employment relationship was also associated with what is perceived as a golden age of prosperity in the West (Tonkiss 2006). However, at the end of the twentieth century, there is a received wisdom that the long-run sustainability of the traditional employment relationship is no longer possible, and that fundamental and dramatic transformations in work and employment are taking place as a result of a more competitive and unstable environment (Sennett 1998; 2009).

## 1.2.2. Supposed challenges of the 'new'

Prominent social scientists have played a leading role in the construction and dissemination of narratives of historical discontinuity in modern employment. 'No-long term', the 'individualised society', the 'network society', a 'political economy of insecurity', are all terms pointing to the idea of how risk, mobility and uncertainty prevail in the lives of workers in contemporary societies and the product of thinkers of the highest calibre such as Richard Sennett, Zygmunt Bauman, Manuel Castells and Ulrich Beck. According to these narratives of dramatic change in employment relations, it is unlikely to be employed with a single employer in a long term contract today (Sennett 1998) because organisations cannot protect their workers from the uncertainty of external turbulences any more (Cappelli 1999). In addition, the extinction of communist regimes in Eastern Europe diminished the political force and programmatic credibility of socialist-oriented organisations in the West, including those related to the labour movement. But this narrative of change and historical discontinuity has an optimistic aspect: workers in new industries, those belonging to the so-called 'knowledge economy', are more autonomous and empowered, their careers do not depend on organisational membership any more (Osterman 1996; Pink 2001; Reed 2009) and they can take advantage of this boundary less environment to move freely among organisations (Pink 2001).

In a sense, it is argued that all these factors together have triggered the adoption of non-standard forms of employment such as temporary, part-time or self-employment (Geary 1992; Harrison and Kelley 1993; Harrison 1994; Smith 2001; Barley and Kunda 2004; Marchington et al. 2005). However, despite the coherence of these narratives of historical discontinuity, there is no consensus about such a decline of the traditional employment relationship (Jacoby 1999; McGovern 2007; Strangleman 2007; Doogan 2009; Halford and Strangleman 2009).

Three are the most common and persuasive arguments against the decline of the traditional employment relationship thesis: i) the problem of considering mass production as a universal system in previous decades; ii) the problem of not considering work as a complex social activity; and iii) the lack of significant statistical information to confirm the thesis of dramatic change. With respect to the first point, it is argued that the rhetoric of change is based on a wrong idea, this is, the supposition that mass production systems and traditional employment relationships were something universal and dominant in the world of work during the post-war years (Pollert 1988; Silver 2003). It is even argued that Taylor himself often complained about the lack of accuracy in following his methods by many firms (Pollert 1991). Moreover, even those prominent proponents of radical transformations have argued that it was mostly white-collar workers who were more likely to receive the benefits and protection of internal labour markets (Sennett 1998; Cappelli 1999; 2000; Sennett 2009).

On the other hand, the erosion of work as a social activity is related to the idea of labour as a commodity – that loyalty and commitment are no longer seen as valuable assets in organisations, and that labour is simply mobile and transferable following only economic criteria. However, as a society requires more information and 'knowledge' activities (Smith 2001; Baldry et al. 2007), the importance of security and reliability in managing the information grows more significant, and the commitment and loyalty of the workforce become crucial (Jacoby 1999; Baldry et al. 2007). Even in those cases where workers might possess high skills and autonomy, 'knowledge' workers seem to still be interested in organisational membership as a way to secure stability in their careers (Donnelly 2009). Also, it seems that much of the obsession with undertaking strategies such as numerical flexibility is often inspired by an oversimplified vision of labour, where employment levels are exclusively determined by labour costs, a tendency that has been reinforced by the ruling of financial principles inside organisations (Lazonick 2002). (Table 1-1 presents a summary of the two models of employment relationship extracted from McGovern et al. 2007).

**Table 1-1. Two models of the employment relationship**

| Employer policy | Organisation-oriented | Market-oriented |
|---|---|---|
| Labour market | Low turnover; permanent employees are differentiated from temporary workers and on-site subcontractors. | High labour turnover; hire and fire according to demand; 'numerical flexibility'. |
| Career | Organisational career; Lower-level entry points; Formal job ladders; Firm-specific skills; Promotion from within. | Inter-organisational ('employability'); Multiple entry points; Limited ladders; General skills; External hiring – use of recruitment agencies. |
| Remuneration | Wages fixed by administrative principles; use of appraisals; individual, group and organisational performance. | Wages fixed according to market signals, e.g. the 'going rate'. |
| Fringe benefits | 'Single status'; Harmonisation of benefits. | Fringe benefits for 'core' staff 'Status divide' between blue-and white-collar staff. |

Source: Extracted from McGovern et al. 2007:38.

Another powerful element in this debate, it is the privatisation agenda taking place for many governments around the world in recent decades. In this sense, it is argued that the commercial pressures of the private sector logic are forcing recently privatised companies to reshape employment conditions into a format that allows work intensification (O'Connell Davidson 1993). However, ignoring the importance of the commitment and loyalty of the workforce seems to be a serious limitation to praise the short-term economic advantages offered by flexible employment relationships (McGovern et al. 1998; Jacoby 1999; McGovern 2007; Strangleman 2007; Halford and Strangleman 2009).

## 1.2.3. Employment relationships in the context
## of inter-organisational settings

As mentioned, there is a coherent narrative between the flexible firm model and labour outsourcing in recent times. However, it is not new for organisations to divide their workforce into different segments, with workers at the periphery being used as a buffer to 'protect' workers at the core during difficult business times, as this practice has been identified before the flexible firm model emerged (Piore 1970; Doeringer and Piore 1971). However, what seems to be new about the flexible firm model is that peripheral segments and workforces can be completely externalised and subcontracted to other organisations. To do so, the employment relationship has to be adjusted because this externalisation process seems incompatible with the 'rigidity' of 'traditional' forms of employment that were oriented to keep employees within the organisation. In this regard, it seems logical to consider that much of the concern about labour outsourcing and labour flexibility is its numerical rather than functional profile: workers are more likely to be subcontracted as a means of reducing costs, following the financial logic identified by Lazonick (2002), rather than as a means of pursuing empowerment or a higher-involvement strategy.

On the other hand, understanding outsourcing as an activity in which a service or product is produced under the specifications of the client firm implies that the subcontractor cannot carry out this activity entirely on its own, and still pursues its own interests in negotiation and coordination with the client company (Lorenz 1988; 1992; 1999). This is perhaps one of the most critical points in the discussion of outsourcing. As mentioned earlier, Stinchcombe (1990) noticed that outsourcing is neither a classical hierarchical arrangement nor a pure market transaction but something in between, a type of agreement that requires a certain degree of coordination and trust (Sako and Helper 1998), or, as DiMaggio (2001:4) suggests: "New forms of coordination – 'relational contracting' – have emerged that entail much less commitment and control than bureaucracy, but more binding ties than simple market exchange." Therefore, the effects of new organisational forms on employment relations and work seem to deserve special attention because of their complexity and powerful implications (Marchington et al. 2005).

In this regard, the undertaking of labour outsourcing as a numerical flexibility mechanism implies that there are considerable tensions and problems between organisations. This outsourcing process implies that the subcontracted workforce is a buffer to protect permanent workers from turbulences in the market (Atkinson 1984; Harrison and Kelley 1993; Harrison 1994) but also to protect the client firm against workers' demands and union formation (de Buen Lozano 2005; De la Garza 2005). Therefore, there is a considerable power and risk asymmetry in outsourcing relations (Stinchcombe 1990; Marchington et al. 2005) and this asymmetry works against the trust and cooperation needed to establish the type of efficient relationships expected in a flexible firm model (Lorenz 1988; 1992; Sako and Helper 1998; Lorenz 1999).

In addition, organisations often have mutually exclusive goals and incentives when outsourcing; client firms prefer customisation and subcontractors prefer standardisation, which is the classic case in customer-oriented arrangements (Korczynski 2002; 2009). Client firms pursue customisation because they want to reduce the negative impact of losing control over an activity that was previously undertaken inside the organisation, while subcontractors prefer standardisation as it is the best way to compensate for the risks they assume in absorbing the responsibilities of the client firm in the administration of the subcontracted labour force.

As a result of these tensions between organisations, workers are exposed to fragmented employment relations that are dispersed among different employers whose demands and interests are divergent in critical aspects. What are these aspects? In relation to the administration of the labour force, client firms and subcontractors are likely to have disagreements and tensions over the recruitment and selection process, training, operation, supervision, monitoring, pecuniary compensation and termination of the relationship. In fact, the entire administration of the labour force in a subcontracted firm is likely to be the source of disputes between the two organisations.

However, these tensions between organisations in outsourcing arrangements could be more problematic in front-line services where the customer–worker interface adds another layer of dispersion into the equation. Therefore, the purpose of the following section is to identify those particularities of front-line service work that challenge outsourcing.

## 1.3.  Service work and outsourcing

### 1.3.1. Defining service work

For Daniels, a British economic geographer, the "service industries have long been the Cinderella of economic geography" (Daniels 1993:1), in the sense that services are one of the least understood economic activities yet they are crucial for the prosperity of modern societies. With the advent of capitalism, the old agricultural-based feudalism was substituted with a manufacturing system, but services were not relegated to the margins. Even then, there was always an intense debate about service work, its characteristics and the kind of contribution services make to society. According to Korczynski (2002), there have been several attempts to define service work, dating back more than two hundred years:

> The original theorists and supporters of the emerging capitalist system were keen to draw out these differences because they saw manufacturing as synonymous with capitalism (think of cotton mills, for instance) and services as remnants of the feudal society that they wished overturned.
> (Korczynski 2002:4)

Service work was almost unanimously regarded as inferior to manufacturing work. Korczynski (2002) observes that this was the prevalent opinion among some well-known social scientists more than two centuries ago, as demonstrated by this paragraph from Adam Smith in *An inquiry into the nature and causes of the wealth of nations* written originally in 1776:

> The former, as it produces a value, may be called productive; the latter, unproductive labour. Thus the labour of a manufacturer adds, generally, to the value of the materials which he works upon... The labour of a menial servant, on the contrary, adds the value of nothing... The services [of the menial servant] generally perish in the very instant of their performance, and seldom leave any trace of value behind them.
> (Smith 1985:314-315)

Arguably, within the context of manufacturing capitalism, service work has 'suffered' the consequences of not showing the physical transformation that factory work offers to the human eye. In many ways, service work is also considered to be a simple extension of manufacturing work (Levitt 1972) in the sense that services mean the transportation, trade and distribution of manufacturing goods (Daniels 1993). However, the main problem with understanding and observing service work is its 'intangibility'. This intangibility is problematic for economists and geographers alike as it seems to be more difficult to measure labour productivity for services than for manufacturing. For this reason, geographers propose an economically-based set of definitions for services in four different groups: service industries, service products, service occupations and service functions (Gershuny and Miles 1983:4).

Also, from the terrain of economic geography, Browning and Singelmann propose another four-fold classification of activities: i) producer services; ii) distributive services; iii) social services; and iv) personal services (Browning and Singelmann 1978). These classifications have an economic and spatial profile and capture the role of different service activities in the value chain of the economic system; this enables people to understand how services are connected to other economic activities, especially manufacturing, and to measure the value added of service work to the aggregated production. These attempts to make labour productivity quantifiable in services demonstrates the need to compare manufacturing and service jobs in order to test the perceived wisdom that good manufacturing jobs are being replaced by bad service jobs in contemporary societies (Gershuny and Miles 1983; Noyelle 1990; Stanback and Noyelle 1990; Daniels 1993; Garza 2006; García 2009). This seems to be the fundamental question for many social scientists about services: what is the contribution of service industries and service work to our society? Do these activities create 'value'? Does the predominance of service industries represent a fundamental change for societies? Are we moving towards a society plagued by bad service jobs whose economic contribution is minimal, where the skills required are low and employment conditions are precarious?

If the analysis of services is confined to the 'tangible' measure of labour productivity many of the essential characteristics of service work, and their implications, are difficult to observe. Here is an interesting but controversial example. There is little question that the labour productivity of footballers has varied considerably over the last hundred years; nowadays footballers are stronger and faster than ever. At the same time, the sport is still played by teams of 11 members each and the rules have not changed significantly. On the other hand, salaries of footballers are amazingly different. Today, footballers could earn millions of pounds, something that was impossible years ago. Is this explained by dramatic increases in footballers' productivity only? For me, the answer is no. The explanation is more about the emergence and development of the advertising industry that has been created around professional sports; it is about image, reputation and marketing. Therefore, the influence of customers' perceptions and participation is considerable in the emergence and development of service industries.

Economics-based typologies of services tell us almost nothing about the intricacies of the customer–employee interface and its major implications for employment conditions and workers' experiences. Service work is considered to be a continuation, an appendix of manufacturing and agriculture, so service workers can provide only a complementary output to the goods already produced by other more 'tangible' activities. Therefore, to explore the full dimension of service work it is important to consider more abstract characteristics. Korczynski (2002) identifies a set of five general features of service work:

- *Intangibility.* In general, physical transformations tend to be absent in service work and this makes it difficult to observe how service work 'adds value' during the labour process.
- *Perishability.* This is the 'temporal' nature of service work. This type of work cannot be stored to be used in the future.
- *Variability.* In some cases, service work implies a direct and constant interaction with customers. When this occurs, there are significant limitations to the standardisation of the labour process because uncertainty increases.
- *Simultaneous production and consumption.* In customer service interaction the 'production of goods' and their consumption occur simultaneously.
- *Inseparability.* Customers are part of the production process in the case of interactive service work. In this type of work employees and customers cannot be conceived of separately.

Although useful, these characteristics are hardly applicable to all forms of service work. Look at the case of one type of professional service. For example, accountants need to obtain a considerable amount of information from their individual clients and process it, but this does not necessarily mean they have a direct and continuous interaction with their customers. After an initial meeting between the customer and the accountant, the bulk of the work can be done by the accountant in isolation. But continuous interaction between service providers and their customers is an essential part of other service work, for example by teachers, health care staff and call centre operators. This example draws our attention to the importance of categorising service work by type of interaction with customers, an approach suggested by Leidner (1993), who identified three sub-categories of service work:

- Where interaction with customers is a crucial part of the process even though it is not part of a product being sold or provided (e.g. salespeople in call centres).

- Where the product exists apart from the relationship with customers, but some interaction is expected to make the product more enjoyable (e.g. flight attendants).
- Where interaction with customers is inseparable from the product being sold or delivered (e.g. teaching) (Leidner 1993:26).

Therefore, the characteristics of many service jobs largely depend on the type of interaction the service provider has with the customer. In this regard, sociological analyses seem to be well positioned to understand the nature and implications of the customer-orientation of service work. As mentioned earlier, for a long time service work was considered inferior to manufacturing work, but there could be also an element of sexism behind this assumption as service work is frequently excluded from the rights and benefits obtained in male-dominated activities; it seems that men are less likely to carry out front-line service work than women (especially if household activities are also considered). In the past service work has mainly been carried out by women, often at home (invisible to the public sphere) and largely unpaid (Walby 1990). For example, it is common to see how similar service activities are perceived in a different way when they are carried out by different genders in opposite contexts (public/private), such as cooking or cleaning (Grint 2005). Nowadays that service industries are the most important source of employment in modern societies; has the emergence of a service-oriented economy changed these social pre-conceptions?

The increasing importance of service work is attracting more attention from scholars and somehow forcing a change in interpretations. For the first time in modern capitalism, since 2006 service jobs represent the biggest share of total employment at global scale[4] according to the

---

[4] For Daniels (1993) there are six ways in which we could understand the expansion of services in recent decades: i) the growth in demand for discretionary consumer services following the growth of per capita output; ii) the steady emergence of a role for producers of intermediate services in the value added to a good or service; iii) the trend towards the external purchase of services by non-service firms using outsourcing; iv) the adoption by producers of effective marketing, distribution, after-sales maintenance and servicing of their products, and by governments to invest in social and community services or infrastructure such as telecommunications; v) the more specialized demands of the entertainment and financial industries; and vi) the ability of service producers to create new products and markets in areas such as securities, junk bonds, reinsurance, debt swaps, Euro-markets, value-added services and data transmission and manipulation (Daniels 1993).

International Labour Organisation (2007). The service-dominated society has emerged at a time when there are substantial numbers of women entering to the labour market, while a free-market ideology prevails, and while there are increasing levels of education, intense international competition, accelerated technological innovation, and rapid changes in demand. Interestingly, these are the factors mentioned earlier as responsible for the rise of the flexible firm paradigm. In this case, it is argued that these elements have given birth to the 'post-industrial society', 'the knowledge economy' or the 'new economy' (Bell 1973; Reich 1991; Daniels 1993; Castells 1996).

It might be possible to find some substantial differences between these concepts; however, for the aims of this research it is enough to consider that all of them relate to a transformation into a service-oriented social structure where the idea of working with people rather than things has become the most popular depiction of work for young generations (Reich 1991).

In general, academic research on service work identifies two main concerns: deskilling and precarious employment conditions. The topic of precarious employment conditions has been already discussed as part of the change in the employment relationship. Now, I will turn my attention to the challenges of deskilling in service work. It is argued that the service industry results in many unskilled jobs (Noyelle 1990), that the introduction of IT systems to support and monitor workers has negative impacts on workers' autonomy (Garson 1988), that routine work is common, and that the principles of deskilling mass production applied to manufacturing (Braverman 1974) seem to be extended over the service workplace (Ritzer 1998). In this regard, the romantic and optimistic image of the knowledge economy as a place where workers are encouraged to use their intellectual capacities more intensively (Reich 1991; Castells 2000) is only true for a small portion of individuals.

Within the body of literature concerned with the skills required by modern front-line services it is possible to find a particular emphasis on how service work demands a great deal of control over customer–worker interactions. The point of debate here is the extent to which this control is actually achieved and how it affects workers. Some authors suggest that a great and damaging level of control over workers' emotions and their interactions with customers is exerted through the design of modern front-line service work[5] (Hochschild 1983; Ritzer 1998).

---

[5] According to Hochschild (1983), emotional labour is now a key component of service work, and this can be understood as service employers controlling personal emotions in exchange for a salary, that is, the subordination of employees' feelings

This level of control over customer interactions triggers a very interesting question: is it possible to control the customer–worker interface to the point of absolute standardisation? If the answer is affirmative, then it is possible to conceive and design front-line service work as a variation of manufacturing work, as it has been suggested by Levitt (1972). Ritzer, in his work *McDonaldization thesis* (1998) deserves special attention here. According to this author, the US company McDonald's epitomises the rationalisation logic of bureaucracies identified by Max Weber.[6] To be successful, this rationalisation of the labour process requires minimum workers' skills as well as customers' docile participation. Ritzer goes even further when arguing that most of the jobs recently created are in fact 'McJobs': low-skilled and highly dependent on customer subordination to bureaucratic rules imposed by business organisations.[7] As a result of this, the whole society is being transformed.[8]

Therefore, if front-line service work can be controlled satisfactorily – the rationalisation logic – then there is little question that the outsourcing of front-line services would bring only minimal tensions and risks for the organisations involved.

Nonetheless, there is still no consensus about the existence of this absolute control and predictability in service work, and the customer–worker interface plays a critical role at this point. It is suggested that, despite the attempt to control their interactions with customers, workers are ultimately responsible for how they treat customers (Leidner 1993). To illustrate the importance of autonomy for front-line service workers

---

to the rules dictated by the job. Hochschild criticizes the dehumanizing nature of emotional labour and claims that emotional labour in the service economy is an extreme case of worker alienation where employees are at risk of losing autonomy over their own emotions.

[6] Ritzer says that the McDonaldization process involves four main rationalization dimensions: efficiency, calculability, predictability and control (Ritzer 1993; Ritzer 1998).

[7] Other authors have shown that only a tiny fraction of the total jobs in the US falls into the description offered by Ritzer (Herzenberg et al. 1998).

[8] In this regard, it is possible to appreciate certain links with Robert Reich's work, *The work of nations: preparing ourselves for 21st century capitalism* (1991), where the author states that there are three types of workers: routine producers, in-person servers and symbolic analysts. According to Reich, symbolic analysts who solve and identify problems by manipulating symbols are the 'winners' in today's societies. Those workers who are educated and can use their knowledge to supply a service will be given the highest incomes. Contrarily, those workers who have no knowledge to sell will be engaged in routine jobs in factories or in-person servers (such as waiters and cashiers) under bad employment conditions (Reich 1991).

Leidner (1993) explored two cases of service areas where there is a high level of routine work: fast-food restaurants and insurance sales. Using these two experiences, Leidner discusses how direct interaction with customers imposes limits to the *routinisation* and standardisation of the labour process. Her evidence suggests that employees in insurance sales are able to select and perform diverse sales strategies autonomously depending on the type of customer. Moreover, in certain circumstances, employees perceive *routinisation* as a tool to solve problems (especially during critical situations such as long queues, complaints, etc.) rather than as a restriction to their autonomy.[9] However, Leidner does not hold an optimistic view of *routinisation* in interactive service work, but her critical vision considers the different contexts where the customer-employee interaction takes place and how participants interpret it.

In the same vein, Korczynski argues that the pressures for standardisation and customisation in service organisations have given birth to a customer-oriented bureaucracy where employees are able to move across different combinations of standard and routine services or more careful and personalised attention depending on the customer. Who decides which customer gets what? Some authors have argued that there is a direct relationship between the type of managerial system applied and customer segmentation (Batt 2000; Batt and Moynihan 2002). In other words, high-involvement managerial practices are more likely to be applied to those employees associated with high-income customer segments.

Interestingly, customer services are frequently targets of outsourcing practices, which means that at least two organisations have to 'understand' customer services in 'the same way'. As mentioned before, these are 'relational contracts' (DiMaggio 2001), where organisations have to negotiate the type of service delivered. In this regard, the contradiction of customisation versus standardisation (Korczynski 2002) arises and creates tensions and frictions between subcontractors and client firms. To look at these problems more carefully, the next section examines the case selected for this research: call centre work.

---

[9] The work of Leidner (1993) offers an opportunity to recognise openly the advantages of routinisation in modern service work from a critical point of view. She also reports that some customers might feel comfortable when obtaining services in an environment that has predictable and standardised procedures.

## 1.3.2. Challenges for outsourcing in service work: the case of call centres

Front-line service work in call centres involves a customer–worker interface that puts additional pressures on the relationship between subcontractors and client firms. Other categories of front-line service work such as fast-food restaurants (like McDonald's) or retailers (like Wal-Mart) have received considerable attention in recent years (Ritzer 1998; Lichtenstein 2006). They are highly visible, iconographic elements of western societies (Lichtenstein 2006). Call centres companies, on the other hand, and contrary to other emblematic representations of the front-line service economy, prefer a status of quasi-anonymity (Micheli 2005). Anybody living in a big city could name half a dozen retailers or fast-food restaurants even if they have never visited them, but nobody could name at least one call centre company, although they are likely to receive a call from one of these centres at least once in their life. This is an undeniable characteristic of call centres: they are ubiquitous but have a furtive presence in everyday modern life. More importantly, despite this 'invisibility' call centres have become the 'voice' and representation of many firms with their customers (Fluss 2005) and, in many cases, this process takes place through subcontracted organisations.

It is also argued that call centres epitomise the characteristics of service work in the new economy (Deery and Kinnie 2002; Glucksmann 2004). The intensive use of labour and IT systems in supporting and monitoring workers make call centres an ideal case of study to analyse contemporary service work. Interestingly, the pioneering works on call centres were also the most pessimistic. Garson's (1988) and Fernie and Metcalf's (1998) used terms such as 'twentieth century panopticons' (Fernie and Metcalf 1998) or 'electronic sweatshops' (Garson 1988), to highlight the role of IT systems in narrowing worker's autonomy and discretion over their own work.

However, there is certain consensus about the heterogeneity of work and employment conditions in call centres at the moment, at least in the British literature. The existence of such heterogeneity has largely been documented by numerous scholars in different contexts, such as the United Kingdom, Australia, Ireland, Japan and the United States (Frenkel et al. 1998; Frenkel 1999; Taylor and Bain 1999; Batt 2000; Kinnie et al. 2000; Batt and Moynihan 2002; Houlihan 2002; Taylor et al. 2002; Mulholland 2004; Taylor and Bain 2007). Some of these investigations suggest the existence of a hybrid managerial approach in call centres that combines the standardisation of processes (to reduce costs) and the customisation of products (to satisfy customers) (Frenkel et al. 1998; Korczynski 2002). On the other hand, Batt (2000) suggests the existence of a continuum of different managerial approaches according to the whole variety of market segments in call centres.

In this regard, Batt argues that customer segmentation determines the choice of any of three managerial approaches: a) the classical mass production model; b) the professional service model; and c) the mass customisation model. The mass customisation model is regarded as a hybrid that gains from the advantages of mechanisation in mass production and from the quality service of professional models (Batt and Moynihan 2002). Batt and Moynihan (2002) explain that mass production models prevail in the organisation of work servicing residential customers; that professional services are used to attend large businesses; and that there is a match between small businesses and mass customisation models where there is a combination of efficiency and quality for the customer. Since servicing residential customers and small businesses might employ the largest proportion of people in call centres it would be obvious to suppose that mass production strategies could prevail in call centres (Batt 2000; Batt and Moynihan 2002).

In the same way, some authors recognise the heterogeneity in managerial strategies, but disagree about the appropriateness of considering call centre managerial systems to be undifferentiated hybrids of *routinisation* and customisation (Taylor et al. 2002). The empirical research of Taylor et al. (2002) suggests the limits to this heterogeneity in call centre work: "our final conclusions are that *routinisation*, repetitiveness and a general absence of employee control are the dominant, although not universal, features of work organisation" (Taylor et al. 2002:136). These authors report that even workers servicing high-income customer segments tend to experience low levels of control over their pace, breaks, planning and targets at work. Their overall conclusion is that, despite the visible quality-oriented approach of some call centres associated with high-income customers, in general, levels of less discretion or control over work are common in the industry (Taylor et al. 2002). In summary, it is possible to argue that there is a general consensus about two characteristics of work in call centres: a) the organisation of work in the industry is heterogeneous and largely associated with customer segmentation strategies; b) despite this heterogeneity, a sort of mass production approach prevails due to the importance of standardisation in those segments that dominate the industry, that is, those oriented to relatively low-income markets such as residential customers or small to medium sized businesses.

There has also been significant research looking at the extent to which call centre work might be shaped by the public or private orientation of the organisation (Glucksmann 2004; Collin-Jacques and Smith 2005; Smith et al. 2008; van den Broek 2008), pointing to the importance of external agents and macro policies over the administration of the workforce inside organisations. Also in the connections with the social structure of the communities where these call centres might be embedded, the experience of work in call centres has been examined through the lens of gender inequality (Belt 2002). In summary, the literature on call centre work is still growing and our knowledge about working conditions in this sector has advanced significantly over the last few years.

For my investigation, two are the most relevant themes in the call centre literature as a case study of service work in the new economy. On the one hand, the analysis of call centre work in the context of inter-firm relationships, outsourcing in particular (Marchington et al. 2005; Taylor and Bain 2005; Batt et al. 2006; Kinnie et al. 2006; Doellgast 2008; Kinnie et al. 2008) and, on the other hand, the analysis of call centre outsourcing and offshoring in different institutional settings like the United Kingdom (Kinnie et al. 2006; 2008), India (Taylor and Bain 2005; Batt et al. 2006; Russell and Thite 2008), the United States (Batt et al. 2004; 2006; Doellgast 2008), Australia (Russell and Thite 2008; Paulet 2009), Germany (Doellgast 2008) and at a global level (Batt et al. 2007). In general, all these studies agree that employment conditions tend to be worse in outsourced and offshore call centres than in their 'in-house' counterparts. These findings contradict the results expected by the classical economics rationale: according to the efficiency maximisation logic of outsourcing, each economic entity has to concentrate its efforts in the area where it gets maximum returns – where this company is more competent and able to maximise its profits and labour productivity.

If this logic is true, then all the companies would be exploiting their core advantages, obtaining maximum returns and productivity. These enable firms and workers to produce higher quality products at competitive prices because of the achievement of economies of scale and specialisation (Lacity and Hirschheim 1993), a virtuous circle! In this sense, working in a subcontracted firm that specialises in a peripheral area for the client firm must, potentially, be an attractive option for those workers who do not belong to the core of the firm.

However, the findings presented in this book indicate that outsourcing arrangements are not as efficient as they are supposed to be due to asymmetries that generates distrust and lack of cooperation between the organisations involved. However, the impact of tensions between organisations in outsourcing arrangements has begun to emerge in the literature in call centres just very recently (Batt et al. 2006; Kinnie et al. 2008; Deery et al. 2010).

In addition, most analyses of the call centre industry are concentrated on developed economies and India. I am not assuming that all these developed economies represent a homogenous group; on the contrary, many contributions to the study of call centre work have been made from a comparative perspective between different models of capitalism, from market to coordinated economies (Doellgast and Greer 2007; Doellgast 2007b), but they are frequently focused, like many institutional analyses, on rich economies (Thelen and Hall 2009). In this respect, the role and importance of all service work, not just call centre jobs, in developing countries have been largely ignored by most of the literature, even when most of these countries have service-oriented economies and a large internal market (just look at the cases of Brazil or Mexico in Latin America), and have attracted considerable foreign direct investment associated, in many cases, with offshoring practices in recent years.

## Conclusions

The study of outsourcing has attracted considerable attention in the social sciences. A large portion of the literature seems to be focused on costs and coordination because most of the debate about outsourcing takes part within the analysis of the boundaries of the firm where transaction costs indicate the separation between hierarchies and markets. On the other hand, the sociological critique of this perspective seems to emphasise the role of power asymmetries between organisations to explain how risks are unequally distributed in inter-firm relationships, and how less powerful players might be forced to accept market mediated arrangements that do not necessarily represent lower transaction costs. However, the implications of these difficulties between subcontractors and client firms over workers' experiences remain relatively unexplored. This chapter identifies two reasons to explain this lack of attention. On the one hand, most of the research on outsourcing has been undertaken in the manufacturing context where the customer–employee interface does not exist as a key component of the experience of work. On the other hand, most of the analysis of outsourcing in services has been focused on the quantitative and more measurable aspects of employment conditions (such as salaries and benefits), paying less attention to the experience of work that tends to be much more abstract and subjective.

This research argues that this gap deserves much more attention for several reasons. On the one hand, it is argued that the emergence of the flexible firm model – and the flexibility paradigm in general – is blurring the boundaries between firms, fragmenting employment relationships and dismantling hierarchies. In this context, the administration of the labour force is becoming more and more a disputed terrain between at least two different employers: subcontractors and client firms. These problems seem to affect workers' identity, satisfaction and, in turn, productivity and wages. On the other hand, these problems seem to affect also the quality of the service provided, affecting customers, subcontractors and client firms. Therefore, the aim of this research is to contribute a better understanding of how workers' experiences and employment conditions in front-line services are affected by outsourcing.

This chapter has discussed how the problems associated with the outsourcing of front-line service work are also fuelling concerns about the characteristics of jobs and employment in services; it is said that good manufacturing jobs have been replaced by bad service jobs, that the 'old' manufacturing model, associated with physical work and machinery but also with the stability of life-time employment and union protection (Tilly 1996; Grint 1998; 2005), is extinct and that the 'new' service model, associated with mental and emotional work, is also strongly connected with precarious employment conditions[10] (Gershuny and Miles 1983; Sennett 2009). Very importantly, the 'old' system was strongly associated with the single breadwinner model, a historic pillar of the patriarch society (Walby 1990; Wajcman 2004; Walby 2007).

On the other hand, concepts such as the post-industrial society, the knowledge economy or the network society (Bell 1973; Reich 1991; Castells 1996) refer to a more advanced production dynamics where 'old' manufacturing jobs are replaced by more sophisticated and knowledge-oriented jobs. In this new industrial order, there would be no more life-time contracts with organisations or the continuation of the single breadwinner model. Now, it is time for independence and mobility, 'employability' has been coined to name the desired characteristics of these new-born workers (Noon and Blyton 2007) whose ethos is more

---

[10] The media also reinforces these perceptions when presenting numerous images of workers in developed countries struggling to keep alive their local factory shops and avoid the relocation of industrial facilities toward the global south, where salaries are considerably lower. At macro level, the media provide and spread figures of large trade deficits, emphasizing the loss of manufacturing capabilities and implicitly arguing that new service jobs are inferior. It is common to see idealistic interpretations of the manufacturing past as a golden age.

individualistic, goal-oriented, and anti-union than their counterparts in manufacturing[11] (Baldry et al. 2007). In other words, in order to face the challenges of intense competition, technical change and rapid variations in demand, organisations must adopt more flexible formats that also affect employment relations (Marchington et al. 2005).

Specifically, most of the fears and concerns over the quality of jobs in the post-industrial society are posed in relation to mass consumption services whose employment conditions and job designs seem to be more exposed than others to the pressures of intense competition and technical change.[12] The outsourcing of front-line segments of customer-oriented industries such as retail, banking, public services, tourism or hospitality work seems to be an effective mechanism in achieving cost reductions. Table 1-2 summarises the main differences between the archetypes of work in the old manufacturing economy and the new service economy.

**Table 1-2. Two different types of work**

| The old manufacturing worker and its context | The new service worker and its context |
|---|---|
| Life-time employment | No long-term employment |
| Single employer | Multiple employers |
| Male | Female |
| Working with things | Working with people |
| The production society | The consumption society |

[11] Much of the social apprehension about the potential pervasiveness of bad quality jobs in the service economy does not come exclusively from criticisms over the low skills associated with service jobs. In a recent publication, *The Meaning of Work in the New Economy* (Baldry et al. 2007), the authors critically examined nine case studies (call centres and software development companies) and concluded that workers in the new economy still experience a combination of gratifying and unpleasant situations but that jobs are more unstable than ever when looking at the type of employment arrangements made. There is an increasing proportion of market-mediated employment relationships in jobs that have been created recently.

[12] Interestingly, it is also argued that these low-quality service jobs might represent a continuation of the type of routine and alienating work that was created by mass production in manufacturing (Gershuny and Miles, 1983; Levitt, 1972).

Therefore, the expansion of mass consumption services through outsourcing arrangements fuels much of the concern about having a service-oriented economy where precarious jobs might prevail (Gershuny and Miles 1983; Daniels 1993; Ritzer 1998; Donnelly 2009).

# CHAPTER TWO

# CONTEXT AND METHODOLOGY:
# THE MEXICAN SERVICE ECONOMY
# AND SELECTED CASE STUDIES

## 2.1. The Mexican context: liberalisation, outsourcing and service work

### 2.1.1. Employment and services in Mexico

Historically, much of the academic research on work and employment conditions in Mexico has been around the manufacturing experience. Also, the central role of the exports-oriented manufacturing industry in the current economic policy has reinforced this tendency (Villarreal 1997; López 1998; De la Garza and Salas Páez 2006; Garza 2006). However, the magnitude of the service economy in employment, gross domestic product and, more recently, its connections with the global economy is making services more attractive and relevant for academic research, local authorities' policies, media coverage and the general public. For example, some years ago the arrival of giant global corporations in the automobile and electronic industries was at the centre of public and academic attention. Now, some years later, the entrance of services corporations (in retail, telecommunications or banking) is perceived as a remarkable event with significant effects for the local economy (Álvarez-Galván and Tilly 2006; Garza 2006; ECLAC 2007).

To start with, it is important to say that many workers in Mexico do not have any type of 'formal' employment contract: the proportion of workers without a formal or written employment contract was about 49% of the total in 2006 (Table 2-1). In these circumstances, the fear of having a job with no contract or not having a job at all is much more of a concern in the Mexican context than having a temporary or part-time employment contract. Therefore, the formal institutional setting is much weaker for Mexican workers than for workers in countries where call centres and other front-line service jobs have been often studied (Ruiz Duran 2005b; De la Garza and Salas Páez 2006; Garza 2006; Batt et al. 2007; Burnett 2009). Mexico is the 13th biggest economy in the world, it is classified as an upper-middle income economy by the World Bank (World Bank, www.worldbank.org, consulted in October 2009) but it is still a society with high levels of poverty and income polarisation (INEGI 2005; ECLAC 2007).

**Table 2-1. Employment contracts in Mexico 2000-2006 (%)**

| Type of contract | 2000 | 2006 |
|------------------|------|------|
| Permanent jobs   | 49   | 42   |
| Temporary jobs   | 7    | 9    |
| Without contract | 44   | 49   |

Source: Presidencia de la República 2006.

However, it is always challenging to find an effective way of speaking about the specific employment conditions that those workers in the service economy face. This is because the service economy encompasses a huge diversity of industries and occupations and their classification has been always problematic, not only in Mexico but in any economy around the world (Gershuny and Miles 1983; Noyelle 1990; Daniels 1993; Garza 2006). In Mexico, like in many other countries, the evidence available[1] portrays a very heterogeneous picture of the service sector with mixed activities and employment conditions (Álvarez-Galván and Tilly 2006; De la Garza and Salas Páez 2006).

In 2007, the service economy absorbed 60.8% of the total employment and about 77.8% of the total female workforce in the country. These figures show a clear contrast with the experience of the primary (agriculture and mining) and secondary (manufacturing and construction) sectors, where women constitute only 4.4% and 17.9%, respectively, of the total workforce (Table 2-2). In summary, in 2007 the service workforce

---

[1] In 2005, the National Institute of Statistics, Geography and Informatics (INEGI) changed the methodology of the National Survey of Employment and Occupation, making the comparison with data collected before that year technically inadequate. However a homologation process was taking place when this book was written.

in Mexico was about 26 million people and about 48% of them were female workers (12.5 million). Therefore, it is clear that one of the main characteristics of service work – and an important distinction from the other two sectors of the economy – is the strong presence of female workers.

Despite its importance, the study of work in the service economy in Mexico remains relatively scarce, particularly in comparison with the study of work in manufacturing where male workers are often the main subject of study (with a few exceptions, such as studies of the 'maquila' industry in the North) (Bensusán and Rendón 2000; Rendón 2003; Álvarez-Galván and Tilly 2006; De la Garza and Salas Páez 2006; Bank Muñoz 2008; García 2009). Therefore, a change in this trajectory is expected in years to come.

**Table 2-2. Mexico: basic employment statistics 2007 (000s)**

| | Total | Primary | Secondary | Tertiary |
|---|---|---|---|---|
| Total | 42,907 | 5,772 | 11,033 | 26,100 |
| Male | 26,841 | 5,072 | 8,165 | 13,603 |
| Female | 16,066 | 700 | 2,868 | 12,497 |
| | | % of total employment | | |
| Total | 100 | 13.5 | 25.7 | 60.8 |
| Male | 100 | 18.9 | 30.4 | 50.7 |
| Female | 100 | 4.4 | 17.9 | 77.8 |

Source: Author's elaboration based on the National Survey of Employment and Occupation (INEGI 2008).

As mentioned, the labour force in service activities is characterised by its huge diversity. For example, workers in services have, on average, more years of formal education than others. Does that mean that workers in services also require higher skills and education to perform their jobs? Not necessarily. This figure can be misleading since it includes professional and technical workers as well as workers with lower skills in hotels, restaurants, and retail activities (Álvarez-Galván and Tilly 2006; Garza 2006; García 2009).

It is worth mentioning here that workers in services, especially those in retail and wholesale trade, are more likely to work longer hours than people in the rest of the economy. For instance, about 28% of the people in the service economy work more than 48 hours weekly (Table 2-3) (INEGI 2008).

**Table 2-3. Mexico: working hours in the service economy 2007**

|  | Workers (000s) | % |
|---|---|---|
| Total | 25,787 | 100.0 |
| Less than 15 hours | 1,833 | 7.1 |
| 15-34 hours | 5,349 | 20.7 |
| 35-48 hours | 10,335 | 40.1 |
| More than 48 hours | 7,423 | 28.8 |
| Not Specified | 848 | 3.3 |

Source: National Survey of Employment and Occupation (INEGI 2008).

Therefore, employment conditions in the service economy in Mexico seem to be polarised, and this diversity allows for the study of multiple employment conditions and different interpretations. On the one hand, it is possible to see professional workers with high skills and relatively good working conditions, those who might resemble the type of employees expected for the new economy in post-industrial societies (Bell 1973; Reich 1991). However, it is also possible to see a mass of female service workers with only a few years of formal education occupying low skill jobs in front-line services such as retail and hospitality (Álvarez-Galván and Tilly 2006; García 2009).

In fact, many of these workers are identified as a kind of 'residual' segment from other activities, a workforce that has been expelled from agricultural and manufacturing activities as one of the consequences of the lack of economic growth and development in many regions of the country (Bensusán and Rendón 2000; Garza 2006; García 2009). As another consequence of this process, there is also a historical tendency of poor rural migrants to come to Mexican cities to work as housekeepers or in the informal economy (Bensusán and Rendón 2000; De la Garza and Salas Páez 2006; García 2009).

A general examination of the Mexican labour market indicates a set of relevant associations between employment conditions in the service economy, urban areas and gender. Table 2-4 shows that more women than men are unemployed, and young women (14-24 year olds) experience higher unemployment rates than young men of the same age. Interestingly, in 2007, Mexico City had a higher unemployment rate for women and men than the national average (INEGI 2008). In addition, Table 2-5 presents more details about employment conditions for women and men in Mexico, and dramatic conclusions can be drawn from them. At national level, 41% of female workers perform their activities employed in precarious conditions by micro businesses; almost 57% had no benefits, 71% did not have a permanent contract and nearly 87% did not have a union. It seems that having a job in Mexico City did not represent a significant advantage for these female workers in general, apart from their income level. In this respect, having a higher income seems to be the only significant benefit for women of having a job in Mexico City rather than working in other part of the country.

**Table 2-4. Mexico: unemployment rates for women and men 2007**

| Place | Unemployment rates (%) for | | | |
| | Women | Young women (14-24 year olds) | Men | Young men (14-24 year olds) |
|---|---|---|---|---|
| Mexico | 3.5 | 7.4 | 3.0 | 5.3 |
| Mexico City | 5.5 | 13.0 | 4.7 | 9.0 |

Source: Adapted from Garcia (2009) based on the National Survey of Employment and Occupation (ENEO), second quarter.

Chapter Two

**Table 2-5. Mexico and Mexico City: employment for women and men 2006**

| | In precarious micro-businesses /a | With low income /b | Involuntary part-time job /c | Without benefits /d | Without permanent contract | Without union /e |
|---|---|---|---|---|---|---|
| ***Women*** | | | | | | |
| Mexico | 41 | 50 | 36.3 | 56.9 | 71 | 87.2 |
| Mexico City | 41.4 | 36 | 32.7 | 52.3 | 65.6 | 86.6 |
| ***Men*** | | | | | | |
| Mexico | 31.1 | 50 | 19.1 | 60.8 | 73.6 | 90.6 |
| Mexico City | 38.9 | 39.1 | 14.9 | 54.1 | 66.6 | 89.2 |

/a People employed in small establishments (1-5 people in retail trade and services and 1-16 in manufacturing) without formal regulation, contracts or benefits.
/b Wages per hour lower than the national median for males (18 Mexican Pesos in 2006).
/c Less than 35 hours per week.
/d Without end-of-the-year bonus, paid holidays or medical coverage.
/e Not affiliated to any union.
Source: Adapted from Garcia (2009) based on the National Survey of Employment and Occupation (ENEO), second quarter.

On the other hand, at national level the situation of men seems to be significantly better than that of women in two aspects: men seem to be considerably less likely to work in precarious conditions in micro-businesses and they are less likely to be involuntary employed in part-time jobs. Apparently, there is no major difference, on average, between women and men in their exposure to low income jobs. However, also at national level, men seem to be more likely to have a job with no benefits, without a permanent contract and without collective representation (Table 2-5, previous page). Again, the greatest advantage of having a job in Mexico City for men is that they might earn a higher income than they would if they worked in other part of the country.

## 2.1.2. Industrial relations and call centres in Mexico

Overall, Mexico's is considered as an emerging economy which means, in institutional terms, that it is neither a market-oriented economy nor a coordinated one because many of its economic institutions are not as powerful as they are in other types of economy. However, over the last decades Mexico's economic policy has been powerfully influenced by liberal and market-oriented economic thought. As mentioned, Mexico followed an import substitution strategy from the late 1940s until the first half of the 1980s. This strategy was based on strong State intervention supported by a surplus in the international trade balance of agriculture. Such a surplus provided a substantial part of the foreign currency needed to buy finished and intermediate goods in other sectors. On the other hand, manufacturing was strongly protected and foreign investment was only allowed in a limited number of sectors. Special regimes operate in some zones (usually at the border with the US) for those industries oriented to international trade (Export Protected Zones) where import and export tariffs were minimal or inexistent (Dussel Peters 2000).

In general terms, it is possible to say that Mexico had, for about four decades, a particular type of Welfare State based on limited political freedom for its citizens and strict control over economic activity. The Mexican Welfare State was part of the strategy developed by the main political party, the Revolution Institutional Party (*Partido Revolucionario Institucional*, PRI) which was in power from the 1930s until the year 2000. This party emerged as a response to the social and political struggles of the Mexican Revolution of the 1910s; as an attempt to stabilise the political regime. Not incidentally, the PRI was composed of four different structures: workers, bureaucrats, peasants and soldiers. The military section eventually disappeared and the nominal category of 'members' of each section was useful in order to include different social classes in each one: workers, managers and capitalists where considered 'equal' members into the organisational structure of the party. For non-Mexicans, the name of the party might seem contradictory having the words 'Revolution' and 'Institutional' at the same time, but this was exactly the intention of the political elite in Mexico, to re-conduct the Revolution's struggles and fights into institutional channels instead of armed conflicts.

For many years, the system seemed to be efficient in allowing each section of the membership to have proportional representation among the seats in the federal Congress, local governments and congresses, and the allocation of ministries with each new president every six years. Although the Mexican Constitution allowed the formation of other political parties, the PRI had all public resources, strong connections with the economic elite and rarely lost any election and, when this happened, it was willing to use the force or electoral fraud (Reading 1986).

The Mexican Industrial Relations system comes directly from this regime. Unions and workers were a fundamental part of the political and social structure of the system. The Mexico's Workers Federation (*Confederación de Trabajadores de México*), the CTM, was an essential and powerful part of the PRI and it exercised, in practice, almost a monopoly in collective labour contracts in Mexico. The current Mexican Federal Law, dates back from the 1971 and it is based on the 123 article of the Mexican Constitution created in 1917. The Mexican Federal Law has 1,010 articles; it gives the right to have a union to any establishment with more than 20 employees; establishes a working week of 8 hours per day for no more than 6 days per week; and provides pensions and social security for workers. Importantly, the law also establishes a three-party conflict resolution council (employers, workers and the government) known as The Referee and Conciliation Meetings (*Juntas de Conciliación y Arbitraje*). In practice, most of the major companies in Mexico (at least those with 20 or more employees) had a collective contract with a union associated with the CTM or the PRI, even though a large majority of workers might be not aware of it (call centres included). Therefore, there is no real significance of these unions for most workers. On the other hand, independent unions are relatively scarce and suffered from the unfair competition of the CTM. In the seventies, a number of independent unions emerged and some CTM unions split out to form autonomous unions (De la Garza 2006). Eventually, the National Union of Workers, UNT (*Unión Nacional de Trabajadores*), was formed to confront the CTM. However, in recent years the UNT has been also criticised for its lack of authentic autonomy and for its close connections with other political parties

(Reynoso 2005). The emergence of a visible and relatively independent labour movement in Mexico was also part of a democratic movement at national scale that took place in the country towards the end of the seventies and the beginning of the eighties.

In terms of levels of industrial conflict, Mexico seems to be in line with global trends. In a research comparing 42 countries (including developed and developing economies) Wallace and O'Sullivan (2006) found a dramatic decline in strikes since 1980. In a comparison between two periods (1981–1985 and 1996–2000) of the 42 countries studied, eight showed an increase and 34 countries a decline in the number of strikes. Mexico appears in the group of countries experiencing a decline (a reduction of 3,612 for the second period) far more than the US (282), below the UK (5,284) and India (6,143) and similar to Peru (3,089) one of the other Latin American countries experiencing a decline in strikes when comparing the two periods (Wallace and O'Sullivan 2006). In terms of working days lost, which is considered another indicator of labour resistance and conflict, Wallace and O'Sullivan indicate that there is insufficient data for 1981 in the case of Mexico (excluding this country for the analysis of the first period) but, for the period 1996-2000, there was a decrease in working days lost by almost 300,000 (Wallace and O'Sullivan 2006).

For Wallace and O'Sullivan it is clear that there has been a major decline in the extent of strikes and their impact (as measured by working days lost) in the last few decades. However, according to these authors "the fact that there has been such a substantial decline at a global level suggests that national factors are insufficient to explain the trends" (Wallace and O'Sullivan 2006:13). Structural changes in the economy (from manufacturing to services), the new composition of the labour market (with an increasing female workforce, migrants and non-standard workers like students), and the impact of neo-liberal ideology in the political economy, seem to be crucial factors to explain the decline in strike activity and collective bargaining.

The information collected by Wallace and O'Sullivan comes from databases of the International Labour Organisation (ILO) which, in turns, receives the statistics from country members. As these authors indicate, there is considerable variation in terms of how these statistics are collected and processed across different countries (Wallace and O'Sullivan 2006). However, it seems that there is a problem of comparison not only across different countries but also across the methodologies used by different institutions within the same country. In Mexico, for example, using the information generated by the Ministry of Labour (STPS 2010), it is possible to contrast the tendencies identified by Wallace and Sullivan (2006). In terms of strikes, the total number has suffered a decrease since 1983, from 230 to only 21 in 2008 (having a peak in 1986 of 312). At industry level, there are significant differences between manufacturing and services. In 1983 there were 124 registered in manufacturing and only 29 in services, while in 2008 manufacturing registered 9 and services 6 (STPS 2010). It is true that the declining tendency identified by Wallace and O'Sullivan (2006) is also confirmed by these data but the number of strikes reported is considerable lower.

Also, despite the prevalence of non-democratic unions, the union federations associated with the PRI are still the main source of industrial conflict in Mexico. In 1983, of the 230 total strikes, 174 were generated by members of pro-government unions while only 56 were of independent unions. In 2008, of the 21 total strikes, 13 were generated by members of unions related to the governing party while only 8 were of independent unions (STPS 2010).

On the other hand, the number of collective contracts in Mexico has increased from 4,334 in 1994 up to 5,477 in 2008, that is, an increase in 1,143 (26.4% more); the highest proportion in the manufacturing sector in 2008 (1,953) while services is still far below (536). Nonetheless, union density and collective bargaining in the country have decreased in relative terms. There are no exact figures available but, taking into account that, during the same period, the total number of establishments in Mexico moved from about 2.5 million to about 5 million (that is, a 100% increase), it is clear that collective bargaining has not increased at the same pace that establishments were created. Nonetheless, it is important to be cautious with these figures because a large proportion of establishments in Mexico are micro or small firms (that is, have less than 50 or 20 employees, depending on the classification); therefore, workers in these firms have not the legal right to form a union. In any event, the lack of reliable information and the significant variation in terms of firm-size classification across different Ministries (Economy, Labour and Industry) makes difficult to analyse the trajectory of union density and collective bargaining in Mexico at macro level.

In Mexico, call centre work has been considered terrain for the Telephone Workers Union. The only independent union in Mexican call centres is at Technotronics whose story is described later in this book. The rest of the call centres in Mexico have collective contracts with unions belonging to the CTM, and have a weak connection with workers. In fact, all the workers interviewed for this research were not aware of the existence of any collective contract. Moreover, despite most call centre workers have a contract for services (self-employed) the collective agreement (in order to provide social security for them) is negotiated by these unions but there is no intervention at all from workers. That is, this collective bargaining is non-democratic and, as mentioned earlier, there is no real significance of these unions for workers.

At international level, it would be reasonable to expect a relatively low presence of collective bargaining and union activity in the call centre industry. This is because of the high flexibility of the industry and because call centres' affordable technical requirements would allow them to move across different geographies in order to avoid the higher labour costs associated with collective bargaining (Batt et al. 2009). However, some authors have found unexpectedly high collective bargaining and union activity at global level but with considerable variations among countries (Batt et al. 2009). According to the authors of the Call Centre Global Report, just below 50% of the call centres in their sample had some form of collective representation and up to 35% were covered by union agreements or unions plus work councils (Batt et al. 2009; Batt and Nohara 2009). The sample consisted of 2,500 establishments in 17 countries including liberal market economies, coordinated market economies and emerging economies. Not surprisingly, call centres in coordinated economies seem to be more likely to have unions and collective bargaining than call centres in liberal market and emerging economies (Batt et al. 2009; Batt and Nohara 2009). In this respect, the Mexican experience confirms an international pattern: collective representation is present in call centres but in a limited scope. Also, the differences among employment conditions in different types of market economies confirm the influence of macro-level institutions and firm-level mechanisms in shaping employment conditions (Doellgast et al. 2009; Holman et al. 2009; Shire et al. 2009; van Jaarsveld et al. 2009). In general terms, call centre workers in Mexico, and the subcontracted segment specifically, seem to be at the low end of the spectrum, this is, with low wages, almost no benefits and without effective collective representation despite the paternalistic approach of the Mexican Labour Law. Nonetheless, at national level, call centre jobs in Mexico remain a competitive job option for many local workers (IMT 2007).

## 2.1.3. Liberalisation and labour outsourcing in Mexico

As mentioned, there is a tendency to ignore the experience of developing countries in analyses of the service sector and its workers. The explanation for such an omission is mainly based on the misleading conception that developing countries are exclusively pools of cheap labour but not post-industrial societies, in other words, that poor countries are observed as places for production rather than consumption of the commodities traded at global scale (Krugman and Obstfeld 1997; Cowie 1999; McMichael 2004; ECLAC 2007). However, many of these countries, especially those frequently categorised as 'emergent economies', such as Mexico, Brazil or India, have a services-oriented economic structure and are avid consumers of imported final goods (Stiglitz 2003; ECLAC 2007).

During the 1980s, Mexico was immersed in the wave of liberalisation that took place in many countries around the world (McMichael 2004; Tonkiss 2006). In this Latin American country there was a transitional period from the imports substitution model (generally known as ISI) to exports oriented industrialisation (generally known as EOI) in the second part of the 1980s (Dussel Peters 2000). The substantial external debt, large fiscal deficit and hyperinflation levels during the late 1970s and early 1980s were interpreted by Mexican authorities as incontestable 'symptoms' of the decline of the imports substitution model in place since the late 1930s (Aspe 1993; Villarreal 1997). To carry out this transition, Mexico's government radically changed its rhetoric in only a few years, from embracing trade protectionism to promoting free-trade agreements, but with the same goal in mind: to achieve a higher level of competitiveness for the local industry and to create long-term sustainable jobs for the population (Aspe 1993). While the imports substitution model was used so the state could directly intervene in order to support local industry, the exports oriented model mainly supports trade liberalisation and free market mechanisms (Dussel Peters 2000; De la Garza and Salas Páez 2006).

In pursuing the liberalisation strategy, Mexico joined the General Agreement on Tariffs and Trade (GATT, the predecessor of the World Trade Organisation) in 1986; and an ambitious privatisation programme took place. Also, national pacts between workers and employers were sponsored by the government to control salaries and prices; public expenditure was significantly reduced (under the accounting premises of the World Bank and the International Monetary Fund); and the Mexican Congress passed a set of legal reforms to relax business regulations (especially those related to foreign direct investment) (López 1998; Dussel Peters 2000). In summary, the Mexican version of the exports oriented industrialisation strategy essentially followed the same free market principles that were promoted by the 'Washington Consensus' (Dussel Peters et al. 2003). In 1994, the liberalisation strategy in Mexico reached one of its main goals: the North American Free Trade Agreement (NAFTA) took place in association with the United States and Canada.

With the liberalisation regime, Mexico achieved a record number of historical exports; the fiscal deficit was reduced; and inflation, rate interests and currency exchanges were stabilised during the 1990s (López 1998; Fujii 2006). Also, the country attracted large amounts of foreign direct investment in manufacturing. This situation is congruent with the opinion of the Economic Commission for Latin America and the Caribbean (ECLAC), in the sense that Mexico remains an *efficiency-seeking inward FDI* destination. This is a type of investment geared towards exports to third markets (especially those of the United States) and has been primarily located in electronic, automotive and apparel industries in the country (ECLAC 2007). In general, under the premises of free market initiatives Mexico succeeded in increasing its share of the global exports market and created a relatively stable and attractive environment for business (Dussel Peters et al. 2003).

However, there are also substantial criticisms to the liberalisation strategy. The exports boom lasted only until 2001 and it is argued that it was not closely related to the modest economic growth experienced by the country in those years (Dussel Peters 2000; Fujii 2006). In addition, despite the exports dynamism, Mexico experienced systematic trade deficits due to larger imports. For some commentators, Mexican industrial capabilities have become largely subordinated to the global strategies of foreign companies (Dussel Peters et al. 2003; Dussel Peters 2008). As a result of global commodity chains mechanisms (Gereffi and Korzeniewicz 1994; Gereffi 1999), large amounts of raw materials and components were imported into the country for assembling and then re-exported to the U.S. and Canadian markets. In this context it has been argued that because emerging countries like Mexico are not producing goods for internal consumption, but for its trading in external markets, they are chained to a systematic dependence on imported consumption goods (Dussel Peters 2000; Stiglitz 2003; McMichael 2004).

On the other hand, the economic stability achieved did not trigger higher levels of economic growth and only a small portion of the local industry base and geographic regions have been linked to exports-oriented activities (Dussel Peters 2000; Dussel Peters et al. 2003; Fujii 2006). This economic model has also been criticised for not creating new employment positions at the pace and quantity required. Every year, one million workers enter the local labour market but only about 350,000 jobs have been created per year by the formal economy during the last 10 years (Fujii 2006; García 2009). As a consequence, informal activities are a growing proportion of gross domestic product and total employment. Some authors calculate that up to 40% of GDP and employment comes from the informal economy (De la Garza and Salas Páez 2006; Fujii 2006). In fact, one of the main challenges for the Mexican economy is not the rising proportion of temporary, part-time or service contracts but the immense proportion of workers without any kind of legal protection at all (De la Garza and Salas Páez 2006).

There was also an important wave of foreign investment in services, or what the ECLAC calls *market-seeking inward FDI*. In 2006, for instance, Mexico received US$18.9 billion of FDI and 38% was invested in services (ECLAC 2007), a proportion that has been stable over the last few years (about 40%), apart from 2001 when 79% of the FDI in Mexico was spent on services, due to the effect of the acquisition of the Mexican bank Banamex by Citigroup (ECLAC 2007).

How to explain the entry of multinational corporations of the service sector into the market of a relatively poor developing country, especially when talking about a country like Mexico whose consumption levels could be strictly constrained by its annual GDP per capita of US$8,340 (according to the World Bank in 2007), and which has 40% of its total population living in poverty (INEGI 2005)? During the 1990s, Mexico suddenly became the target of world-class names such as America Online, *Telefónica de España*, BBVA, HSBC and Wal-Mart. Overall, there are two main reasons to explain this interest in the Mexican market: the removal of restrictions for foreign capital was successful in attracting foreign companies, and the size of the country and its income polarisation allows the existence of a large lower and upper middle class, which can be targeted by Mercedes Benz, as well as Wal-Mart or McDonald's.

Many of these arguments are strongly connected to formal reforms of the regulation of capital mobility in Mexico, but there are few arguments about similar changes in the labour market. As mentioned in the section about industrial relations in Mexico, the current labour regulation dates back to 1971 and does not explicitly recognise different types of contractual arrangements that are common nowadays, such as outsourcing (Alcalde Justiniani 2005; de Buen Lozano 2005; De la Garza 2005; Reynoso 2005). In more than 1,010 articles on labour law there is no mention of the words 'outsourcing' or 'subcontracting'. However, the same law recognises that there are circumstances in which a single employee might have multiple employers, but all employers are equally responsible for the rights and obligations contained in the employment relationship and contract (De la Garza 2005; Reynoso 2005). Fortunately, labour arrangements under outsourcing regimes are now receiving more attention from unions (de Buen Lozano 2005; De la Garza 2005; Micheli 2005; Reynoso 2005).

Is it possible that the labour regulation has been left behind from the rest of the structural reforms in the country? Is it possible to have a paternalistic labour regulation as part of a free-market-oriented economic policy? What has been the role of labour and its local institutions in the attraction and emergence of FDI and the creation of new industries such as call centres? Actually, the findings of this research suggest that the emergence of new service industries such as call centres in Mexico can be largely explained by this apparent 'contradiction': the combination of a deregulation process for capital mobility that allowed banking and telecommunication companies to expand into other businesses and the lack of enforcement of the labour law that make call centres an attractive industry for investment and business expansion (in addition, of course, to the large pool of workers with the right skills for the industry.

### 2.1.4. The emergence and expansion of a new industry: a brief history of call centres in Mexico

Many of the multinational corporations that entered Mexico during the liberalisation process were involved in processes of mergers and acquisitions with local companies (ECLAC 2007). This was the case for banks such as Citigroup or BBVA, or retail trade companies such as Wal-Mart (Ramírez 1999; 2002; McKinsey 2003; Álvarez-Galván and Tilly 2006; Garza 2006). After these initial steps, most of the foreign companies eventually undertook vertical disintegration (Dussel Peters et al. 2003); in many cases, customer services were regarded as the lowest point in the organisational structure and targets of this disintegration. Call centres were considered a fundamental part of these services and were eventually moved out from the organisations. As part of this process, the emergence and expansion of the call centre industry, and its subcontracted segment specifically, were driven mainly by the strategies of giant telecommunications and banking companies (IMT 2006). In Mexico, all the big players of the call centre industry – Phonemex, Telvista, Technotronics or Sitel – have strong connections with giant telecommunications or banking firms such as *Teléfonos de México*, *Telefónica de España*, *Banco Santander* and BBVA. Indeed, the market targeted by call centres is still dominated by these two sectors (IMT 2006; 2007). In 2007, about 340,000 people were employed by the call centre industry and 95,000 of them were allocated to any of the 120 companies of the outsourced segment (IMT 2007).

There is no any specific industry association for call centres in Mexico and they do not belong to any major industrial association. However, call centre companies and their staff in Mexico have a very active social and organisational life. In many ways, the Mexican Institute of Teleservices is responsible for it. The *Instituto Mexicano del Telemarketing* (Mexican Institute of Telemarketing) was founded in 1991, but it changed its name to *Instituto Mexicano de Tele-servicios* (Mexican Institute of Teleservices; IMT) in 2007. According to the director of the institute, the original goal of creating the institute was two-fold: to train the personnel needed for the telemarketing industry, and to promote marketing services across call centres and their clients. Some years ago, a group of large call centres and the IMT were thinking about the possibility of joining the *Cámara Nacional de la Industria Electrónica, de Telecomunicaciones e Información* (National Association for the Electronics, Telecommunications and Information Industries; CANIETI). However, they decided not to join any association until the industry would be strong enough to defend its interests as a unique and solid group. At that time, as a recently created industry, they were concerned about the possibility of not being heard or taken into account within any major industry association (interview with the general director of the IMT). Here, as we can see, the argument of power asymmetries, coordination and trust emerges as an important factor in inter-firm relations and networks.

The IMT holds two annual congresses that are key events for staff of the companies in the sector. One takes place in March and is based in Mexico City; the second is in September and based in Monterrey (a northern industrial city). The IMT publishes a bi-monthly business magazine called *Contact Forum*, which contains information about human resources practices, IT solutions, training opportunities, job vacancies and other services, and has news from the industry. Recently, the IMT has been encouraging the adoption of a formal certificate for the operation and management of call centres, a type of national standards intended to increase the quality of services offered and the employment conditions in the industry. The IMT recently obtained the patent of this certification in a procedure at the Mexican Institute of Industrial Property (the institution responsible for the use of copyrights in Mexico).

Importantly, the IMT has established a set of annual prizes, including for the best technology, best human resources practices, best customer relations management and best new company in the sector. Through its magazine *Contact Forum*, the IMT calls for nominations in each category and each company votes. During the annual congress celebrated in Mexico City, the prizes are handed out during a gala dinner:

This is one of the reasons why the IMT is successful without being the official association representing all call centres. It is because they are excellent in marketing. They always get the attention of companies to participate in prizes or events. The IMT creates a 'nice' visibility for the sector. They project a very sophisticated image of the industry and people love that.
—Owner of a small call centre.

There is no question that the IMT plays a crucial role in the life and projection of the industry and that its initiatives tend to raise the profile of call centres and the services delivered. However, the IMT is still a private organisation and most of its resources are aimed at those who can afford them.

## 2.2. The research design: a case study approach

Carrying out empirical and qualitative research entails some important challenges at different levels. Very often, qualitative research has to respond to concerns and criticisms related to external validity, the extent to which the conclusions obtained from the analysis of a specific case of study can be generalised (Silverman 2001; Bryman 2004), or the extent to which the case study selected is representative of the entire population. The challenge is even bigger when the information available about a specific case study is scarce and incomplete, which is not uncommon in the social sciences where absolute control over experiments is impossible (Silverman 2001; 2004). In this regard, the guide of intuition can be useful when building a research strategy, selecting a research design and making use of different methodological tools in particular contexts.

To undertake this research, a case study approach was selected based on the type of research questions formulated, references in the literature and resources available for this investigation. It is frequently argued that there are not better or worse types of research designs or methodological approaches *per se* because each type might be useful for particular kinds of research questions, the resources available, and the existing knowledge derived from previous research (Yin 1994; Hakim 2000; Silverman 2001; 2004). Nonetheless, other authors might consider important to make clear distinctions about the attributes of different *types* of social research, such as quantitative or qualitative research (Bryman 2004). In any case, in the social sciences, any research design is expected to be a rigorous test of a well-defined thesis independent of whether the approaches are qualitative or quantitative (Merton 1959; King et al. 1994; Hakim 2000).

In this research, the call centre industry was chosen as a case of study of labour outsourcing in the service economy. This is an exemplifying case study in the way defined by Bryman: "cases are often chosen not because they are extreme or unusual in some way but because they will provide a suitable context for certain research questions to be answered. As such, they [exemplifying cases] allow the researcher to examine key social processes" (Bryman 2004:51). The profile of call centre work is emblematic of the new economy and the presence of multiple clients of different backgrounds is a fruitful terrain to explore workers' experiences and employment relations in a context of intense inter-organisational arrangements and interactions (Moss et al. 2008).

The type of research questions formulated by this thesis, about how workers' experiences and employment conditions are affected by subcontractors' problems of coordination and negotiation with client firms, required a close and careful examination that seemed more suited to a qualitative strategy, especially when dealing with a relatively small number of observations. The analysis of how the entire labour process takes place, its tensions and problems in a multi-employer site like call centres required the elaboration of primary observations and data. Therefore, I decided on a period of intensive fieldwork to collect the information.

There were several other reasons to follow this type of research design. There are no public statistics or detailed descriptions about non-standard forms of employment in service work in Mexico yet. In particular, there is no detailed information about employment and work in call centres in Mexico yet, and almost all the information available is collected, processed and distributed by the Mexican Institute of Teleservices. Being a private company, its procedures and methodology to gather the information are not open to public scrutiny, so a case study approach was better suited to build an in-depth knowledge of the industry and its workers. Most of the sociological literature on front-line work and call centres has been written using case studies (Glucksmann 2009; Paulet 2009). As mentioned earlier, I believe that this type of approach is particularly well suited for collecting information about workers' experiences and employment relations when multi-employers and organisations are involved. However, I also wanted to enrich my primary observations, notes and data by using secondary data analysis to provide the reader with a more general view at macro/industry level.

This research did not collect longitudinal data but a snapshot of work and employment relations in subcontracted call centres at one particular point in time. Nonetheless, this case study approach allowed me to become familiar with the recent history and evolution of each organisation studied, building a more solid and informed analysis. This helped to compensate for some of the disadvantages of not using a more quantitative-oriented longitudinal analysis. This point has been particularly useful when discussing the origins and evolution of call centres in Mexico and when the historical importance of the firms and participants chosen becomes more revealing. The companies selected to be studied in this research meet the criteria developed by Noyelle[1] about how to draw generalisations from a case study approach:

> Typically firms selected for case studies tend to be 'lead' firms: they are often more progressive in the introduction of new technology than their competitors, are often gaining markets shares over their competitors and, not unlikely, are performing better financially. Not surprisingly then, they often precede others in organisational innovation, new uses of human resources, new skills, and new training. But the way in which leading firms are changing usually points to changes other firms might be likely to undergo if they are to survive in a transforming market environment. In that sense, case studies of lead firms are extremely useful as long as we remember the limitations of their findings.
> (Noyelle 1990:229)

Thus the cases of subcontracted call centres presented in this research are a good theoretical example of the critical elements identified by the literature on outsourcing and service work: a) they are leading companies in the sector in terms of workforce size, revenue, and diversity and prestige of their clients; these call centres offer a huge diversity of services for many different client companies, from credit card sales for banks to technical support for customers of software firms; b) these call centres operate in an environment where interactions between customers and workers are an essential part of the service or product delivered; c) they carry out a service activity subjected to the tensions between the standardisation of processes and the customisation of goods/services; d) they undertake a type of service interaction that is supported and monitored using IT systems largely affecting workers' self-discretion and autonomy; e) the Mexican call centre industry operates in a setting of intense competition, fast technical change and shorter product cycles where client companies and subcontractors often pursue contradictory goals; and f) there is a significant presence of women and young college-

---

[1] When analysing skills, wages and productivity in the service sector using case studies, Noyelle defends the advantages of looking at 'leading firms' rather than any other type (Noyelle, 1990:229).

educated workers in the call service industry.[2] Finally – and this is one of
the main areas where this research is likely to make a contribution to the
existing literature – the research also explores in more detail the
administrative structure of call centres in the sixth and final empirical
chapter, by looking at the role and experience of managers. In most of the
cases, the administrative structure of call centres comprises 5-10 per cent
of the total workforce. Staff in administrative positions benefit from
having good career opportunities and relatively good employment
conditions, and yet it was in this segment of the workforce where I
detected the highest levels of tension and dissatisfaction. These results
seem to contradict the findings of many studies about work in the new
economy where higher levels of autonomy tend to be associated with
higher level of satisfaction in workers (Baldry et al. 2007). However, the
most interesting thing about the managers' case is that, contrary to what
happens in the rest of the subcontracted organisation, the boundaries of the
firm seem to be re-established in managerial circles, where higher levels of
commitment and loyalty are needed in order to protect and support the
expansion of the firm.

## 2.3. The four organisations selected

The companies selected for the study can be considered leaders of the
industry in Mexico and the Spanish-speaking world and are representative
of the services offered by call centres in Mexico City and the entire
country. They were selected after considering the information available for
the industry, taking into account the advice and discussions with
specialists and consultants from the IMT in informal conversations and
recorded interviews, and the conditions of accessibility to the firms that
were faced during the fieldwork. The goal was to have access to a group of
organisations that: a) were leading companies in the country – taking into
account the advantages of looking at leading firms as stated by Noyelle

---

[2] However, it is important to be aware of the 'real' dimensions of the 'call centre
phenomenon' in Mexico in terms of employment. Despite its explosive expansion
over the last years, the call centre workforce, and more specifically the portion
allocated in the outsourced segment, comprises only a tiny fraction of all
employees in the country. Other relevant and traditional sectors such as
manufacturing (7.5 million) or construction (3 million) employ a much larger
segment of the workforce, and other service activities employ even more people
(for example, Wal-Mart, the biggest supermarket store in Mexico, employs slightly
more people than the entire outsourced call centre segment).

(1990); b) had a large diversity of client firms; and c) also included a good variety of categories of jobs for the workforce.

After a series of emails, phone conversations and even face-to-face conversations with executives and directors of several firms, four organisations were selected. The managers of the four organisations declared their commitment to provide me with unrestricted access to their employees, and confidentiality in handling information was agreed in all cases. In order to protect the identity of the participants, their names and those of their organisations have been changed and appear here as: Phonemex (a foreign firm, the largest call centre company in Mexico); KPM (a large Mexican competitor); Datatech (also a foreign firm and the largest help desk in Mexico); and Technotronics (the only company with a 'real' union in the industry). These companies' profiles are described in the following sections.

### 2.3.1. Phonemex: the Spanish giant

The main case of study in this research is the Spanish company Phonemex. Phonemex is the most important call centre company in Mexico, and in the Spanish and Portuguese world when measuring revenues and employment (IMT 2007). This company operates globally with other subsidiaries dispersed across the world in Latin America, Asia, Africa and Europe. Very importantly, Phonemex belongs to the Spanish telecommunication giant *Telefónica de España*, and many of Phonemex's contracts come from this company and other subsidiaries in the same holding. For example, in Mexico City, Phonemex operates the call centre of *Telefónica de España* 'in-house', so it is one of the rare cases in the industry where the call centre company is allocated 'inside' the facilities of the client firm. According to one corporate director interviewed (in Spain), Phonemex was created as a business opportunity to obtain quick financial returns in the stock market:

> At the beginning the board of directors was interested in the creation of an entire group of spillovers, make the companies grow up quickly, and then selling them immediately in order to take advantage of favourable conditions in the stock market at that time. However, the results have been excellent and the company became profitable very soon. Now, we continue with the expansion process and I must say that this is the only spill-over which remains in the corporation after almost ten years.
> —Corporate Director, Phonemex.

Phonemex was set up in the Mexican market in 2001. At that time there was just one client firm, five workstations and only 20 employees, including agents, supervisors, managers and directors. In 2009 Phonemex employed more than 24,000 workers in almost 12,000 workstations distributed in ten units located in four different states within the country and providing services to more than 55 firms in different industries such as banking, insurance, airlines, software, retail, education, electronics and pharmaceuticals (Expansión 2009). More recently, Phonemex has become one of the top 500 companies in Mexico in terms of revenues (rank 252) and employment (rank 26!) (Expansión 2009). Phonemex should be consider a central piece for the understanding and analysis of the call centre industry in Mexico in many respects: it is not just the biggest employer but also the most influential actor in the sector; the company has the most experienced managerial group (most of them previously employed by its rival Technotronics); and it has been persistently ranked near the top of the Great Place to Work list.

### 2.3.2. KPM: a Mexican competitor

The second company is the Mexican company KPM, which is a large firm that was created in 2001 by five Mexican shareholders, all of them with previous experience in the financial industry and coming from the same organisation. One of the shareholders and a current corporate director explained how this common background in the financial sector was crucial in creating the new company:

> We all worked together in a big foreign bank in Mexico City [Citibank-Banamex]. It was in this bank where we witnessed how telemarketing services were introduced and became important for financial services. Actually, some of us got directly involved in the process. We learnt a lot from that experience but, more importantly, when we left the bank we were convinced that call centres were a very attractive business opportunity in the country.
> —Corporate Director, KPM.

Six years later, KPM operates three different centres, two of them in Mexico City and the third one (created in 2006) in a provincial state. In total, KPM employs about 1,500 people and has about 15 different clients, all of them from the banking and insurance sectors. The corporate director did not talk openly about how KPM managed to have so many clients from the financial sector, but my best guess, after listening to the whole interview again and revising my fieldwork notes, is that he and his partners used the business and social connections created alongside their careers in the bank to get some clients for their call centre afterwards. Also, according to my own observations and conversations in the field, KPM is one of the most active organisations in the social and organisational life of the sector.

### 2.3.3. Datatech: the high end customer segment

The third organisation is Datatech, a Dutch company of helpdesk services. This company is located in a very exclusive zone of the metropolitan area of Mexico City known as *Interlomas*. The centre is part of a global corporation focused on business software solutions. The centre in Mexico was originally created to provide technical support to just one client in the United States. After some months in operation, however, the headquarters went on expanding its services, hoping to attract more clients with business interests anywhere on the American continent. The company already had two similar units, one in Europe and the other one in South Asia. This is how one corporate director explained the origins and expansion of the operations in Mexico:

> In 2003, people at the headquarters finally realised that the outsourcing of helpdesk services could be a profitable business for the company in this country. Mexico was selected due to the successful experience we had with one client but also because Mexico represented the best combination of cost and quality for the firm. In Mexico we have a great pool of skilled people.
> —Corporate Director, Datatech.

In 2009, Datatech had about 500 employees and more than 25 clients in the financial, software and pharmaceutical industries. Despite its relatively small size Datatech has one of the highest revenues in Mexico (rank 479) (Expansión 2009). The company provides services in Spanish, French, Portuguese and English, uses the highest security measures and imposes the most restricted access in the industry that I observed during this research, characteristics that reinforce its image as a high-tech organisation. In many ways, Datatech has the highest profile of labour skills and clients and the location of the firm in the *Interlomas* area makes a powerful status statement about the company: it projects the image of exclusiveness and technical sophistication.

### 2.3.4. Technotronics: home of the only union in the industry

The fourth and final source of information was the company Technotronics, which is a subsidiary of the Mexican giant Telmex (*Teléfonos de México*, Telephones of Mexico), a telecommunication company which dominates the local market and is expanding rapidly to other Latin American countries under the brand name *América Móvil* (BBC 2009). Telmex belongs to the holding *Grupo Carso*, whose major shareholder is Carlos Slim, one of the richest men in the world (BBC 2009). Technotronics was one of the few subcontracted call centres that had a union and was perhaps the only one with 'real' union representation for workers. This company only provides services to companies in the same corporate holding (*Grupo Carso*) since the call centre is not allowed to have any kind of 'external' clients; this restriction was imposed by the board of directors after the company was unionised in 1998.

After completing a first round of exploratory interviews with unionised workers, I lost contact with the union, executives and managers of Technotronics. However, the information collected in informal conversations with members of this company was extremely valuable. In spite of its lack of commercial openness and its minimal involvement in the institutional life of the sector, the information about this company and its relations with the union are crucial to understand the expansion of the industry and the characteristics of employment conditions. Table 2-6 shows some relevant indicators of the call centre industry in Mexico.

## 2.4. The unit of analysis: accounts and job categories

'Account' is the concept used in Mexican call centres to name the contract with client firms and 'platform' is the term used to name the specific physical space in which the services for individual clients are undertaken. In practice, managers and workers in call centres tend to use these terms at random. Another frequent expression in the Mexican context is 'campaign'; however, 'account' is still the most popular term and it is also a regular expression in the Anglo-Saxon literature on call centres (Taylor and Bain 1999).

**Table 2-6. Mexico: general indicators of the call centre industry 2007**

| Dimensions | | |
|---|---|---|
| No. of workstations | 214,000 | |
| Total employment | 341,000 | |
| No. of companies | 21,262 | |
| Proportion of the Latin American industry | 29.5% | |
| **2006 employment growth** | | |
| Mexico | 21% | |
| Latin America | 15% | |
| Worldwide | 6% | |
| **Establishment size** | | |
| No. of workstations | Companies | % |
| < 20 | 16,500 | 77.6 |
| 21-100 | 4,400 | 20.7 |
| > 100 | 362 | 1.7 |
| Total | 21,262 | 100.0 |
| **Cost structure** | | |
| Human resources | 63% | |
| Telephone lines and internet | 19% | |
| Technological infrastructure | 9% | |
| Other utilities | 9% | |
| **Industry structure** | | |
| | Companies | Employees |
| In-house | 21,142 | 246,000 |
| Outsourcing | 120 | 95,000 |
| Outsourcing segment | | |
| No. of workstations | 20,885 | |
| **Outsourcing as proportion of the    industry:** | | |
| Employment | 31.2% | |
| Workstations | 9.8% | |
| Sales | 33% | |
| **Other indicators** | | |
| Workstations oriented to offshoring services | 34% | |

Source: Mexican Institute of Teleservices 2007.

**Table 2-7. Accounts selected in Phonemex**

| Client industry | Outsourced service | Call & contact type |
|---|---|---|
| Financial | Retail credit approval (sales) | Processing information |
| | Automobile credit approval (sales) | Processing information |
| | Banking services (customer services) | Inbound |
| | Insurance services (sales) | Inbound |
| Airlines | Ticket sales & customer support | Inbound |
| | Ticket sales & customer support (bilingual service) | Inbound |
| Telecommunications | Mobile phone services (sales & customer service) | Inbound/outbound |
| Electronics | Computers, audio & video (sales, customer service & technical support) | Inbound |
| Software | Business software solutions (sales, customer service & technical support) | Outbound/Inbound |

Source: Interviews by the author.

In order to explore in detail the outsourcing of front-line service work when multiple organisations are involved, I took advantage of my access to the large and diverse company Phonemex. Within this firm I selected nine different accounts and studied: a) the type of service provided embodied in the type of job design; and b) the client firm industry. In the first dimension, the three basic job categories of front-line service work in call centres were included: a) sales; b) customer services; and c) technical support. These categories illustrate the diversity of work performed in call centres: inbound and outbound calls, information processing and, more recently, contact through email and chat. In the second dimension, the accounts selected were in financial, airline, telecommunication, electronic and software services. The cases of financial, airlines and telecommunication client companies have been included due to their historical connections with the creation and evolution of call centres (Micheli 2002; 2007; Moss et al. 2008) and because these industries often have the largest number of employees within the outsourcing units. Aside from these three historical industries in the sector, electronics and software have been added because, in spite of employing a small proportion of the total workforce, they were reported to be significant contributors to the gross revenues of call centres (Micheli 2002; IMT 2007; Micheli 2007). Table 2-7 provides an overview of the accounts selected in Phonemex.

Because the aim of this research is to analyse service work and outsourcing in the new economy, and particularly the effects of inter-firm relations on workers' experiences and employment conditions, I decided to select just a small number of call centres but with multiple clients in order to focus my attention on employment conditions across different accounts but within the same organisation. I considered that this strategy would be the best way to avoid the effects stemming from the variation in many subcontracted companies. To this effect the accounts selected in the other three companies (KPM, Datatech and Technotronics) were chosen as a comparison group with those already chosen in Phonemex. Table 2-8 presents the accounts selected in the other three companies.

**Table 2-8. Accounts selected in other commercial firms**

| Client industry | Outsourced service | Call & contact type |
|---|---|---|
| Financial (KPM) | Credit card sales | Outbound |
| | Credit card sales | Outbound |
| | Insurance sales | Inbound |
| Software (Datatech) | Software business solutions (technical support) | Inbound |
| Telecommunications (Technotronics) | Internet and phone services (sales, customer service & technical support) | Inbound/Outbound |

Source: Interviews by the author.

The structure of the entire research design at industry level is presented in Table 2-9, which shows how the research design was inspired by the relationship between client companies and internal job designs. I used two axes for including these dimensions; the vertical axis is for job categories and the horizontal axis is for client firm industries. It must be highlighted that breaking down call centre jobs into different categories was crucial for the analysis because each one represented a clear and distinctive job design, different levels of interactions with the client firm, and the potential for different experiences and employment conditions, at least in theory.

**Table 2-9. Structure of the research design**

| Client industry & job category | Financial | Airlines | Telecom. | Electronics | Software |
|---|---|---|---|---|---|
| Technical Support | – | – | Technotronics | Phonemex | Phonemex Datatech |
| Customer Service | Phonemex | Phonemex | Phonemex Technotronics | Phonemex | Phonemex Datatech |
| Sales | Phonemex KPM | Phonemex | Phonemex Technotronics | Phonemex | Phonemex Datatech |

Source: Interviews by the author.

## 2.5. Research methods and data collection tools: interviews and observation

During the period from October 2006 until March 2007, a total of 65 interviews were carried out with workers, supervisors and managers (including corporate directors, human resources managers and unit directors) from the four different companies previously introduced: Phonemex, KPM, Datatech and Technotronics. Interviews took place in nine different facilities, all of them in Mexico City, with the exception of the one for Datatech (which is located in *Interlomas*, in the metropolitan area of the city). All the interviews were carried out face-to-face at the respondent's workplace. In addition, I spent periods of about 8 hours in the workplace where I took notes about the interactions between agents, supervisors, coordinators and managers while doing the interviews. In the cases of agents and supervisors, I selected respondents from those having breaks for meals, smoking or leaving the office after their shifts. In the case of managers and coordinators, I circulated an email through the organisation and they were selected according to their availability and account profile. All the interviews were carried out in private rooms; after obtaining consent from the respondent they were recorded and I transcribed all of them. Table 2-10 shows how the interviews were distributed among the different companies and participants.

**Table 2-10. Respondents by organisation and position**

| By organisation | Managers/a | Supervisors | Workers | Total |
|---|---|---|---|---|
| Phonemex | 9 | 10 | 19 | **38** |
| KPM | 2 | 2 | 4 | **8** |
| Datatech | 3 | 3 | 5 | **11** |
| Technotronics | 2 | 1 | 5 | **8** |
| Total | 16 | 16 | 33 | **65** |

a/ Including corporate directors, human resources and unit managers.
Source: Interviews by the author.

In addition to the interviews with people whose jobs were directly related to call centres, I undertook another 18 interviews with other relevant informants, such as union officials (from two different national unions); Ministry of Labour officials (one from the federal government and the other from the city government); four academics and researchers (three of them from the National University and one of them from the Metropolitan University); two consultants (both specialised in labour issues); five industry representatives (all of them members of the Mexican

Institute of Teleservices, including the president); and three other informants of mixed background: a client company representative; the corporate director of a company, who did not consent to the recording of the conversation; and a corporate official in a large staffing agency (Manpower) which has close business connections with call centres. All these interviews (with the obvious exception of the one that was not recorded) were also transcribed. Table 2-11 summarises the profiles of these additional respondents.

**Table 2-11. Other respondents**

| By profile | No. |
|---|---|
| Union officials | 2 |
| Ministry of Labour officials | 2 |
| Academics & researchers | 4 |
| Consultants | 2 |
| Industry representatives | 5 |
| Other relevant informants | 3 |
| Total | 18 |

Source: Interviews by the author.

In order to gather the information, a set of different semi-structured interviews was designed for managers, supervisors and workers. In accordance with the research questions, the interviews covered four areas: a) labour history and socio-demographic profile of the respondent; b) a description of the current job (including job design, monitoring systems and compensation schemes); c) interactions with the client firm; and d) an evaluation of the respondent's own work in a broader context or perspective. Also, the respondents were asked to complete a brief questionnaire during the second section to provide information about levels of discretion and autonomy at work. The questionnaires contained between 19 questions (for managers) and 27 questions (for workers). They interviews lasted, on average, 65 minutes and the contact details from most of the respondents were collected to have the opportunity of following up questions.

# Conclusion

In order to analyse the effects of inter-firm arrangements on work and employment relations this research undertook the study of subcontracted service work using call centres in Mexico City as an exemplifying case of study. According to Bryman, the main advantage with the use of an exemplifying case is it will "provide a suitable context for certain research questions to be answered" (Bryman 2004:51). As mentioned earlier, the profile of call centre work as emblematic of the new service economy and the presence of multiple clients of different backgrounds is a fruitful terrain to explore work and employment relations in a context of intense inter-organisational arrangements and interactions.

In view of the existing literature on outsourcing, service work and employment conditions in subcontracted call centres are a good case study for different reasons. First, because call centres are an environment where interactions between customers and employees are a crucial part of the service or product delivered. More importantly, within this environment there are significant tensions between the standardisation of process (pushed by call centres) and the customisation of services (pushed by client firms). Second, this sector faces intense competition, faster technical changes, and shorter product-cycles where the pressures for reducing labour costs are considerable; this is a crucial reason for the use of non-standard forms of employment. Finally, a significant proportion of women and young college-educated employees work in this sector, and they are also some of the most vulnerable sectors of the population in the labour market.

The four companies selected are leaders in the industry, in the country, and the Spanish-speaking world (Phonemex is the biggest Spanish-speaking call centre company in the world), and all of them offer a large diversity of services to multiple client firms (with the exception of Technotronics, which is restricted to provide services to other subsidiaries of *Grupo Carso*). Within these organisations the research design was inspired by two variables or units of analysis: job categories/designs and accounts. There are three different front-line job categories in call centres: sales, customer service and technical support; and the accounts correspond to the different client firms from different sectors: financial, airlines, telecommunications, electronics and software. In order to gather information from these job categories and accounts, three different questionnaires were used to carry out semi-structured interviews with the respondents (workers, supervisors and managers). Interviewees were asked to explain their labour history and socio-demographic profile, to describe their current job (including job design, monitoring systems and compensation schemes); to describe their interactions with the client firm; and to evaluate their work in a broader perspective or context.

Finally, it is important to consider the relevance of Mexico as the institutional setting for the analysis undertaken in this investigation. It seems that the emergence of some new service industries in Mexico – such as call centres – has been certainly triggered by the deregulation of capital and the lack of institutional protection for labour. These two factors combined would increase the economic returns from investments in labour-intensive industries. Since the mid-1980s Mexico has experienced an intense period of liberalisation reforms aimed at attracting foreign investment and accessing international markets (Aspe 1993; Dussel Peters et al. 2003; ECLAC 2007). As a result, Mexico's manufacturing exports grew substantially during the second part of the 1990s and started to decline at the beginning of the current century (Dussel Peters et al. 2003; ECLAC 2007).

Furthermore, the attraction of large amounts of foreign investment and the arrival of multinational corporations in manufacturing and services have not generated employment at the rate needed: almost one million people need jobs every year while only 350,000 are created (Ruiz Duran 2005; De la Garza and Salas Páez 2006; García 2009). On the other hand, labour legislation has remained largely untouched since the 1970s although several modern practices such as outsourcing are not covered by it (Bensusán and Rendón 2000; De la Garza 2006; García 2009). In sum, the weak institutional setting of a developing country like Mexico, offers a valuable scope to test the impact of new and flexible inter-firm arrangements on workers' employment conditions.

# CHAPTER THREE

# OUTSOURCING AND MULTI-EMPLOYER
# RELATIONSHIPS:
# PROBLEMS AND CHALLENGES

## 3.1. Outsourcing: conflict and cooperation
## in multi-employer relationships

As discussed in the first chapter, one of the main challenges in outsourcing is the definition of the boundaries of the firm (Coase 1937; Williamson 1979; 1981; DiMaggio 2001; Marchington et al. 2005). Outsourcing is understood as an arrangement for the production of goods or services under the specifications of the client firm. In practice, when the product acquired is not firm-specific, organisations might use spot contracts, whereas in services where outsourcing implies repeated interactions and negotiations between organisations, relational contracts seem to be more suitable (Kay 1995). This is because the provision of a service might be a complex activity and requires direct interaction with customers, but also constant interactions with the client firm as a source of support and information. Intuitively, it seems that the outsourcing of services might require a high degree of monitoring and coordination between the organisations involved. Is this relationship dominated by conflict or cooperation? Or both? According to the flexible firm model, any type of flexible arrangement between organisations must be based on strong cooperation and coordination (Piore and Sabel 1984; Castells 1996); however, other approaches would emphasise the role of asymmetric power and information as a source of either intense competition (Porter 1998) or constant conflict and tension between organisations (DiMaggio 2001; Marchington et al. 2005).

During the interviews for this research, call centre managers insisted that they were entirely responsible for managing the labour force, from selection up to termination of contracts – they neither required nor allowed major assistance or intervention from the client firm. Thus there was no room or even reason for external intervention from the client firm; it was against the criteria of efficient specialisation (Perrow 1986; Lacity and Hirschheim 1993; Porter 1998). Nonetheless, these call centre managers also said (normally at the end of the interviews, when they had greater trust in me) that it was not easy to achieve complete sovereignty over the workplace and most of them accepted that one of the big challenges in their relationship with client firms was to maintain independence over the operation of individual accounts:

> There are some clients who want to enter into 'our kitchen' and we need to push them out and sit them down, tell them that they have to enjoy the meal, tell them that we are the chefs and that everything is going to be fine. We have to persuade them that we are the experts and that they should trust us; because this is exactly the reason why they contracted us, that's the idea behind outsourcing! Isn't it?
> —Manager, Datatech.

Therefore, it seems that conflict and tension exist alongside trust and cooperation in the outsourcing of call centres as it has been also identified in manufacturing (Lorenz 1988; 1992; Sako and Helper 1998; Lorenz 1999). These tensions between client firms and subcontractors revealed that the two parties lacked common goals. We already know that client firms tend to demand higher levels of quality in the service while call centres seem to be more inclined to focus their efforts on maximising the total number of calls answered (Korczynski 2002). According to the staff in the Mexican Institute of Teleservices (IMT), a major source of conflict has to do with the type of agreements between organisations about how the service is charged:

> At the beginning, some years ago, during the late 1990s, call centres charged by the number of seats or workstations available at the accounts. Later, clients realised that this was very inefficient, due to the demand peaks during the day and across the year. Sometimes, they had 100 agents when only 50 were needed. Now they tend to be more focused on the number of calls answered... Therefore, there is much pressure now on agents to answer as many calls as they can... and, well, this is pushing quality down. More recently, there are some efforts, from both sides, to reach an intermediate point for service agreements between quantity and quality.
> —Consultant, IMT.

In front-line service work, the administration of the labour force and provision of services are closely related. According to the IMT (2007) and information from global studies (Batt et al. 2007), about 60 per cent of total costs in call centres are labour costs. Therefore, careful administration of this area can lead to cost reduction and influence the quality of the service. If the two organisations have a 'common' workforce, why is there so much resistance from the subcontractor to giving up some control to the client firm? My own observations and responses from managers suggest that the fundamental reason for this has to do with the multi-employer profile of the site, specifically, because subcontractors wanted to avoid tensions *among* and *with* employees. The next quote illustrates this:

> We do not allow clients to get involved in how we manage and pay our people. We know that they are looking for cost reduction... but we need to keep the balance and equality inside the organisation. To do so, we use the external labour market as a reference. We want to compensate our people fairly and impartially but at the same time we need to avoid salary inflation inside the organisation.
> —Human Resources Manager, Phonemex

However, the relationship between call centres and client firms needs to be flexible and call centre managers cannot simply ignore the opinions or 'recommendations' from client firms about the managing of the workplace, and a relational contract seems to be the appropriate way of dealing with these tensions. In some cases, as a way of building up trust between the parties, call centres 'reserve' a physical space (inside the workplace) for the client firm representatives: "Our clients know that they are welcome at any time. Actually, they know that they have a seat next to *us*, an office in *their* accounts. Our clients know perfectly well that they are allowed to come whenever they want" (CEO of Phonemex for Mexico and Central America). Nonetheless, despite the efforts to build an environment of cooperation and trust, tensions between client firms and subcontractors remain a distinctive characteristic of the day-to-day operation of subcontracted workplaces.

For example, when administering the account, client firms seemed to be particularly concerned about the turnover rate and its potential implications for the operation. Interestingly, the same manager who had previously declared that the call centre had total responsibility over the administration of the workforce, blamed client firm representatives for high turnover rates in a further statement:

> In call centres, we understand turnover as a seasonal problem due to the large proportion of students we have here. But sometimes they [the clients] get scared because turnover increases, so they come into my office saying:

"I am having too much turnover!" [She shouts] and then I say: "So, be nice
with them".
—Human Resources Manager, Phonemex

The situation in this account could be considered typical according to
my other conversations with human resources managers in call centres.
Without exception, managers insisted that they were the only ones who
had absolute responsibility for the whole administration of the workplace.
However, as the interviews progressed and the level of trust with the
researcher increased, these managers admitted that, in fact, client firms
and their representatives were key determinants of the work experience
and employment conditions, and that these representatives actually interact
with employees in the subcontracted workplace:

Bancomer [a bank] as a client is very 'cool' [in English in the original],
and Telefónica [a telecommunications company] is... well... [long pause
and she smiles]. In both cases we have the client representative 'living'
with us [this means that the client firm representative had an office, a
'physical' space in the account located in the subcontracted call centre].
But in one of the cases Ana [Bancomer's representative] comes out of her
office and cheers them, dances, she does whatever she needs to do in order
to support them. But in our Puebla branch [with Telefónica] it is not the
same thing. Over there, the client representative comes out and... SNAP!
[she makes a whip sound]... shouts at everyone that the account is not
reaching the goals.
—Human Resources Manager, Phonemex

These tensions and conflicts between call centre managers and client
firm representatives have significant effects on workers. For example,
workers realised that there were notorious differences over employment
conditions and work experiences among accounts. In many cases, even
those workers who had not joined the company yet, who were only
candidates, appeared to be informed of this situation thanks to word-of-
mouth and social networks operating at the recruitment stage, something
that has been previously detected in other analyses of call centre work
(Fernandez et al. 2000; Castilla 2005) and was characteristic of older
industries (Grint 2005). It is interesting – and surprising – that this rather
unsophisticated and ancient form of recruitment persists in the supposedly
hi-tech service economy. It is evident that workers and candidates get a
great deal of information from the social network. For example, candidates
used this information to pursue a job in their preferred account:

Some job applicants do not want to work in particular accounts due to the reputation of clients. Candidates tell us things like: "I was told that you have vacancies at Bancomer, US Airways and Sony, I am only interested in these three, these are the ones where I want to work... I am sure about this, so do not send me to any other".
—Human Resources Manager, Phonemex

Therefore, despite the constant claims of call centre managers about their total independence in the administration of the workforce, there is no doubt that client firms played a significant role in shaping workers' experiences and employment conditions within the subcontracted workplace. Moreover, the administration of the subcontracted workforce seems to be a disputed task between both organisations.

### 3.1.1. Tensions in multiemployer sites: distrust during recruitment and selection

The first point of tension between organisations in relation to the administration of front-line services is very simple and straightforward: it is about which workers will be recruited and selected to carry out the service; and this is not a trivial issue. For the client firm, these workers will represent the voice of the company and shape customers' impressions and experiences. However, subcontracted firms seem to be concerned about how to fit the new workforce into the complex mosaic of different services and clients that they have without causing major disturbances (Baron and Kreps 1999). Here, the transaction cost approach seems to be useful in predicting which services would generate more tensions than others. According to Williamson, those operations involving more firm-specific skills would result in higher transaction costs of monitoring and securing information (Williamson 1979; 1981), and this type of operations would tend to be internalised or regulated with relational contracts when using the market. The evidence collected in this research seems to confirm this view, since higher levels of tension and interaction between companies occur more frequently in customer segments of higher revenue and where there is more service specialisation, such as technical support for large companies (as in Datatech, the Dutch helpdesk). Among subcontracted call centres, software and electronic clients are more likely to participate in the final selection of job candidates than banking and airline companies. However, all the companies, in one way or another, showed some interest in the way the subcontracted staff is selected.

Very often, the client firms allow call centres to make the initial round of interviews; after this process the main candidates are shortlisted and, at this point, client firm representatives from software and electronics companies are more likely to join a selection panel in order to make the final decision about who would be hired; this practice might not be very pleasant for subcontractors. According to call centre managers, this practice could have some negative side-effects on candidates, who might feel over exposed during the selection process:

> Some clients want to participate in the final stages of the selection process in order to make sure that the people we are choosing have the profile they are looking for... that's fine for us... However, they do not understand that it is not necessarily good to put too much pressure on people during the interview and screening processes. Just think about this for a second... sometimes you have a little kid, he is very young and this is his first job interview in life, and he has to be sitting in front of four old guys asking him all sorts of questions! Like a professional exam! [The exam required to get a Bachelor's Degree in Mexico.]
> —Human Resources Manager, Phonemex

However, these negative side-effects on candidates were not the only undesirable outcome of sharing the responsibility of selecting staff with client firms. During the period of interviews and observation, I also detected that call centre managers avoided joint staff selection procedures because frictions and tensions with the client firm could be noticed by workers. Unexpectedly, workers could be aware of the tensions between the two 'employers', the two sources of authority and power in the workplace. As mentioned, these tensions seem to increase in the higher levels of customer service and revenue for the firms, especially in technical support services provided by highly skilled workers:

> The most difficult thing I've ever done in human resources was the setting up of the Microsoft account. It was difficult because we did not understand each other very well. These guys were looking for 'Hollywood stars', not for ordinary agents. For call centre work your basic tool is the telephone, you will be at the phone most of the time in order to transmit and receive information, but candidates for technical support in Microsoft get mad with this kind of job description... After our initial selection we had a final round of interviews with Microsoft representatives in the panel. At the very beginning of the interview, people from Microsoft asked the candidates: "Did they tell you what a call centre is about and what type of work you will do?" Of course we did! But the candidates used to say "No"... only to create confusion between the clients and us! You have no idea how bad it was.
> —Human Resources Manager, Phonemex

Nevertheless, tensions among call centres and client firms at the entry point, during recruitment and selection of workers, were just the beginning. Once workers are selected, more tensions and divergences between organisations and employees emerge during training and operation stages.

### 3.1.2. Diverging expectations and results:
### training and operation

When a candidate is selected, he or she starts a training period that might last from only one week up to three months, depending on the job. However, most jobs, those in sales and customer services, do not require more than two weeks of training, as is the case in Britain (Taylor and Bain 1999; Taylor et al. 2002; Taylor and Bain 2007). When workers were asked what type of skills they believe were more appreciated by call centres and their client firms in selection and training, technical/ professional or 'social/soft' skills (such as verbal skills, being able to one's control temper, and patience), the majority of workers said that social skills seem to be more appreciated by both call centres and client firms:

> At the beginning I thought that both were important... I thought that first, because they wanted to know if one had the minimum education they were looking for, people with certain education... then, after the interview, the first filter, they wanted to look at my verbal skills and how I was when interacting with other people... so first they looked for education and then for social skills. Finally, in training everything was about product information... but soon you realise that, the real thing you will need, it is a type of special talent, social talent I would say, for sales.
> —Outsourcing worker, Phonemex Wal-Mart

Workers seem to be confused about the meaning of 'social skills' or 'verbal skills' for this type of job. At the beginning they appeared to be confident about their abilities to speak to others or 'make friends', but suddenly they realise that these abilities are much more demanding than they had expected, and that they might need some training and to use prepared speeches in the form of scripts. This is something that Leidner (1993) notes in her study of insurance sales workers. In positions within sales and customer services there is much stress on workers developing social skills so they are able to handle potentially difficult interactions with customers such as complaints, or 'seducing' unresponsive customers; but even following the scripts is not an absolute guarantee of success:

I think verbal and social skills are the most important tools for this job. I
believe they wanted a good handling of the product, the information and
how to deal with the customer, that you show some experience and
knowledge... At the beginning I needed much time to talk to my customers
because I did not know how to adapt the script to different situations and I
was always trying different ways and making mistakes... but it does not
matter how hard you try, if the other person is in a hurry they do not care
about you so you need to develop special skills to catch people's attention.
The way you talk has to be good and you need to have answers for all their
questions... the script is not always enough. Well... I suppose that some
years ago they would be more concerned about my computer skills. But
now, come on! Most people know how to use a computer but we do not
know how to talk to people! So, I think now they are more interested in
how you present the product and teaching you how to manage the
relationship with customers.
—Outsourcing worker, Phonemex BBVA

The previous paragraph taken from an interview with a sales agent
reveals that for some workers interacting with people in the 'right way',
using the appropriate social and verbal skills, was actually a more complex
task than mastering some of the technical skills needed for using
computers. For this reason, the training period often seems to be focused
on the internalisation of the scripts and procedures to deal with customers.
This is not exactly the same type of training explored by Hochschild in her
case study on flight attendants (1983) but it certainly shows the
importance of emotional labour in the way workers are encouraged to
create the 'right' impression on customers.

However, tensions and problems between subcontractors and client
firms tend to emerge once again at the operation level. It seems as if call
centres and their clients were pursuing different outcomes:

When training they teach you the characteristics of the product and how to
sell it. A week later you need to pass the exam, if not... goodbye... Everything
depends on your learning capacity I guess... If you are a good and quick
learner it is OK, because you will know the product and how to sell it, really.
In the company they want you to make as many calls as you can but the client
[firm] is more interested in the form or how you treat the customer; they are
more concerned about the impression we made on customers.
—Outsourcing worker, Datatech Sybase

Therefore, there is no question that scripts play a crucial role in the
interaction between workers and customers but the extent to which these
instruments satisfied the opposite demands for standardisation and

customisation of the two organisations involved *per se* is not clear enough. As Leidner (1993) suggests, it is important not to underestimate the relevance of scripts and observe them as simple routine mechanisms of workers' and customers' alienation. Scripts also provide agents with a sort of 'comfort zone' where they might feel secure and more relaxed in their interactions with other people and they can adapt these scripts to the goal they prefer: either customisation or standardisation. On the other hand, the use of scripts guarantees a minimum level of service and quality for customers (Leidner 1993).

Interestingly, it is not only the level of tension and conflict between organisations that increases in higher customer segments. Also, levels of workers' resistance to scripts and training procedures seem to increase in job designs that require higher skill levels and more formal education (in technical support services). Technical workers seem to resist the idea that they should be subject to the same 'rules' that apply to staff in other job categories in call centres. These workers are more likely to believe that other skills and procedures are more significant for their jobs, unlike their counterparts in customer services and sales:

> For the type of work I am doing here… for this category… I would say that the most important thing is the technical skills you may have. At least it was my impression in the first interview. In the second place, let's say it was the academic level, and then verbal and social skills last. If you do not have technical skills you are not suitable for the technical training you need here, as simple as that. Here we do things with electronics, not just answer the phones…
> —Outsourcing worker, Phonemex Sony

Technical workers in support services seem to be particularly sensitive to the received wisdom that call centre work is low-skilled. During my interviews and interactions with staff, most technical workers insisted that they were different from other call centre workers, that the skills needed in their work were more sophisticated and their customers were different, more demanding and more prestigious. Not incidentally, these workers were also the best paid but the most dissatisfied, and they were uncomfortable with the popular image of call centre workers. They had different expectations, they were older and better educated and they did not like the idea of being stereotyped as 'call centre boys'. Moreover, technical workers seem to be the group of workers that exploit the conflicts between subcontractors and client firms the most. For example, in my informal conversations with technical workers, they often mention that when they receive contradictory orders from subcontractors and client firms (about the type of treatment or amount of time they should dedicate to customers) they choose the option that is more convenient for them (in terms of time available, revenue obtained, or empathy with the customer). If any of the two 'bosses' (either subcontractors or client firms) complain, technical workers' simply say: "The client firm representative [or the internal supervisor] told me to do so".

In summary, evidence from this research suggests that technical workers seem to have more power – and even obtain certain advantages, when exploiting the tensions and contradictions between subcontractors and client firms. According to McGovern (1998), technical occupations have traditionally been considered secure, not only because they were normally assigned to white collar positions in primary labour markets, but because the apparent exclusivity of the workers' knowledge gives them a better bargaining position in the labour market. In Mexico, as in the Irish case study explored by McGovern (1998), the inflation of credentials, the over-supply of skilled workers, and vertical disintegration practices such as outsourcing have created a more demanding labour market; this is giving organisations the advantage of hiring only the individuals with top qualifications and higher levels of academic performance, even in this secondary labour market of call centre outsourcing.

Overall, it is very difficult to appreciate the tensions between call centres and their clients in recruitment, selection, training and operating in a monolithic way. There is an important division between the three basic job categories in two groups: sales and customer services on the one hand, and technical support agents on the other hand. Workers in the first group appreciate their social skills and networks as an 'open' advantage; they suggest that these abilities and relations are something 'inclusive', something to share with people in Human Resources, and with their friends and acquaintances in the external labour market. They use these abilities to learn more and to socialise with others, and they are a source of satisfaction. However, technical workers play down the importance of social and verbal abilities and appreciate social networks in a restrictive sense. They insisted that their social or 'professional' network was exclusive and closed, to the point that it was inaccessible even to human resources managers. Also, technical workers claimed that technical skills were much more important than any other ability in the workplace in order to complete the tasks they have. In saying so, they try to create a different image for themselves in relation to the rest of the workers in call centres, because technicians do not need to be nice or empathetic simply because they have superior knowledge.

Findings of this research suggest that these problems of cooperation and negotiation between subcontractors and client firms affect workers' experiences and employment conditions. This can be seen most clearly in the levels of loyalty and commitment of employees at work.

### 3.1.3. Problems for loyalty and commitment

For Korczynski (2002), one of the most distinctive characteristics of service work is the tension experienced by workers because of the demands of loyalty and commitment from customers and managers. However, in outsourced services like the call centres analysed in this research, tension increased because workers had to deal with three different sources of power and authority instead of two: customers, call centre managers and client firm representatives. So, who won workers' loyalty and commitment, and how? Workers, as a group, did not offer uniform answers about this. Here is an example:

> I identified myself more with Phonemex [the call centre] because they pay my wages and it is with their people that I deal on a daily basis. But we all have different opinions in that respect.
> —Outsourcing supervisor, Phonemex BBVA-Bancomer

At the beginning of the research, I expected that most employees would have the same opinion when asked about this subject. In the end, workers are physically located inside the call centre, receive their wages from this organisation and interact with other call centre staff most of the time. However, as the fieldwork progressed, other interesting opinions emerged:

> I feel more identification and loyalty towards Metlife [the client firm] because I am much more involved with the work and the information that I process for them. KPM [the call centre] is the organisation where I am physically, where I work, but they have many different clients. I believe that as an employee one is much more involved with one's particular area and client.
> —Outsourcing worker, KPM

Initially, in order to explain these unexpected viewpoints, I believed that identity and loyalty were more influenced by the social status assigned to particular brand names among clients. Workers in the account of a world class firm, such as American Express, would be more likely to display commitment and loyalty to this brand than would those employees who were working in the account of less known and prestigious clients, such as the Mexican retailer Soriana, for example. Also, I considered that there was a chance that more respected brand names would be more successful in internalising their organisation's culture and corporate missions than others, which would give them better control over the emotional display of workers (Hochschild 1983). Banking, telecommunications, electronics and software clients seemed to have a better and more powerful status for workers than the rest of the companies:

> I feel closer to Bancomer [the client]... because their processes are better, they have good planning and organisation. I mean, they do things better, they are a better company and everybody knows that, don't they? I mean their brand has more prestige.
> —Outsourcing worker, Phonemex BBVA Bancomer.

However, some workers also claimed to have a higher level of loyalty to the client firm, not because it represented a higher status but simply because it was the client firm's name – an essential part of the 'raw material' that employees were using all day long. These employees insisted that the work they did was for the client company primarily and not for the call centre, even in situations where the client was 'invisible' in the account:

> I identify myself mostly with Telefónica [the client]... even though I do not know anybody from Telefónica! Anyway, I feel more identified with them because my work is for them. When a customer calls me he or she does not know that I am in Phonemex, I talk to him or her as a Telefónica employee; I talk about its offers, its services, and the company. About Phonemex I do not mention even the name!
> —Outsourcing worker, Phonemex Telefónica

These views would constitute a good example of the alienation in emotion work described by Hochschild (1983) in the sense that workers perform the role assigned to them using the emotional script and personification they are entitled to undertake in the name of the client company. However, and as mentioned before, workers did not all agree about which company they were most loyal and committed towards in their work. The status provided by the reputation of the client firm seemed to be important for some workers, while others were more loyal to the company that they represented in their daily work. However, many workers insisted on the importance of the *physical* presence of the client firm and interactions with their representatives:

Definitely I feel more identification, loyalty, commitment toward Datatech [the call centre] really; I am pretty sure about that... On the other hand, with General Electric, well, we do not have much contact, not at least at my level. We certainly know some medium level managers from General Electric but basically we do not have any contact with them, at least not the type of regular contact that creates some sort of special affinity.
—Outsourcing worker, Datatech General Electric

In the end, most workers recognised that they were situated at a middle point between two employers, and that they had to figure out how to manage a good relationship with the two:

In my case I would go for both because at the end, Sony's well-being is Phonemex's well-being... and my job is for the two organisations... I cannot take sides because I would damage the other side in a way... Actually, you know what? When I am doing my job I feel more like working for Sony but then I realise that I am working in Phonemex and surrounded by Phonemex staff, so the balance changes all the time.
—Outsourcing supervisor, Phonemex Sony

There is no question that there was great confusion about who was the 'real' boss in subcontracted workplaces. The tensions and problems between client firms and call centres generated a special environment where workers displayed different levels of loyalty and commitment to their work and organisations depending on various factors such as status and prestige or the frequency and quality of interactions with these organisations. It seems that, against this apparently chaotic background of loyalty and commitment, many workers are able to gain some advantages for themselves, such as being able to choose the account where they are allocated.

However, it is important to know the extent to which these apparently chaotic relationships, interactions and divided loyalties and commitments really 'damage' the production process and affect workers' experiences and employment conditions. To find this out was a big challenge since I had no opportunity to compare the views of workers 'in-house' with those of workers outsourced in call centres. Instead, I explored the experience of downsized workers, who had previously worked in one of the client firms and were outsourced to an external call centre. In doing so, I collected information from workers contrasting their experiences of working in different places and situations.

## 3.2. The paradox of outsourcing:
## the core importance of downsized workers

As mentioned, the connection between vertical disintegration of banking and telecommunications companies and the emergence of call centre subcontractors is fundamental for understanding the dynamics of work and employment relations in Mexico. Downsized subcontracted workers are crucial for call centres because they are a source of knowledge and experience not only for the organisation but also for younger workers. The workers who were downsized and moved to 'peripheral' areas can be a core factor in the success of the outsourcing. Moreover, in many respects, the experience of downsized workers is useful to enable one to observe the effects of problems and tensions between client firms and subcontractors. These downsized workers were particularly easy to find in the accounts of banking and telecommunications clients. They were usually in their late 20s and early 30s, most of them married, with children and they used to have a 'permanent' post in one of the client firms. To analyse the experience of downsized workers and how they illustrate the potential effects of problems and tensions between subcontractors and client firms, this section looks at the information provided by a key informant.

Mauricio Martínez was an employee in Phonemex; he was 30 years old at the time of the interview (2007). He was married, and had a 5-year-old son. Mauricio had completed all the courses in the School of Management at the University of Mexico but had not taken yet the professional exam in order to obtain the Bachelor's Degree, so like many call centre workers he had not completed his college education. Mauricio arrived in Phonemex in September 2002 as a customer service agent. Before that, he worked in customer services in Bancomer (a Mexican bank recently bought by BBVA, a Spanish consortium). In September 2002, this division of the bank was subcontracted to Phonemex, workers included. This is how Mauricio describes the process:

> The same day Bancomer was firing me Phonemex was hiring me. A month before that, we had a meeting in which we were told about the reasons for the outsourcing. They talked in terms of the specialisation advantages that will be brought about by Phonemex and they wanted to know whether we would be able and keen to move to Phonemex. Also, the bank wanted to know to what extent Phonemex was able to provide us with a good job offer in order to retain us in the new account... A good offer compared with what we were getting for working in Bancomer. So, a month later we went into a room with a big table to sign our termination agreement; on the

other side of the room there was another big table, Phonemex's, but hiring people for the 'same' job. It was very impressive to see how most people were moving around the room signing termination agreements and new employment contracts immediately.

Since March 1999 Mauricio had been in a full-time job at Bancomer. In Mexico, as in many other parts of the world, banks enjoy the reputation of being good employers as they offer advantageous benefit plans. When Bancomer was bought by BBVA in 2000, a restructuring process began. This process consisted of vertical disintegration and the contracting out of entire sections of the bank such as internet banking or customer services. During this period Mauricio was moving around in different areas of the organisation trying to avoid redundancy. However, when he was in internet banking (Bancomer.com) the bank decided to move the whole section out with a subcontractor. Interestingly, when Mauricio was moved to Phonemex he was upgraded to the position of 'integrator', which is a halfway position between agent and supervisor, a type of link between the subcontractor and the client firm. In this job, Mauricio had two main areas of responsibility. First, he was responsible for the design of scripts and work processes for the agents. The job design and processes had to comply with ISO 9000 quality standards as they were agreed between the bank and the call centre – it was the bank who asked for this certification. To perform this part of the job, Mauricio was in permanent contact with the bank, especially when new services or any other sort of changes in design were introduced. When this happened, call centre agents need immediate training to be made familiar with those changes. In fact, every time a change took place, Mauricio had to visit the bank's central offices (outside Phonemex, of course) to receive training and feedback, then came back to Phonemex to disseminate the new information among customer service agents. The second part of Mauricio's responsibilities had to do with the monitoring of how scripts and processes actually worked. Again, he had to stay in permanent dialogue and contact with Bancomer's representatives and Phonemex's supervisors in order to make the adjustments needed. Additionally, if an agent could not help a customer, Mauricio had to be available to provide back office support. Finally, Mauricio was also in charge of registering the amount hours of work undertaken in the account – which was essential to process the bill for the client firm.

Therefore, there is no question that the relationship between client firms and call centres subcontractors requires close communication and interaction, as has been reported in many other cases (Lorenz 1988; Sako and Helper 1998; Lorenz 1999). The crucial thing here though is that Mauricio was chosen for this position because he knew the bank very well and this was an important factor in building up trust and communication between organisations:

> When we were downsized and outsourced, the bank was in the process of analysing which areas could be externalised. So, they started with areas of low risk, such as credit card sales, because it did not imply the transfer of vital or secret information from the bank. Because the relationship with Phonemex went so well, they just decided to continue with other peripheral areas, such as internet banking, Bancomer.com, where we are now, and I was chosen as integrator because I know the bank very well.

Mauricio believed that the bank made use of outsourcing for the three reasons commonly mentioned: capacity, specialisation and cost reduction. At least he was told that it was for specialisation reasons that Bancomer moved part of its operations to Phonemex. However, Mauricio did not see any major positive changes in the quality of the service and productivity levels. According to him, they had a level of service of 97 per cent (this means that 97 out of 100 calls were answered in less than 6-7 seconds) which is considered a good response level according to the industry standards. However, Mauricio considered that the main problem is the quality level of these responses. He thought that the main explanation for their poor quality had to do with the lack of homogeneity in skills and experience of the group of employees in the account. To explain this situation better, Mauricio made a distinction between two groups. He called the first group "people of Phonemex origin", referring to those workers who were contracted directly by the call centre to work in the bank account, but who had no previous experience in banking services. Mauricio called the second group "people of Bancomer origin", referring to those workers who had been downsized from the bank and moved to Phonemex, like himself. Here we have his general explanation:

> People of Phonemex origin are about 21-22 years old and without any kind of professional experience. On the other hand, outsourced staff from the bank has careers of about 10-15 years in banking services. So, many of these guys from the bank were over 30 years old... As you can see, the difference between supervisors from Bancomer and supervisors from Phonemex was considerable and this has a very important impact on the account... to be completely honest with you, most of these guys from Phonemex, including young supervisors, always received orders from us, even from our agents, or at least, they learnt from what we did. We were so good in doing our jobs that we did not need any kind of retraining at the beginning of the outsourcing, only continuing with our jobs but in a different place, that is, in Phonemex... Nonetheless, the main challenges

are the frictions and tensions and differences between the staff hired by Phonemex afterwards and those downsized workers from Bancomer like me.

What were the tensions between these two groups of workers? According to Mauricio, most of the tensions had to do with differences in job expectations and the commitment to service quality and efficiency. Mauricio said that many staff of Bancomer origin were "professional and committed" to their jobs, that they kept the standard of professional banking services. They were people with a "serious personal and professional project". On the other hand, people of Phonemex origin were less committed, were irresponsible and lacked "mature personal and professional projects".

As the account became bigger, many agents of Bancomer origin were promoted to the category of supervisors. Paradoxically, one of the consequences of this systematic upgrading of ex-Bancomer agents to call centre supervisors was that the proportion of high skilled entry-level agents dropped dramatically and the quality of service suffered negatively. Also, this problem was aggravated because there were not enough supervisors of Bancomer origin to cover all the supervision posts needed. According to Mauricio, an experienced agent from Bancomer was able to deal with 100 or 130 calls in 8 hours, providing a very good level of service and accuracy of information to customers:

> Nowadays an agent from Phonemex working 8 hours probably answers between 40 and 60 calls maximum per day... Well, this is only a supposition based on my own numbers because Phonemex employees only work between 4 and 6 hours in Phonemex. In Bancomer, 80 people were enough for this job and now we need up to 180 workers to do the same thing.

Mauricio believes that the lack of strong commitment and a less 'mature' attitude have negative effects on the performance of young workers in Phonemex. For example, he said that even when employees have all the information and tools to do their work, in the end, they always ask him how to perform their tasks, which seems to waste time and resources in producing blueprints. Mauricio says that this situation was like communicating through a 'broken phone', meaning that there was a bad flow of information among staff in the account. Mauricio mentioned that supervisors and agents did not speak the same language, because workers did not read the handbooks. In conclusion, according to Mauricio, Phonemex is selecting very "low quality entry-level staff":

They are very young [workers of Phonemex origin] and they do not want
to learn new things here. That's a problem because we need to deal with
complex processes and information that is updated all the time. For
example, these guys do not like reading and they have low expectations in
these jobs; they only want to make some money in order to buy things or
pay for holidays but do not want to make any extra effort. That is, to read
more and to study the manual, to know exactly what they are doing.

According to Mauricio, these tensions have increased the turnover rate.
He explained that about four or five workers (there were up to 180 in the
account) left the account each month, but when they were part of
Bancomer, before the outsourcing, no more than two or three people left
the place each year. Mauricio's arguments and opinions depicted a
negative image and landscape for young workers in those places where
they have to share responsibilities with older and more experienced
workers. Also, Mauricio insisted the lack of commitment and loyalty from
younger workers might create serious problems, such as fraud:

Integrators and supervisors have a password to access confidential
information of customers. It is used only in exceptional cases and always at
customers' request. However, some agents were asking me for passwords
more than usual. In the end, we found that they were committing fraud.
The curious thing is that there was no way in which the bank could have
punished me and other supervisors for this due to the way the system is
organised here... I mean, there was no way of finding any specific clues or
traces to blame me or any of my colleagues for what happened because
using these passwords is an integral part of our daily routine. So working
for a subcontractor protected me! If I were working as bank employee they
would have sacked all of us immediately! Afterwards, another colleague
and I designed an interface to protect key information and restrict agents'
access all the time. I did not receive any extra compensation for this, but
this is my job and I feel satisfied and safe with the solution we designed.

After looking at the problems between different groups of workers in
the subcontracted workplace and the negative effects on service quality,
productivity levels and even the risk taken when handling customers'
information, an obvious question emerges: is this type of outsourcing
sustainable? Why not just re-internalise this section and services if all
these problems arise? When I asked Mauricio these questions, he said:

The discussion has come up in the bank because of the quality problems
and the low levels of service provided that I told you about before.
Sometimes there are rumours about the consequences of the many
criticisms we get... I still have friends working in the bank and they told

me that they always receive complains about the call centre service... To be
honest, sometimes the bank itself is responsible because it takes too much
time to resolve some critical problems... I do not know... for example,
sometimes the bank imposes a period of up to three-four weeks for credit
and debit card replacements. This is ridiculous! When customers call us
asking for a replacement and we inform them that they might have to wait
for up to one month, they get mad! And they are right.

It is important to reflect a little bit further on the importance of
downsized workers in the outsourcing of call centre services. Their
experience demonstrates that the allocation of labour in subcontracted
arrangements is far from being a simple technical or administrative
decision even when considering the three basic arguments of capacity,
specialisation and cost-reduction (Harrison and Kelley 1993). It is clear
that labour outsourcing might bring significant cost reductions but it also
faces many challenges and constraints due to the nature of workers'
expectations, of client companies' demands and of call centre managers'
problems of authority. All these factors combined might damage the
quality of the service.

One of the fundamental reasons why outsourcing contracts might
persist despite the inefficiencies and problems between organisations and
the workforce is the use of cost reduction arrangements such as non-
standard contracts for workers. In this way, outsourcing in Mexico can be
supported by the use of contract for services (de Buen Lozano 2005; De la
Garza 2005; Reynoso 2005). In these contracts, workers do not enjoy full
labour rights and employers have only limited responsibilities, which
reduces the costs of contracting Mexican labour even further (De la Garza
and Salas Páez 2006).

## 3.3. The contract for services as a competitive advantage in outsourcing

At first glance, most of the evidence collected about the relationship
between client firms and call centre outsourcing seems to validate the idea
that outsourcing allowed firms to focus their efforts and resources on their
core businesses and transfer peripheral activities such as customer services
to subcontracted call centres. In this regard, it seems that outsourcing
allows costs to be kept to a minimum via specialisation. However, when
outsourcing takes place there is a considerable degree of tension and
conflict between the subcontractors and client firms involved, as we have
seen in the previous sections of this chapter. Such a level of conflict and
distrust raises questions about the extent to which the outsourcing of front-

line service work reduces costs mainly based on a more efficient use of technology and specialisation.

According to the information presented, it is possible to see how these tensions among client firms, call centres and workers might erode the quality of service and productivity levels. However, many client firms might accept this 'damage' since 60 per cent of the total costs in call centres are labour-related (IMT 2007) and outsourcing might significantly reduce these costs when using additional mechanisms other than specialisation and making efficient use of technology.

Another way in which labour costs can be significantly reduced comes from the type of contract signed by workers, and this is a crucial determinant of inequality at work in recently created service industries. Most workers in Mexican call centres have a type of contract called *contrato por obra determinada* or 'contract for a fixed task' (Barajas Montes de Oca 1995; Micheli 2005). This is a type of labour contract that was designed to reduce the responsibilities of employers and to link workers exclusively with the tasks they perform *but not* with the organisation that employs their labour power (Alcalde Justiniani 2005; de Buen Lozano 2005; De la Garza 2005; Micheli 2005; Reynoso 2005).

In practice, these could be considered a kind of contract for services of the type identified by Hogdson (1998). For example, those workers in one of the companies analysed in this research had a contract for the fixed task of selling flight tickets in a call centre for a US company. If the contract between the call centre and the airline finishes, then the contract for those workers who are in the airline account would automatically expire without major obligations for any of the employers. This system has been used for a long time in Mexico and it helps organisations to achieve the labour flexibility they are looking for (Alcalde Justiniani 2005; Bouzas 2005; De la Garza 2005; Micheli 2005; Reynoso 2005).

However, many unions and activists have challenged the legality of this form of contract. According to my interviews with labour lawyers in Mexico City, this type of contract contravenes the Mexican Constitution and national laws:

> The Mexican Constitution and the Labour Law do not consider the figure of outsourcing. All of them are employment relationships before the law, even if you do not have a contract. Any relationship of subordination in exchange for a salary is considered an employment relationship under the Mexican law, and workers must receive all the benefits and protection stated by the Constitution and its laws. All these arrangements such as contracts for services are mainly designed to avoid legal responsibilities.
> —Labour lawyer, Mexico City.

Despite these claims, the contract for services is largely used in Mexico even at public offices (Bouzas 2005). During the fieldwork for this research, officials from the Ministry of Labour in Mexico City explained me that the government is one of the main users of this type of contract for the outsourcing of catering, cleaning and security services in public buildings. This is one of the biggest challenges for economic and social policies in Mexico. As mentioned above, there have been almost no changes to the labour law in Mexico since 1970 (de Buen Lozano 2005). In formal terms, the labour law in Mexico is based on the assumption that workers constitute the weaker part of the employment relationship (Reynoso 2005; De la Garza 2006). When examining the legislation, it is possible to perceive that workers are automatically protected when they enter into any kind of subordinate relationship in exchange for a salary (Bensusán and Rendón 2000).

However, in practice things are very different. There is no question that one of the great economic advantages of Mexico is its large labour supply; Mexico City offers an excellent supply of young and competent workers for call centre jobs. It seems that call centre employers prefer flexible contracts with these workers in order to avoid labour costs associated with unionism while compensating for the economic inefficiencies that might emerge in the operation of subcontracted services. Therefore, it is possible to argue that the use of low-paid contracts for services is also evidence suggesting that outsourcing is not as technically efficient as neoclassical economists would predict: the reduction in the cost of labour would compensate for the problems and bottlenecks between call centres and client firms.

## Conclusion

Over the last decades outsourcing has occupied a prominent place in business and neoclassical economics literature as a remedy against almost any risk or challenge of our times, such as unexpected changes in demand or intense competition, as a mechanism to expand the boundaries of the firm establishing collaborative networks and distributing risks (Watanabe 1971; Atkinson 1984; Piore and Sabel 1984; Harrison 1994; Castells 2000). At the same time, outsourcing is frequently criticised as a mechanism that does not provide workers with safety and stability in exchange for the loyalty and commitment they have towards firms (Tilly 1996; Sennett 1998; De la Garza 2005)

Initially, managers interviewed in subcontracted call centres argued that no intervention is required or allowed from the client firm. This view corresponds to the theoretical assumptions made about the logic of outsourcing arrangements (Williamson 1979; 1981; Lacity and Hirschheim 1993). However, as the fieldwork of this investigation progressed, this research collected much evidence about how client firms might play a central role in the administration of the labour force, disputing the authority of the subcontractor at different stages: recruitment, selection, training, operation and compensation. The central divergence between organisations in the outsourcing of front-line services seems to be the dilemma of customisation versus standardisation (Korczynski 2002; 2007; 2009). On the one hand, the main interest of client firms is the customisation of services to achieve higher levels of quality in order to satisfy and retain their customers – this is how they maximise the benefit of outsourcing customer services. On the other hand, subcontractors are more interested in the standardisation of processes as the most efficient way to reduce costs – and compensate for the risks they are assuming as subcontractors. These opposite goals of the organisations involved in outsourcing seem to have an impact on workers' experiences and employment conditions. The tensions derived from these divergent goals seem to increase as we move towards front-line services for higher-income customer segments which are undertaken by highly skilled workers.

One of the great challenges of this chapter was to provide convincing evidence that these tensions and problems have effects on workers' experiences and employment conditions that, in turn, have significant effects on their levels of service quality and productivity. This task was not easy. It was not possible to compare 'in-house' versus subcontracted call centres at the same time in order to look at the specific effect of the interaction between client firms and subcontractors in the administration of the labour force. Instead, this research looked at the experience of downsized workers in order to provide an *ex ante, ex post* landscape of the effects of outsourcing. The findings suggest that divergences between client firms and subcontractors in the administration of the workforce might have a negative impact on the quality of the service and productivity levels. Particularly, it seems that subcontractors' incentives for creating internal labour markets are minimal, so they attract mostly young and inexperienced workers to the call centre. On the other hand, downsized and older workers – previously allocated in the client firm – are more likely to be responsible and committed to their jobs, partly as a consequence of their previous experience as full-time, permanent workers.

Therefore, it is worth asking to what extent outsourcing can be truly efficient when one considers the significant level of conflict and tension in the administration of the subcontracted workforce within the organisations involved. To address this concern, it is important to highlight the role of non-standard forms of employment in outsourcing as a competitive advantage. Specifically, it seems crucial to look at how the contract for services – which reduces employees' salaries and benefits, and restricts security at work – is used in Mexico. One can argue positively that the dramatic reduction in labour costs is possible not just because there is a more efficient allocation and organisation of work but also because of the reduction of workers' salaries and benefits, which is possible thanks to the use of contracts for services instead of standard labour contracts (De la Garza 2005; Reynoso 2005). In other words, that the use of contracts for services complements the efficiency in the allocation and organisation of labour, and both together trigger the reduction of costs. More pessimistically, it is also possible to argue that the true importance of the contract for services is that this type of contract acts as a substitute for efficiency in the outsourcing relationship.

I am certain that for the organisations involved, there is a balance between the efficiencies to be made from outsourcing and paying low wages when using outsourced labour. To consider this in more detail, it is important to have more information about the organisation of work and specific employment conditions with different client firms. In this respect, the next chapter presents the cases of different job designs and the organisation of work.

# CHAPTER FOUR

# THE ORGANISATION OF WORK
IN MULTI-EMPLOYER SITES:
SIMILAR JOBS BUT DIFFERENT EXPERIENCES
OR THE 'VISIBLE HAND' OF THE CLIENT FIRM

## 4.1. The service dilemma: standardisation versus customisation and the organisation of work

Is it possible to have absolute control over the interactions between customers and employees in front-line service work? If the answer is yes, we would be implying that the complete standardisation of front-line service work is possible. If the answer is no, we would be implying that it is plausible that workers' autonomy and self-discretion are essential to perform front-line service work. In many ways, this is one of the leading themes of the debate about the rationale and profile of the labour process in call centres. The use of IT systems to help and monitor workers' performance on the one hand, and the uncertainty added by customers' presence on the other, have led researchers to analyse how different production and managerial systems are used in call centres (Deery and Kinnie 2002; Hannif and Lamm 2005; Kinnie et al. 2006).

In chapter one, it was mentioned that early studies of call centre work emphasised the role of IT systems in reducing workers' opportunities to exert control over their own work (Garson 1988; Fernie and Metcalf 1998). As a result of this, call centre work, and much interactive service work in general, was regarded as a continuation of the manufacturing mass production model (Levitt 1972; Giddens and Birdsall 2001). However, these interpretations have been criticised because of their monolithic appreciation of call centre work, ignoring the complex heterogeneity of job designs and clients within the industry. Many authors have pointed out the importance of customer segmentation practices. Frenkel et al. (1998) and Korczynski (2002) suggest that a hybrid managerial approach that combines the standardisation of processes (to reduce costs) and the customisation of products (to satisfy customers) is the type of production system dominating the organisation of work in call centres. Related to this, the work of Batt (2000) makes an important contribution. She suggests that there is an association between the type of market segment targeted and the managerial system chosen, arguing that customer segmentation strategies define the choice of any of the three managerial approaches: a) the classic production model, b) the professional service model, and c) the mass customisation model. The mass customisation model is regarded as a hybrid that gains from the advantages of mechanisation in mass production and from the quality service of professional models. Batt and Moynihan (2002) assign each of these systems to each of the three customer segments that are common targets of call centres: a) residential customers to mass production; b) small businesses to mass customisation; and c) large businesses to professional service.

However, there are authors who disagree that production systems in call centres can be considered to be undifferentiated hybrids of standardisation and customisation (Taylor et al. 2002; Taylor and Bain 2005; 2007). Taylor et al. (2002) report that even workers servicing high-value customers tend to have low levels of control over their pace, breaks, planning and targets at work. From this perspective, the nature of work in call centres, with the use of IT systems to supervise and monitor labour performance, plays a crucial and determining role in narrowing employees' opportunities to exercise higher levels of control and discretion over their work.

Nevertheless, relatively little attention has been paid to the role of client firms in this process. Despite the claims that mass production and standardisation systems prevail in call centres, the analysis of even minimal variations in managerial approaches in the administration of the labour force might allow a better understanding of the tensions between organisations and the use of controlling mechanisms over workers in inter-firm relationships. Batt's seminal work on call centres (Batt 2000; Batt and Moynihan 2002; Batt et al. 2004; Batt et al. 2006; Batt et al. 2007), for example, emphasises how different types of customers influence managers' selection of particular production systems, but she does not examine the influence of client firms.

The findings of my own research suggest that it is crucial to look at the experience of work in the same type of job category but oriented to a different client to understand how subcontractors deal with the difficulties of having a large diversity of client firms in the same place.

**Table 4-1. Basic characteristics of job categories in the Mexican call centres studied**

| Job category | Market & task | Skills & education | Typical Compensation |
|---|---|---|---|
| Sales | Credit cards for mass markets (outbound calls) | Routine work & high school | - Up to 75% of the salary might depend on productivity bonuses;<br>- Contract for services;<br>- Few opportunities for promotion. |
| Customer service | Airline tickets for mass and middle class markets (inbound calls) | Semi-autonomous work & college education | - Up to 30% of the salary might depend on productivity bonuses;<br>- Contract for services;<br>- Few opportunities for promotion. |
| Technical support | Software solutions for high-income markets (inbound/outbound calls) | High-skill work & engineering degrees | - Up to 20% of the salary might depend on productivity bonuses but it is common to see employees with a 100% fixed salary;<br>- There are also some employees with permanent contracts;<br>- Some opportunities for promotion within the subcontracted firm or even in the client firm. |
| Supervisors | All the markets and services | Autonomous work & college education | - Up to 30% of the salary might depend on productivity bonuses (and it depends on the team's productivity);<br>- Contract for services;<br>- Few opportunities for promotion within the subcontracted firm or even in the client firm. |

Source: Interviews by the author.

As mentioned, this chapter explores four different job categories in call centres: sales, customer services, technical support and supervisors. The first job design is related to credit cards sales. This activity includes two accounts, American Express and *Banco Santander*, and each one employs about 100 workers, both located in KPM. The second job design is related to ticket sales and customer services for two airline companies, both located in Phonemex. One of the accounts employs about 100 people who work for the Mexican airline Volaris while the other account has about 60 workers who provide services for the US low-cost airline US Airways. The third job category, technical support, includes two accounts servicing sales and technical support for two foreign software companies, Microsoft and Sybase. The Microsoft account is located in Phonemex while the Sybase account in Datatech. Finally, the information on supervisors is drawn from all the services considered in this research. The basic characteristics of these categories are summarised in Table 4-1.

## 4.2. Sales

Sales work has the lowest status of the jobs in call centres (Batt 2000; Taylor et al. 2002; Batt et al. 2007). Workers in sales tend to have the lowest level of skills, are not educated beyond high school level, have minimum experience in sales, have only basic grammar and speaking skills, and need no more than a rudimentary knowledge of computer software (to fill in forms) and telephonic devices (enabling them to carry out the simple tasks of dialling a number or transferring a call) (Taylor and Bain 1999). In general, sales workers were the youngest category of staff in most of the companies studied (18-22 years old). The recruitment process is largely based on the social networks of the employees, who are frequently asked to invite friends and acquaintances to submit job applications. The training period tends to be short (about a week or so) and is focused on product information. My observations and information provided by staff at sales accounts show that there is almost no interaction with the client firm on the job and that the relationship between client firm representatives and outsourced managers and supervisors tends to focus on the evaluation and discussion of the quantitative components of service level agreements. Finally, sales agents are likely to receive the lowest salaries in the industry and productivity bonuses are an important part of their total wages. However and perhaps surprisingly, my observations and information given by the staff involved also suggest that there were relatively high levels of workers' satisfaction in these accounts something that contradicts the findings obtained by other researchers (Taylor and

Bain 1999; Baldry et al. 2007). In order to analyse this case in more detail I selected two different accounts of credit cards sales in different outsourced companies.

The primary goal of the day for agents in sales was to earn a bonus, but agents in sales accounts struggled to reach the daily quota that would allow them to get the desired 'price'. In the call centre KPM, there was an account that offered services for American Express; agents held a contract for services and had a six-hour, five-day schedule, organised in two shifts: the first from 9am to 3pm and the second from 3pm to 9pm. Work was organised individually and agents were assembled in groups of no more than 15 individuals headed by one supervisor. Staff was on average 18-22 years old and the account was dominated by single, lower-middle-class students from public colleges in Mexico City. Employees received a base salary the equivalent of £100 per month plus a bonus of £3.20 per pre-approved card (the information collected from customers had to be checked by the Credit Bureau; if it was correct, the transaction was considered pre-approved and then had to wait for American Express's authorisation). But this mechanism was new:

> The system has changed a lot, I used to make a lot of money, up to 12,000 pesos [£600] monthly... and this was only through the bonus. It was a lot of money to me, but now it is impossible to make it. It changed because some guys were lying and filling the system with false information... I mean, some people used to call their friends and acquaintances to sell cards using false information.
> —Outsourcing worker, KPM American Express

It should be noted that agents in this account faced a market restriction because at one point the client company (American Express) decided to use another call centre to target more urban areas across Mexico. As a result of this decision, sales agents felt frustrated because they believed that the market in Mexico City was already saturated. This was the main source of stress reported from agents in this account. The second source of stress was related to system failures; to perform their jobs, agents needed remote access to the client firm's information system to check products and services, and to fill in databases with customers' information. Agents pointed out that the connection was often slow or broken and it was not possible to conclude the transaction quickly once customers had agreed to buy the card. Indeed, agents considered that this delay could make customers to change their mind about purchasing the card. Therefore, the trust and cooperation required by inter-firm relations (Lorenz 1988; Sako and Helper 1998) seems to fail at some critical points.

According to the interviews and my observations, agents in this account did not have daily contact with American Express managers or any other staff from that firm, but occasionally had visits from them, when they came to distribute souvenirs or give short motivational talks. Despite not having regular contact with client firm representatives, most agents were aware of the implications of having a job in a particular account, rather than one of the others within the outsourced call centre. An agent explained how this affected his salary:

> Now my salary is low, especially in relation to those guys who are working in the account of Banco Santander, on the other floor. We do exactly the same thing but they have better bonuses because they are still receiving the bonus for sold cards instead of the pre-approved card arrangement that we have here. The system did not change for them because they did not have the same problem we had.
> —Outsourcing worker, KPM American Express

Most of the agents claimed that they had higher levels of autonomy and discretion over their work because client firm representatives never monitored their performance directly. Therefore, employees could decide how to use the database and the number of calls to make every hour, at least during the first days of the month when there was less pressure to reach monthly target sales. In general, employees in the American Express account did not feel intimidated by monitoring procedures, especially after some weeks of experience. Employees recognised that the client firm had a lot to do with the way work is organised and compensated in the account. For example, all of them said that American Express was responsible for the reduction in the scope of potential customers to be targeted by the account and that this had negative consequences on employees' wages. Finally, employees spoke repeatedly about the job and salary conditions of workers in other accounts: it was common that agents compared their schedules, salaries and benefits with workers in other accounts rather than with co-workers. Thus it is evident that subcontracted workplaces with multiple clients offer a unique opportunity for workers to compare their working conditions with their peers (Gartrell 1982).

*Banco Santander* had the other account selling credit cards in the same call centre (KPM). Again, sales agents had a contract for services and they worked eight-hours five days a week. It took them up to one month to be proficient in their jobs. As in American Express, employees are 18-22 years old on average, and most of them are single, lower-middle-class students from public schools in Mexico City. In this account, employees received a monthly base salary the equivalent of £100 plus a bonus of about £4 per credit card sold independently of any validation of data from the Credit Bureau. To motivate agents, there was a daily target to sell three credit cards; if agents sold three credit cards in less than eight hours, they were allowed to go home. The bonus was assigned individually and no competition was encouraged among agents. Agents worked on their own, assembled in groups of no more than 15, headed by one supervisor.

It is important to bear in mind that workers in American Express complained that agents in this account (*Banco Santander*) were receiving better salaries for doing exactly the same job within KPM. Although this was true most of the time (because the base salary was the same but the bonus was higher and more easily reached by agents of *Banco Santander*) workers in *Banco Santander's* account were subjected to a different managerial approach. Agents in this case appeared to be subjected to stronger supervision and monitoring measures than their counterparts in the American Express account. As a consequence, the turnover was higher in *Banco Santander's* than in American Express's account (about 10 per cent versus 7 per cent monthly). As has been shown by Taylor et al. (2002), employees often complain that client firm representatives are not interested in the well-being of the sales agents; instead they are concerned about the sales figures reported from the account even though the service level agreements also include service quality.

Routine and close monitoring prevail in these two high-volume, low-value accounts; the standardisation of processes is a priority; and there is almost no opportunity for workers to exercise self-discretion and provide a tailored service to their individual customers. The service level agreement between American Express, *Banco Santander* and KPM was based on results, in this case on the total number of credit cards sold (or pre-approved). Because the pressures for standardisation appear inevitable in these cases, a type of mass production approach seems to dominate labour management in credit card sales in call centres. These findings from Mexico are in line with the evidence presented by authors such as Batt (2000), Felstead and Jewson (1999) and Taylor and Bain ( 2007) from many other call centres around the world, including the United Kingdom, the United States, Australia, Japan and India, among others. In other words, process standardisation and low levels of employee autonomy and discretion seem to be common when servicing high-volume, low-income markets in call centres in markedly different institutional settings. Therefore, it seems that the high-volume, low-value nature of credit card sales activities imposes significant limitations on the possibilities of workers to adopt more personalised interactions with customers through higher levels of discretion. Importantly, it seems that tensions between client companies and call centre subcontractors remain low in this area. However, the absence of tensions and conflicts between organisations does not necessarily mean that workers' experiences and employment conditions are not influenced by the client firm.

In these two cases, the apparently simple task of selling credit cards ultimately required trustworthiness in the process of collecting information from customers, and the economic incentive of the bonus was insufficient to obtain that trust. As a consequence, client companies had two different responses to this challenge and, interestingly, neither included modifications in the level of the bonus. On the one hand, the American Express account approached the matter indirectly by changing the compensation system, making it dependent on the evaluation of a third party (the Credit Bureau). In other words, American Express introduced a type of bureaucratic control on workers when imposing new rules for getting the bonus.

On the other hand, the *Banco Santander* account increased the levels of monitoring and supervision over gathering information from customers. Thus it followed a more direct approach, using supervisors more intensively and tightening technical control over the labour process using IT technologies. Not surprisingly, even though workers in the *Banco Santander* account enjoyed higher bonuses and greater flexibility in their working schedule (thanks to the daily target plan), they also suffered more stress and higher turnover rates than their counterparts in the American Express account. Therefore, despite having very similar activities and job designs, it is possible to see different solutions by managers in these two accounts as they deal with similar problems in the same subcontracted workplace.

In summary: a) workers in both accounts perform essentially the same tasks (outbound calls and sales); b) the service is oriented to the same customer segment (mass markets of low and middle-income levels); c) employees receive the same base-salary; and d) employees are organised in similar ways. At the same time, workers in both accounts: a) have a different bonus system; b) have a different kind of interaction with supervisors and personnel from the client firm; and c) have a different turnover rate. These differences, despite their obvious impact on workers' experiences, did not appear to stem from different production systems but from variations in the same mass production approach as standardisation in the processes is still the rule in both cases. The elements explaining most of the variance in workers' experiences and satisfaction seem to be the type of interactions they have with the client firm and, interestingly, their relationship with supervisors. These two findings were not expected in a system that: a) has an outsourcing rationale of non-involvement from the client company with regard to the subcontracted labour force (Lacity and Hirschheim 1993) and b) is supposed to be highly standardised and lacking of personalised styles of supervision (Fernie and Metcalf 1998; Taylor and Bain 1999).

## 4.3. Customer services

Customer services jobs are generally considered to fall roughly in the middle between sales and technical support services in the hierarchy of call centre jobs (Batt 2000; Taylor et al. 2002). Salary levels tend to be in an intermediate position between those for sales and technical support staff and the proportion of the bonus as a part of the base salary is less than that obtained by sales staff. Employees in customer services normally have been educated to college level (if sometimes unfinished) and tend to perform semi-autonomous tasks in their jobs. Workers in this category frequently deal with a set of pre-configured tasks that customers choose from a system menu, but it is not uncommon that customers might demand responses to unexpected problems. The average age of workers in this category is 20-24 years old – slightly higher than for workers in sales activities. Unlike staff working in sales, customer services agents essentially deal with incoming calls, which gives them a different balance of power in the conversation with customers. In sales or outbound calls, agents are the active party of the relationship because the call was initiated by the agent who has a sales purpose; customer services or incoming calls are normally initiated by customers and these calls are normally longer and more complicated than calls relating to sales. During the interviews and observations for this research, workers in customer services commonly displayed more stress and dissatisfaction than agents in sales tasks.

Again, many people are recruited to customer service work from the social networks of current employees (Fernandez et al. 2000; Castilla 2005), but workers previously employed in the client firm are usually chosen to fill these positions (following vertical disintegration practices like outsourcing). The training period varies from only one week to one month depending on the amount of information needed to perform the services in the account (the training period might increase substantially if the service is provided in other languages, like English, for example). The interaction with the client firm in the workplace tends to be more frequent and agents are expected to be more committed with slightly higher quality standards. Most of the interaction between client firm representatives and staff from the subcontracted company is still based on the evaluation of quantitative elements of the service level agreement (Taylor et al. 2002).

Nevertheless, workers in this type of accounts commonly stated that the most demanding and stressful aspect of their work is the lack of updated information to answer customers' enquires; once more, the relationship and flow of information with the client firm seems to be critical in shaping the experiences of workers in the workplace.

Customer service agents also have different benefits than sales agents. Although the bonus for customer services agents is not as important as it is for sales agents, most of the organisations were moving to piece-rate systems in their attempt to increase productivity levels. In Phonemex, there was an account that provides customer services for the Mexican low-cost airline Volaris. Here, agents received inbound calls from customers who wanted to purchase tickets or make arrangements in case of cancellations or changes. Agents had a contract for services and their work schedule was of six-hour, six-day a week. Their monthly salary was the equivalent of £65, the lowest in Phonemex, but the bonus could be up to 75 per cent of the base salary depending on productivity and adherence to service quality standards. In this account, the bonus was assigned individually and the maximum level could be reached only by the three best sellers for each supervisor (there are 20 agents per supervisor). In addition, employees could obtain a single round-flight ticket if they were one of the top ten sellers in the account every three months, and all-included holiday packages were awarded to the top ten annual sellers of flight tickets. Unsurprisingly, this system provoked intense competition and tension among employees. For example, agents were not supposed to break down sales individually: if a customer purchases five tickets this operation should be registered as a single sale (not five), so one call represents only one potential sale. But some agents divided single operations involving multiple tickets into individual sales, and this situation created confusion and problems with reservations.

In addition, workers were instructed not to develop relationships with customers, which led to paradoxical situations, as observed elsewhere by Korczynski (2002). In facing the pressures of a dual system where efficiency and quality are supposedly prioritised, workers had to introduce themselves to the customers using their first name, but were instructed not to direct customers to specific workers because this was against management goals of efficient call-handling (Korczynski 2002). However, in the attempt to increase their sales and receive better bonuses, the agents interviewed acknowledged that breaking down sales and developing relationships with customers were common practices in the workplace:

Well, you are not supposed to break down sales... it is against the rules!
But some people do so and they increase their sales disproportionately...
That's not fair for the rest of us... Also, some others recommend customers
to ask for them personally in case they need more tickets in the future, and
this... again... is not fair on the others.
—Outsourcing worker, Phonemex Volaris.


In the Volaris account, the main source of surveillance for workers was
peer pressure, reinforcing the idea that piece-rate systems encourage
competition and rivalry between workers rather than cooperation, and this
in turn helps to discipline and control workers. One of the workers
interviewed reported that the main tensions in the workplace were the
frictions among staff because they had to compete with each other for the
bonuses and for this reason they continually observed and monitored the
performance of their peers. However, agents in Volaris were also aware of
how and when they were electronically monitored, but some of them
appreciated these mechanisms as a way to increase service quality for their
customers. Interestingly, many agents in this account complained about
the lack of reliable information from the client firm in order to perform
their work. Workers said that customers themselves were an important
source of updated information about the services offered by the client
company (such as seasonal discounts that were not communicated to
workers in the call centre). Like many people in inbound services, agents
in this account did not feel they had a great level of discretion and
autonomy over the pace of their work and their break times, because they
could not control the flow of calls (Fernie and Metcalf 1998; Taylor and
Bain 1999; Kinnie et al. 2000).

Another account in Phonemex provided customer services for the
American low-cost airline US Airways. Agents received inbound calls
from customers in the United States who wanted to purchase tickets, make
cancellations or changes, or make other general customer service inquiries.
Employees maintained that they became proficient in their job within
approximately one month. One of the most important and distinctive
characteristics of this account was that all services were provided in
English because they were dealing with customers in the United States.
Like all the previous accounts (American Express, *Banco Santander* and
Volaris), workers in the US Airways account had a contract for services
and usually worked eight-hour days, six days a week. On average they
were 20-24 years old, slightly older than workers in credit card sales, and
the workforce is dominated by single, middle-class and upper-middle-class
students from private colleges in Mexico City. The base salary was the
equivalent of about £290 a month plus a bonus of up to 30 per cent,

depending on individual productivity and service quality. Agents did not receive any tickets as a premium or bonus, but they knew that agents in the Volaris account did. Some of these agents thought that improving their English-speaking skills and problem-solving abilities are the most important skills they acquire through this job:

> Every day we speak in English to people in the US in order to get solutions to the problems our customers have. They are very kind to me and very often I receive the information and the support I need. However, I have never seen someone from the client firm in person... perhaps they speak personally to my boss... or they visit the president of the company, but never agents in this floor!
> —Outsourcing worker, Phonemex US Airways

In this account, employees did not experience the same frictions and tensions between each other because bonuses were assigned individually and workers did not have to compete to get them. Workers in this account had frequent telephone contact with representatives of US Airways in the United States, but never met them in Mexico. I observed that the working atmosphere in this account was more relaxed and even friendlier than in Volaris, although the staff was doing exactly the same type of work.

As it has been detected by Korczynski (2002), agents commonly identify their interactions with customers as their main source of satisfaction but also as a significant source of stress. Some interviewees described experiences where they showed not just professional commitment to their customers but also emotional empathy:

> I have plenty of nice experiences in this job, but the happiest one was when I helped an old lady to find another flight after she had a cancellation. She was desperate and I spent about two hours or so making calls and looking for a solution until I got one. She told me that my mother would be very, very, proud of me... and I cried.
> —Outsourcing worker, Phonemex US Airways.

The previous statement is an excellent example of the type of evidence that Bolton and Boyd (2003) would use against Hochschild's suggestion that there is no chance of having authentic and autonomous feelings when carrying out this type of work (Hochschild 1983). In this case, the worker in the account of US Airways displayed the type of emotional management described as 'philanthropic' by Bolton and Boyd (2003) because he did not pursue any type of economic incentive for the extra work and time he dedicated to solve the problems of the customer, but was guided mainly by empathy; it was a kind of gift.

The clash between the standardisation of processes and the customisation of products for workers in customer services and in sales seemed to be very important. In many ways, this middle-value, high-volume activity involved efforts to tailor attention and lower cost operations simultaneously. Workers in these accounts and services had a higher level of skills (including a second language); they might perform repetitive tasks but these activities were more complex and even unpredictable from time to time. It is very important to mention here that, as a way of compensating for the lack of control they feel over the flow of (inbound) calls, most workers said that they had more power than outbound agents because the customer was the one "who is calling and requesting a service and help."

This was a type of service demanding high customisation: customers may call in a good mood because they want to plan holidays and business trips, but sometimes interactions between customers and representatives occur under difficult circumstances because of flight delays or cancellations. In the workplace, it was common to see employees interacting with each other, making suggestions and helping each other with information, having opportunities for self-discretion in the way they relocate passengers and deal with some complaints. On the other hand, workers also suffered the pressures of a bonus system connected with productivity levels. In trying to reach maximum sales, workers followed strategies (such as breaking down sales and developing relationships with customers), which created tension and problems among when competing for bonuses and premiums.

In summary, workers in this job category: a) performed essentially the same tasks but in a different language; b) oriented the service to the same customer segment but in different cultural contexts; c) received different base salaries and bonuses; and d) found that there was a different kind of interaction with the client company.

There is no doubt that electronic surveillance and monitoring played a key role in the organisation of work for these customer service representatives; their interactions are closely monitored and even recorded. But it is also true that customer service representatives tended to develop more complex skills and interactions with customers and other co-workers. Credit card sales staff was more likely to work in isolation and with minimal horizontal interaction (with other sales representatives). Those working in customer support services had multiple interactions with other people in the workplace and there were considerable variations in the amount of personal commitment shown by employees. Therefore, workers' autonomy and discretion were higher and more crucial for workers in these accounts.

According to the evidence from the accounts of Volaris and US Airways, the work of customer services agents could hardly be performed within the rigidity of a conventional mass production approach; this confirms the challenges and limitations of controlling front-line service work (Leidner 1993; Korczynski 2009). Here, workers 'break the rules' constantly, in an even more 'sophisticated way' than their counterparts in credit card sales. While sales staff devoted much effort to simulating the validation of customers' information by calling friends and asking them to confirm real customers' data, customer services representatives had to build up more complex resistance mechanisms with customers and co-workers, such as breaking down sales, or making extra efforts to find alternative solutions for customers in difficult situations. The crucial difficulty in understanding why customer services workers seem to break the rules more often and display more complex behaviour is the confusion about who is the 'real client' in the workplace (Cooke et al. 2005; Marchington et al. 2005).

In credit card sales, employees made clear distinctions about who was the client and who was the boss at work. For them, the client was the bank or the credit card company who hired their services whereas the bosses were the managers and supervisors in the call centre; people purchasing credit cards hold a status of quasi-anonymity. However, customer services representatives experienced much confusion about the same issue. During my interviews, workers were often confused by the meaning of the term 'client'. For them, the 'client' was either the client firm (the airline) or the customer of the airline. Very often, the interests of the two 'clients' appeared in conflict and employees felt forced to take sides.

The final outcome seems to depend on many factors (such as the customer's profile or the type of problem) but there was no absolute certainty that customer service agents would 'defend' airlines' interests even when subject to strict supervision and monitoring. How is this possible? Well, when employees take the customer's side they very often invoked their commitment to high quality standards. When this happened, supervisors and managers found it very difficult to reprimand workers. This situation had already been identified by Korczynski (2002). However, it is also true that workers heavily rely on routine behaviours when they feel overwhelmed by calls. Then routine procedures make it easier for workers to perform their tasks and secure a minimum of service quality to customers in difficult situations involving high pressure (Leidner 1993). In summary, it seems that workers in customer services have a larger arsenal of coping strategies to deal with the difficulties of front-line service work in call centres than their counterparts in sales activities.

## 4.4. Technical support

The job of providing technical support in call centre work in Mexico has comparatively high status. On paper, technical support workers seem to have most of the ideal characteristics of service work in the new economy: high skills, autonomy and relatively high education. Workers in technical support services are the best paid in the sector by far, although in one of the cases presented here workers do not receive bonuses but have fixed salaries and are motivated by career opportunities. Most of the positions in technical support tasks are filled by people with college degrees, many of them in engineering, and it is not difficult to find some people with master's degrees. The work performed usually required high skills and some firm-specific knowledge; basic experience in customer or sales services is highly desirable but not critical in the recruitment process. As expected, it is common that workers in this category display high levels of autonomy when performing their tasks, but high levels of dissatisfaction and tension were also observed in some of these cases. A plausible explanation for this situation is that higher levels of education tend to be associated with higher expectations in the labour market. However, as mentioned in previous chapters, technical workers do not seem very comfortable with the image of workers in call centres and hired by subcontracted companies. Not surprisingly perhaps, the average age of workers in technical services is the highest of any category, from 26 years old. The recruitment process for technical workers still relies heavily on employees' social networks, but it is also common that companies visit colleges and technical schools to encourage applications. The training period could take some time: a week or two before starting to work, a month of close supervision on the job, and finally up to 6 or 7 months to be proficient in the job.

Client companies are more likely to display an interest in the management of the technical support workforce. At the recruitment stage, it is common that some client companies reserve the right to carry out the final interviews with shortlisted candidates before they begin working at the subcontracted workplace – something that was mentioned in previous chapters. At the job, client companies tend to focus on the evaluation of quantitative indicators of the service level agreement but discussions about qualitative aspects of the business relationship and services provided are often included.

In this research, one of the accounts providing technical support was located inside Datatech, a Dutch company in Mexico City. This account was a helpdesk service for Sybase, a software company in the United States. The work schedule was of eight-hour five-day a week and these workers were the only ones in the sample who had a permanent contract, which also included a private medical insurance. Most of the agents hold degrees in engineering and some of them had Master in Science degrees from private and public schools in Mexico City; the average age of this group of workers was 26-30-year old and most of them were single, male and middle class. They said that they needed up to five or six months to be proficient in their jobs. In Datatech workers did not receive any kind of bonus but only a salary related to their position in the organisational ladder. Entry-level workers received a monthly salary the equivalent of about £370. In general, this was the case where workers had the best employment conditions for agents – a good fixed salary, on-the-job training and opportunities for promotion.

The call centre manager of Datatech, Rubén Gómez, insisted that the organisation's goal was to retain workers for at least three years, because this period of time was considered "the minimum they need to become proficient with most of the firm-specific skills that they would need to stay even longer in Datatech; I am saying so because we want them to stay with us after all the training they get here". Despite this statement, technical support agents interviewed in this research were not entirely convinced of staying in Datatech for long periods of time:

> Well, I know that the employment conditions we have here are good, especially if you look around and see how many people in Mexico are struggling to get a job, whatever job, even people with postgraduate education... but, I do not know, to be honest, I think it is a problem of expectations. We have invested a lot in our education and we dreamt with working for a huge and well-known company. Datatech is good, and it is also known in the sector, but people outside do not know what is all these about... personally I would like to try to look for a job with our client in the US, instead of staying in the outsourcing.
> —Outsourcing worker, Datatech Sybase

The selection process for these workers in Datatech lasts for only one week and there is no intervention at all from the client firm, perhaps, because this client firm is based in the United States. The training period might last up to three months, but higher technical skills are expected from the candidates from the beginning. Once they are in the workplace, agents have regular interactions with the client company. Supervisors send daily reports to the company in the United States and the following day they discuss the feedback received with their teams. In addition, all the conversations have to be recorded, and a sample of them evaluated and sent to the headquarters for a double and blind evaluation. In general, workers experience constant and job-based interaction with the client firm:

> We have a lot of contact with them [client firm managers] every day. Well, it is also because we are providing services to their own employees and, if there is any problem with our services, they could contact our bosses in the US immediately.
> —Outsourcing worker, Datatech Sybase

Agents in the Sybase account at Datatech identified the workload as the main source of stress in the workplace, especially because most requests are labelled as 'urgent' (problems with software, hardware, networks, security measures, etc.). Employees here think that they are acquiring useful skills because they are getting some expertise in managing the tools of a prestigious company while also improving their English language abilities. However, these technical workers also admit that their autonomy and discretion is limited by the system of incoming calls and requests whose flows are impossible to control.

There is no question that fulfilling workers' expectations might play a fundamental role in order to get their loyalty and commitment, especially from those who work in technical support services, which have higher skills and consequently higher aspirations in the job market. In Phonemex, whose business profile seemed to be less prestigious than that of Datatech, technical support agents were better paid, their salary included an important bonus proportion, and they seemed to be more satisfied that their counterparts in the Dutch outsourcing. In the case of Phonemex, I am talking about those workers who were in the account that provides sales services on behalf of Microsoft. They had a separate, closed space, and workers from other accounts on the same floor were not allowed to enter into the same workspace. Each worker enjoyed a spacious desk, which contrasts with the often limited space other workers had in adjacent accounts. The average age here was 28 to 32-year old, and most of the staff was single and male, with engineering degrees from public and private schools, and a middle-class background. Agents had a contract for services and their typical schedule was one of eight hours, five days a week. Microsoft is involved from the stage of recruitment and demands the right of having the last interview with candidates; in doing so, Microsoft controls access into the account.

Microsoft also provided direct training to the agents, who received a monthly salary the equivalent of £450 plus a bonus of up to 30 per cent depending on productivity and service quality standards. In this account, the bonus was assigned individually and agents did not have to compete to get it. In fact, interviewees often said that they spent part of their free time helping other agents. Agents in this account looked for customers and, to do so, they needed to be familiar with the technical characteristics of the programs and the 'financial' advantages of using these software products. Each agent was assigned particular geographic regions of Mexico as market targets with a list of potential customers; agents spent the day making outbound calls to technical and finance staff in different companies to introduce the product and make deals. Most of the workers in this Microsoft account acknowledged that they knew when and how they were monitored. Arguably, they assumed that this ability (to know the monitoring electronic mechanisms used) is something that is expected from someone with their technical skills. In merely a few cases, employees admitted that they did acquire new skills through performing this job, and most of them do not consider sales skills an asset for their 'technical' careers. The monitoring process and attempting to meet monthly sales targets were the main sources of stress reported in the workplace.

These skilled workers tend to be more resistant to be monitored with the kind of tools they master better than anyone around, but they seem to feel more insecure about their social abilities and verbal skills in interactions with customers. For these reasons monitoring is apparently more painful for them:

> I believe that the biggest challenge for people in this account is finding new clients and making deals with them. This can be a long and arduous process and you need patience. Sometimes, monitoring is not very helpful when you are trying to be convincing to the client because it might not allow you to feel comfortable.
> —Outsourcing worker, Phonemex Microsoft.

Importantly, technical workers felt that they did not enjoy a satisfactory level of autonomy and discretion in this account, contrary to the experience of technical workers in the account of Sybase at Datatech, who recognised a higher level of autonomy in their tasks. As in other cases, technical workers in the Microsoft account felt the pressure to get the sales targets at the end of the month and thought that they were losing autonomy over the pace of work and breaks as the end of the month approached. Most of them acknowledged that they received better salaries than most of their colleagues in the same organisation working in other accounts. Nonetheless, they also admitted that, among people performing the same kind of task for software companies, they were in a worse position because they worked in a subcontracted company; similar views were expressed by their counterparts in Datatech. Agents in technical support services had higher levels of education, and were more likely to speak a foreign language, to receive better salaries and to interact with the client firm. In general, they appeared to be guided by the customisation of products and services rather than the logic of mass production.

In summary, workers in these technical support services: a) perform different tasks, in a different language but for the same client industry; b) orient the service to different customer segments and to different cultural contexts; c) receive different base salaries and bonuses; d) have a different kind of interaction with the client company; e) were the best paid of the workers interviewed in this research (given the high revenue per client); f) had the most stable jobs; but g) suffered the same problems as many of their colleagues in credit card sales (for example pressures to get quantitative targets).

The experience of technical support agents was the most ambiguous of the three categories explored until now. It was expected that these workers would report higher levels of satisfaction and commitment to their organisations and jobs as a result of their relatively higher autonomy and income. However, many of them expressed dissatisfaction and frustration with their posts. If only the pecuniary compensations were considered it would be impossible to explain these manifestations of discomfort; they would be considered irrational. However, if one relates expectations of workers to the importance of loyalty and commitment, then it is possible to understand their dissatisfaction. On the one hand, these workers had comparatively high levels of education and skills; consequently, they were expecting better salaries and bonuses and better opportunities for a good professional career within the organisation. They believed that if the organisation valued them they would be able to stay with the company and be promoted. If this did not occur, these workers believed that they were not important to the organisation. However, most of them were in their early 30s and were becoming anxious about their career opportunities and job stability; they were starting (or already had) families and were looking for long-term contracts.

Overall, the evidence about the experience of work in front-line services in the different categories and accounts presented here seems to confirm that mass production approaches dominate the organisation of work in the call centres chosen for this investigation. In this sense, the Mexican experience is not different from others in developed countries.

Call centre work is largely standardised and subject to intense control and monitoring, even for technical workers with higher skills. These findings also contrast with optimistic narratives about the experience of work in the new economy where more educated workers are supposed to enjoy more autonomy and control over the labour process. Nonetheless, the essence of interactive service work – the constant interaction with other human beings as part of the service produced – is also a source of power and discretion for workers. In other words, the nature of front-line service work offers coping strategies that make stress at work more tolerable and even enjoyable from time to time.

Finally, the evidence presented in these three sections about sales, customer services and technical support activities also indicates that client firms play a significant role in shaping workers' experiences and employment conditions, and that their intervention has real costs for the operation of outsourcing in the form of extra arrangements for recruitment, selection, training and operation. Also, it seems that client firms are more likely to be involved as we moved to customer segments of higher value. In other words, it seems rational for client firms to incur some additional transaction costs for the coordination and operation of subcontracted services in call centres when the return expected from these interventions is higher. Additionally, as this research progressed, supervisors emerge as another fundamental factor in the experience of workers, something that I did not anticipate. This unexpected discovery suggests that, if we want to go deeper in the exploration of labour outsourcing in services and clarify the real effects of client firms' intervention, it is also important to identify the real power and effects of supervisors in the workplace. Therefore, the following section focuses on the experience of supervisors and their role in the organisation of work in subcontracted workplaces.

## 4.5. Supervisors

According to my observations and information collected in the field (through the interviews), call centre supervisors have a crucial and stressful role in administering the workforce and dealing with the problems between subcontractors and client firms. Supervisors play a fundamental part in at least three areas: a) operation: they are responsible for the operation of the services in the accounts – they schedule shifts, assign responsibilities, prepare reports and authorise bonuses for agents; b) support: they are a constant source of support for agents; if an agent could not deal with any specific issue, the call is automatically transferred to a supervisor; and c) communication: they are the bridge between call centre managers, client firm representatives and agents.

Despite all these responsibilities, the salary difference between supervisors and lower front-line workers is not very significant. However, I identified two policies that affected supervisors' salaries considerably. First, a large part of supervisors' salaries (up to 30-40 per cent) was based on the productivity of the whole group of workers under her or his supervision, as explained by this supervisor in KPM:

> As a supervisor you get all the pressure from upper management and clients [companies]. Each time somebody from the client company comes, Banco Santander in my case, the entire floor is in tension, almost in shock... Our interactions with them can be very harsh, they ask for changes each time and never say why are doing this or that! They never give me any convincing explanation. The problem is that we [supervisors] receive our bonuses every three months and they can punish us with discounts on our salaries if our team did not reach the sales targets... This is not fair, and I do believe we are the only account with this policy in the organisation.
> —Supervisor, KPM Banco Santander.

This statement from a supervisor in the *Banco Santander* account at KPM is enormously valuable not just in explaining how supervisors' income is affected by the performance of the group but for other reasons as well. In the first place, it reinforces the idea that bonuses and piece-rate systems are still the main compensation systems for rewarding work in sales (Fernie and Metcalf 1998). Second, this statement also reinforces my argument that client firms play a fundamental role in the administration of the subcontracted workplace despite many statements from different managers refusing to acknowledge this fact. Third, this statement also reveals some of the most obscure but important advantages of the contract for services used by employers in the outsourcing industry: reducing workers' salaries as a mechanism of pressure, something that is illegal in Mexico, at least in formal labour contracts (Barajas Montes de Oca 1995; de Buen Lozano 2005; Reynoso 2005). Here again, the use of contracts for services, as commercial arrangements but not employment contracts, helps to adjust the revenues and expenses reported by the account.

In this regard, one of the characteristics of the Mexican case – which reveals the weak institutional context for employment relations in this country – is that supervisors and agents have a contract with call centres that gives discounts or 'penalties' in accordance with the goals and revenue reported by the account. These types of penalties and discounts are common in trade contracts between companies (Lorenz 1999) but are considered illegal in labour contracts (de Buen Lozano 2005). In this regard, outsourcing seems to be very effective in atomising the employment relationship and eroding workers' rights.

A second policy that affects supervisors' wages is also connected with the pressures from the client firm. As a way of reducing turnover among agents and increasing results, client firms tend to push call centres to a system of productivity-based compensations, especially for workers in sales and customer services. In some cases, workers with attractive bonuses might receive better earnings than supervisors, whose salaries often had a larger fixed proportion and smaller bonuses. This example is illustrative:

Q Is it attractive to be promoted to supervisor in these accounts?
A Well, in my opinion, this is one of the biggest challenges for the account right now. Look, in order to retain people from the bank after downsizing, as I told you before, they offered us relatively good entry-level conditions. However, supervisors do not have such attractive conditions. So, almost nobody wants to be promoted, at least nobody who came from the bank, people like me... The coordinator is around all the time trying and trying to convince agents to accept supervision vacancies but everyone knows that they are paid less.
—Interview with outsourcing worker, Phonemex BBVA Bancomer.

Therefore, filling supervision vacancies was an important challenge for call centre managers; people did not want to take these jobs either because they offered a lower salary or because people were not interested in a long-run commitment with the organisation. The same outsourcing worker quoted in the previous paragraph provided me with a very interesting explanation of the situation when asking how call centres fill the supervision vacancies since almost nobody was interested. As he mentioned in the previous paragraph, coordinators spent a lot of time going around the account and having conversations with agents in order to convince them of taking a supervision position when it became available. When most of the agents pointed out that the main problem with the job was the lower salary, because it depends on others' productivity, they were frequently told: "Yes, but you need to think about your status, you will be more important in the organisation." So the call centre managers tried to persuade agents that although a supervision position did not have a good salary it was better than their current position because of its status, that this type of *service* would be more appreciated by the organisation.

However, this outsourcing worker (who previously worked for the client firm) explained that only young workers were convinced by this type of speech. He said: "I have some experience already, at the bank, about the meaning of loyalty and commitment for organisations; in the end, they just want to get rid of you... or moving you to outsourcing!" In view of this situation, what are the opportunities from promotion and advancement in this organisation for entry-level staff like this worker and other experienced workers in lower positions? Well, another worker had a very interesting viewpoint:

> After some time you get some knowledge of the organisation and how it works. I know that the operational structure, from agents to supervisors, is a dead end... Your possibilities of getting something better from there are almost nothing. Your big chances are to get into the administrative structure. They have much better jobs. So, my strategy is not to be a supervisor but, instead, to remain as an agent, trying to get more knowledge about the administration of call centres or particular accounts, the ones that are more important for the company. To do so, you need to talk to people from the administrative structure when possible, suggest and introduce improvements frequently, showing your face and showing that you can deal with the big picture.
> —Outsourcing worker, Phonemex BBVA Bancomer.

When I asked this worker for the meaning of 'the big picture' he explained that a person must be able to show managers that one understands the entire logic of the call centre business and not only about how one's particular account works. A worker must show that she or he is able to work with all the fundamentals not just in the operation but also in the administration: work with people by phone, but also be able to prepare reports and deal with numbers. When this interview took place, at the beginning of 2007, this worker was an *integrator*, which is a job somewhere in between agents and supervisors, a position of support for supervisors, with similar characteristics but with the same salary advantages that agents had. This position was created to use the experience of 'senior' employees like the one providing answers and information for this section. In a follow-up telephonic conversation a year later, this worker told me that he had been promoted to the administrative structure. He entered as an analyst in the finance department with a permanent contract, paid holidays, end-of-the year bonus, pension plan and private medical insurance.

But it seems that this worker trajectory is an exceptional case. Most of the call centre supervisors interviewed did not have the same expectations or were unclear about how to cross the barrier between operational and administrative posts. Many of the supervisors interviewed reported high levels of stress and frustration. It is important to have in mind that these supervisors were older than entry level agents, and that supervisors were more likely to have family responsibilities and be dependent on the income obtained from their jobs, in other words, they reflect the disparities of power in the employment relationship: a worker depends much more on her or his job than an employer depends on an individual worker.

Therefore it was not strange that some supervisors were under constant stress in order to make as much money as they could; some of them were even dealing with different jobs at the same time:

> Q You mentioned that you have two jobs...
> A Yes, I have two full-time jobs. I work from 7am to 2.30pm in the systems section of the Police Department. At 3pm I start here and I finish at 9pm. Monday to Friday.
> Q How can you manage to have two jobs?
> A Because I have to... I need to pay my family bills. I mean, but I like my job here a lot. My job conditions in the police are good, they are public sector you know... fixed salary and decent benefits, all that kind of stuff... but the environment is horrible, plenty of aggressiveness... here, instead, the environment is softer. I feel better here, it is nice.
> —Supervisor, KPM Metlife.

In summary, it seems that there is a significant gap between the level of responsibility and the compensation obtained by supervisors in the call centres studied. Their work clearly represents a crucial point in the operation of call centres; they monitor and support agents, they correct mistakes in processes and develop new tools, and, very importantly for this research, they act as a communication bridge between agents, call centre managers and client firm representatives.

All supervisors interviewed were likely to believe that members of their groups could display higher levels of autonomy and discretion in their work. They were more likely to believe that their supervision style was relaxed and that they gave workers enough autonomy and control over their own work. Interestingly, most of the workers interviewed confirmed that supervisors were a key figure in the experience of work, that a good and supportive supervisor could facilitate the work for all the people around and vice versa. These findings seem to confirm, for the Mexican case, the crucial role of supervisors in supporting workers' activities and tolerating coping strategies in other national contexts, like the British case (Deery et al. 2010).

On the other hand, several supervisors told me that, in the end, the job design is the most important determinant of the quality of the work for agents. For example, they told me that agents making outbound calls have more 'power' to make decisions about their pace of work, the number and duration of their breaks, and the planning of their daily activities (for example, whether they start with 'new' phone calls or resume conversations with potential customers identified days before). However, almost everyone in the accounts chosen agreed that routine tends to dominate the workplace when the end of the month was approaching and sales targets had to be achieved. Even supervisors had to adjust their managing style of the labour force in accordance with the outcomes expected by the client company and the call centre.

## Conclusion

This chapter analysed job designs in different accounts in order to discuss the influence of client firms on workers' experiences and employment conditions in subcontracted workplaces.

As mentioned in the literature review, one of the central themes in the United Kingdom and United States debate about work in call centres is how to manage the tensions between the standardisation of processes and the customisation of services (Batt 2000; Korczynski 2002). The intensity of this tension seems to be higher in front-line work because of workers' direct interaction with customers. As a result, some authors argue that this type of work imposes many restrictions to *routinisation* (Frenkel 1999; Korczynski 2002). Front-line service work might offer workers the opportunity to exert certain levels of autonomy and discretion, and it seems possible to question the fear of those observers who argue that a strict routine rules interactive service work in a way that resembles manufacturing under mass production systems (Garson 1988; Fernie and Metcalf 1998; Taylor et al. 2002). There is thus no question that the strict control exerted by IT systems and bureaucratic rules plays a prominent role in the experience of work in call centres. Most of the employees in this industry have neither the time nor the resources to offer a tailored service to customers, since call centres prioritise their attempts to standardise processes that allow cost reduction (Taylor et al. 2002; Baldry et al. 2007; Batt et al. 2007). However, a side-effect of the predominance of mass markets in call centres seems to be the deterioration in the employment and work conditions of the staff.

This chapter looked at the different job designs in call centres to explore the implications of customer segmentation on employment conditions and how to manage the tensions between organisations. In general, it was possible to observe how agents in the same organisations and performing essentially the same activities (*e.g.* sales) had different forms of remuneration (wages and bonuses) and different kinds of interactions with their supervisors and representatives of the client firm. Workers with the lowest-status jobs – sales agents – were more likely to have worse employment conditions and to suffer the consequences and pressures of standardisation. However, workers in customer services and technical support also expressed lower levels of satisfaction with their jobs, even though they enjoyed more autonomy.

To what extent were these variations the result of different job designs, the side-effect of different client firms, or the result of different managerial approaches? The evidence collected seems to confirm that tensions between organisations and managerial approaches – in the standardisation of processes versus the customisation of products – increased in the higher value customer segments. First, in low-value, high-volume activities, for example credit card sales, repetitive and low-skilled tasks dominated workers' performance with little variation. Second, in the case of customer support activities (airline services) the level of skills and the complexity of the tasks increase, as do the levels of tension and unpredictability. In the third and final case, where front-line service workers interact with high-value customers, the customisation of products dominates the dynamic of technical support with a certain level of rationalisation for the standardisation of processes in particular tasks.

According to the evidence provided by these experiences, the limitations of mass production models in dealing with the challenges of interactive service work start to emerge in customer services, and client firms seem to put more pressure on subcontractors and workers. Customer service workers 'break the rules' constantly and negotiate with customers and co-workers how to build up more complex resistance mechanisms (such as breaking down sales, or making extra efforts to find alternative solutions for customers in difficult situations). Customer service agents often deal with contradictory demands from client firms and customers, and the final outcome depends on many factors (such as the customer's profile or the type of problem), but there is no absolute certainty that customer service agents will ultimately 'defend' the interests of the client firm, even when the worker is subject to strict supervision and monitoring. It was common for employees to take the customer's side arguing that they were committed to high service quality standards. Among technical support workers there was more evidence about the dominance of a hybrid model designed to deal with demands for efficiency (minimisation of costs) and quality (customisation of products) simultaneously. Nevertheless, it does not mean that these workers suffered less stress, alienation and dissatisfaction in service work; a hybrid model is not necessarily more benevolent.

Most of the literature on call centres shows that there is a positive correlation between levels of autonomy and self-discretion on the one hand and workers' satisfaction on the other (Taylor and Bain 1999; Taylor et al. 2002; Baldry et al. 2007). However, the observations in this research do not demonstrate that there is a clear association between these two variables. As we move closer to high revenue markets, technical positions and supervision jobs, levels of self-discretion and autonomy increase, but the level of workers' satisfaction does not necessarily improve, and even decreases in some cases.

There is a plausible explanation for this: because of the inferior employment and payment conditions for sales representatives (the lowest job category in call centres), workers in this segment do not have much commitment to their work; because of their lower levels of autonomy and discretion, these workers assume that they are not ultimately responsible for customers' satisfaction, and they commonly blame 'the system' if something goes wrong. A kind of compensating mechanism appears to emerge here: if the employer does not provide good employment conditions, workers are not highly committed to their jobs, find them unsatisfying and perform them poorly.

This conclusion is also reinforced by my fieldwork observations. The working atmosphere was good (in general) in credit card sales accounts, where it was common to see workers having a social life within the workplace, even flirting and making jokes most of the time. However, workers with higher skills (and usually attached to services for higher customer segments) and supervisors 'feel the pressure' of having better levels of autonomy and self-discretion, and feel that they are ultimately responsible for customers' satisfaction. Therefore, if something goes wrong, employees in technical support and supervisors feel that they were as much responsible as the system for that problem. Because these supervisors and workers were more attached and committed to their jobs, their satisfaction levels were also much more sensitive to their job performance.

Also, the findings presented here suggest that the idiosyncratic styles of supervisors play an essential role in shaping workers' experiences and employment conditions in call centres. Much of the emphasis of this chapter was on exploring the effects of client firms on the administration of labour and it was not expected that supervisors would have much influence on this. From the evidence collected it is clear that supervisors are essential on at least three fronts: a) operation: when monitoring workers' performance; b) support: when helping employees in difficult circumstances and negotiating schedules and working conditions; and c) communication: when they act as a bridge between agents, call centre managers and client firm representatives.

In summary, employment conditions in subcontracted call centres seem to be much dependent on: a) job designs; b) the influence of client firms (mainly embodied by the figure of client firm representatives); and c) supervisors as the main mediators for negotiation and transmission of workers' complaints and problems. Interestingly, the organisation of work into different job categories and customer segments seems to be an effective means of controlling and disciplining workers while creating vertical and horizontal separations that might erode workers' collective response and organisation.

However, it is noticeable that these separations also create problems and tensions. This chapter provided much information about how workers often complain not just about managerial styles and client firms' demands, but also about the lack of parity in employment conditions among similar jobs. These job designs (in sales, customer services and technical support) seem to alleviate some pressures while generating horizontal tensions between workers in the same job category. How do service-oriented organisations with multiple clients, like call centres, deal with these horizontal tensions? The next chapter looks at social divisions in the workplace in order to address this question.

# CHAPTER FIVE

# CONTROL IN MULTI-EMPLOYER WORKPLACES: THE IMPORTANCE OF SOCIAL DIVISIONS

## 5.1. Call centres and the social geography of Mexico City

Mexico City is the political capital and economic centre of the country. This megalopolis includes 16 different *delegaciones* or counties of the *Distrito Federal* (Federal District) surrounded by a huge metropolitan area composed of counties of the provincial States of Mexico and Morelos. Altogether, about 23 million people live in this space, about 9 million in the *Distrito Federal* and the remaining 14 million dispersed across the metropolitan area (Figure 5.1).

Broadly speaking, it is possible to trace some social divisions geographically: those living in the south and west of the city have, in general, higher income levels and access to better public infrastructure than those living in the northern and eastern areas. Clearly, there are some exceptions, but this spatial division is pervasive in the minds of Mexico City's inhabitants and reinforced by many urban stereotypes. For example, everybody knows that people living in *El Pedregal* (south) or *Polanco* (west) neighbourhoods enjoy a higher income than those living in *La Providencia* (north) or *Iztapalapa* (east). The former are considered wealthy areas, the latter less wealthy.

The largest concentration of subcontracted call centres is located in downtown Mexico City, within *Cuauhtémoc* and *Benito Juárez* counties. These places are characterised by their good public transportation facilities including subway, public and private buses, taxies and the recently created metro-bus. Many of these call centres are located close to the corporate offices and headquarters of many of the call centres' clients, such as banks, telecommunication companies, electronics and software firms (Figure 5-1).

Most call centre workers come from counties in the north-eastern region of Mexico City and the surrounding area in the State of Mexico; in other words, from the poorer, less affluent parts of the city. This area, composed of nine counties, has a high concentration of the 'ideal' pool of candidates for call centre work: college dropouts of between 18 and 30 years old. *Iztapalapa* county, for example, contains 20 per cent of the total population of Mexico City and 13 per cent of those who are at least 18 years old and have not finished college education.

Figure 5-1. Workers and call centres in Mexico City and the metropolitan area

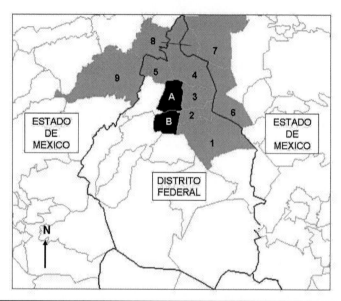

| Destination points | Origin points |
| --- | --- |
| A. Cuauhtémoc (Mexico City)<br>B. Benito Juárez (Mexico City) | 1. Iztacalco (Mexico City)<br>2. Venustiano Carranza (Mexico City)<br>3. Gustavo A. Madero (Mexico City)<br>4. Azcapotzalco (Mexico City)<br>5. Iztapalapa (Mexico City)<br>6. Netzahualcóyotl (State of Mexico)<br>7. Ecatepec (State of Mexico)<br>8. Tlalnepantla (State of Mexico)<br>9. Naucalpan (State of Mexico) |

Source: INEGI 2008 (www.inegi.gob.mx) and the author's interviews.

Altogether, the nine counties surrounding the call centre cluster by the north and east represent 38 per cent of the total population of Mexico City and the Metropolitan Area, a median age of 27 years, and 40 per cent of the population of 18 years or more with unfinished college education (Tables 5-1 to 5-4).

**Table 5-1. Mexico City: total population and median age by county 2005**

|  | Total Population | % of Total | Median Age |
|---|---|---|---|
| Mexico City | 8,720,916 | 100.0 | 29 |
| By County |  |  |  |
| 1. Alvaro Obregón | 706,567 | 8.1 | 29 |
| 2. Azcapotzalco | 425,298 | 4.9 | 31 |
| 3. Benito Juárez | 355,017 | 4.1 | 35 |
| 4. Coyoacán | 628,063 | 7.2 | 31 |
| 5. Cuajimalpa de Morelos | 173,625 | 2.0 | 26 |
| 6. Cuauhtémoc | 521,348 | 6.0 | 32 |
| 7. Gustavo A. Madero | 1,193,161 | 13.7 | 30 |
| 8. Iztacalco | 395,025 | 4.5 | 30 |
| 9. Iztapalapa | 1,820,888 | 20.9 | 27 |
| 10. La Magdalena Contreras | 228,927 | 2.6 | 28 |
| 11. Miguel Hidalgo | 353,534 | 4.1 | 32 |
| 12. Milpa Alta | 115,895 | 1.3 | 24 |
| 13. Tlahuac | 344,106 | 3.9 | 26 |
| 14. Tlalpan | 607,545 | 7.0 | 28 |
| 15. Venustiano Carranza | 447,459 | 5.1 | 30 |
| 16. Xochimilco | 404,458 | 4.6 | 27 |

Source: Elaborated by the author based on INEGI, *Conteo de Población y Vivienda 2005* (INEGI 2005).

**Table 5-2.** Mexico City: 'ideal' labour supply for call centres by county 2005

|  | Population aged 18-year and older with high school finished or some college education | % of Total |
|---|---|---|
| *Mexico City - Total* | *1,348,607* | *100.0* |
| 1. Alvaro Obregón | 103,078 | 7.6 |
| 2. Azcapotzalco | 73,707 | 5.5 |
| 3. Benito Juárez | 120,481 | 8.9 |
| 4. Coyoacán | 146,734 | 10.9 |
| 5. Cuajimalpa de Morelos | 23,697 | 1.8 |
| 6. Cuauhtémoc | 98,436 | 7.3 |
| 7. Gustavo A. Madero | 170,816 | 12.7 |
| 8. Iztacalco | 59,119 | 4.4 |
| 9. Iztapalapa | 185,300 | 13.7 |
| 10. La Magdalena Contreras | 29,804 | 2.2 |
| 11. Miguel Hidalgo | 79,904 | 5.9 |
| 12. Milpa Alta | 7,473 | 0.6 |
| 13. Tlahuac | 30,748 | 2.3 |
| 14. Tlalpan | 103,226 | 7.7 |
| 15. Venustiano Carranza | 64,461 | 4.8 |
| 16. Xochimilco | 51,623 | 3.8 |

Source: Elaborated by the author based on INEGI, *Conteo de Población y Vivienda* 2005 (INEGI 2005).

**Table 5-3.** State of Mexico's metropolitan area: total population and median age by selected county 2005

|  | Total | % of Total | Median Age |
|---|---|---|---|
| State of Mexico | 14,007,495 | 100.0 | 24 |
| Total for the main 4 counties | 4,334,036 | 30.9 | 27 |
| 1. Ecatepec | 1,688,258 | 12.1 | 25 |
| 2. Naucalpan | 821,442 | 5.9 | 27 |
| 3. Netzahualcóyotl | 1,140,528 | 8.1 | 27 |
| 4. Tlalnepantla | 683,808 | 4.9 | 28 |

Source: Elaborated by the author based on INEGI, *Conteo de Población y Vivienda* 2005 (INEGI 2005).

**Table 5-4. State of Mexico's metropolitan area: 'ideal' labour supply for call centres by county 2005**

|  | Population aged 18-year and older with high school finished or some college education | % of Total |
|---|---|---|
| State of Mexico | 1,118,123 | 100.0 |
| **Total for the main 4 counties** | **438,655** | **39.2** |
| 1. Ecatepec | 136,379 | 12.2 |
| 2. Naucalpan | 99,299 | 8.9 |
| 3. Netzahualcóyotl | 109,723 | 9.8 |
| 4. Tlalnepantla | 93,254 | 8.3 |

Source: Elaborated by the author based on INEGI, *Conteo de Población y Vivienda 2005* (INEGI 2005).

Clearly, the concentration of call centre companies in this area is not accidental. Downtown Mexico City is a well-known retail and office space and its location facilitates the commuting of workers from many different parts of the city. Most importantly, this geographical position is also attractive because it frequently works as an intermediate place between workers' households and other destinations such as schools or second jobs, crucial factors in the location of most industries (Holmes 1986; Scott and Storper 1986).

In the interviews, Mexican workers emphasised the importance of location and schedule in the search for a suitable job. In particular, they seemed to be interested in two factors: transportation and food. For example, people interviewed spent, on average between one and one and a half hours in commuting to work and invested about 20 Mexican pesos (approx. £1) in public transportation every day. In Mexico City, each subway ticket cost 2 Mexican pesos (approx. £0.10) in 2006 and the system is not divided by zones, so passengers pay the same price no matter how far they travel. Subway is the cheapest and most efficient form of transport in Mexico City. Other transport could be more expensive (also in 2006), such as Metro-bus (4.50 Mexican pesos, approx. £0.23, for one journey), private bus (minimum 2.50 Mexican pesos, approx. £0.13, for one journey) or taxi.[1]

The other main concern for these workers was where to eat and how much to pay for it. In the call centres analysed, most employees used the dining room facilities of the firm. These usually consisted of spaces with tables and chairs, dispenser machines with candies and sodas, and microwaves to heat the food. I never saw any 'in-house' catering service. Also, it was common to see fliers of fast-food restaurants, *taquerías* (tacos) or *torterías* (Mexican sandwiches) all over the place, and workers went downstairs to the building's entrance to pick up food orders. On average, workers interviewed spent 40 Mexican pesos (approx. £2) on meals daily. Overall, call centres 'encourage' workers to stay within the facilities of the call centre as much as possible during working hours.

This does not seem to be the standard for Mexican offices where most employees usually go out to have their meals and have a pause in the work day. Employees in call centres were encouraged to reduce the time they spent having their meals and many of them were not allowed to go outside for lunch; however, this restriction seemed to be applied only to the lowest category of front-line work. Other workers who had no direct interaction with customers had more freedom to move outside the building during meal times:

> Everything depends on the workload, you know... In fact, we are allowed to go out but, usually, I prefer to call in order to get my food because sometimes I have no time to go to a restaurant or something like that... but ordinary agents, the type who are always at the phone, they cannot go out anyway but we, as back officers, can do so. That's one of the reasons why this job is a little bit better... We have more responsibilities, it is more interesting, so we have some privileges as well, that's why we are allowed to go out but, to be honest, the workload is a strong limitation... So in practice we rarely make use of this advantage.
> —Outsourcing back office worker, Phonemex Volaris.

Time for travelling and meals is crucial for work in call centres, especially in places like Mexico City. If we bear in mind that most of the people in call centres work part-time (no more than six hours per day), that they might spend up to three hours travelling (round trips) and commonly combine this activity with others (such as studies, housekeeping, childcare

---

[1] The minimum salary in Mexico City (in 2007) was the equivalent of about £75 monthly (INEGI 2007). Salaries in call centres varied from the equivalent of £75 (sales) to £400 (technical support) monthly.

or a second job), then time and distance are not superficial issues for these workers.

Despite the physical dispersion among the areas where these workers lived, most of them seemed to have similar characteristics. In general, the typical call centre worker in Mexico City could be described as a young person (between 18 and 30 years old), with college education unfinished, and belonging to a household with a lower-medium class income (about 6,000 Mexican pesos monthly, the equivalent of approximately £300). In short, they are the children of manual workers, low level bureaucrats and people in the informal economy.

As mentioned in previous chapters, most call centre workers are in front-line services with low skills and minimal autonomy, subjected to rigid scripts and constant monitoring from supervisors (either directly or through IT devices). Importantly, workers in these jobs tend to hold many social values and cultural traditions that have been pervasive in the Mexican society for a long time. For example, most workers tend to believe that sales work is more appropriate for women, because they have the 'enchantment' needed to convince customers, whereas more 'aggressive' duties are more appropriate for male workers, such as dealing with difficult customers in tasks related to the managing of unpaid bills. Nevertheless, despite the widespread perception that gender would play a role in the division of labour in call centres, this research did not find major evidence of gender segregation in the workplace, at least in the four categories analysed so far (sales, customer services, technical support and supervision positions). According to the IMT, men and women are evenly distributed in call centres of Mexico City and there is a roughly 50-50 per cent mix across all categories (IMT 2007), unlike the industry at global level where call centre work is dominated by female workers (Batt et al. 2007). This does not mean that there is no gender discrimination in Mexican call centres but this research was unable to find strong evidence for it in front-line services.

Also, in this research I did not found strong evidence that skin colour and other ethnic characteristics that could be 'observed' in workers' way of speaking (such as tone of voice, pronunciation and accent) were of relevance when assigning workers to different categories. This was a little bit surprising since I assumed that skin colour would be particularly important for economic interactions among Mexicans (even if these interactions are undertaken through the phone, that is why the connection with the tone of voice). In Mexico, a lighter skin is considered of higher status. Managers of client firms and call centres appear to be aware of this particular cultural value in the interaction with customers and among employees; so I assumed that employers will consciously divide the workforce bearing in mind skin colour. However, it seems that this physical characteristic was not so clear and relevant in the end, something that seems to be in line with findings for the manufacturing industry in Mexico as well (Bank Muñoz 2008). However, it seems that social bonds, much more than skin colour or gender, were of more importance in dividing the workforce. For this reason, when recruiting new staff employers try to take advantage of these social bonds when asking existing employees to find job candidates among their acquaintances and friends.

## 5.2. The importance of social networks in recruitment

Most of the human resources managers interviewed did not consider temporary staff agencies as a reliable source of job candidates. They preferred to ask employees to 'invite' friends and other acquaintances to apply for the vacancies available. In a context where they might need dozens of people from one day to another the response could be amazing when using the social networks of employees. According to some managers, word of mouth is the most effective way to recruit; most of the time it is enough simply to ask some agents to invite or encourage their friends to apply for a job to have a large number of candidates the following day.

There is no question that social networks are a reliable source of information in connecting job seekers with potential jobs (Granovetter 1973; 1992; Granovetter and Swedberg 1992; Fernandez et al. 2000; Castilla 2005). Here is how one of the managers interviewed explain the situation:

> The company uses four basic mechanisms for recruitment: the internet, going to schools directly, exchange meetings with other companies, and through our own employees. Word of mouth among our employees is the most important and effective way for us to get candidates for our vacancies. We say: 'If you bring people we will give you *Phonemex-kilometres* [points exchangeable for corporate memorabilia].' Then our people go to their schools or neighbourhoods and tell their classmates and friends that there are vacancies here and we get many candidates. We also have contact with some employment agencies. But so far, our young people bring new candidates most of the time.
> —Human Resources Manager, Phonemex.

The crucial importance of existing employees in bringing in more employees and 'controlling' the pool of candidates (Maguire 1988;

Fernandez et al. 2000; Castilla 2005) is corroborated by the responses given by most of the workers interviewed in this research. Specifically, most employees said that they knew that the company paid to announce vacancies in the press and on the internet, but most of the time in order to recruit new staff they asked employees to invite friends or people they knew to work for the company. Using the social ties of existing employees to fill vacancies is a well-known practice in many other industries (Tilly and Tilly 1997). What is surprising in this case is that call centres are supposed to be a relatively high-tech industry of the new economy, where more sophisticated mechanisms would be in place to select new employees. In other words, some practices of the old economy appear to persist in new industries.

However, Alejandra González (the head of human resources in Phonemex) and other human resources managers interviewed said that sometimes employees' social networks are insufficient when there is a massive recruitment drive. She spoke frenetically about the level of recruitment that is sometimes required by call centres. Apparently human resources staff sometimes needs to go out and 'literally' pick as many people as they can:

> Sometimes you need 500 people for next Friday [in three-day time], and that is a 'war recruitment', that is how we call it, 'war recruitment' [she says jokingly]. Then we need to go everywhere to get people, whatever the place! I was telling my staff that we had to go outside and pick some people from the sit-in close from here [a sit-in to protest at alleged electoral fraud in the presidential elections of 2006]. However, we are lucky; Mexico City and its more than 20 million inhabitants is still a suitable place for 'war recruitments' when it is necessary.

However, it would be a mistake to depict an image of call centre companies furiously 'devouring' workers in the market like insatiable job-creating machines. In fact, the flow also operates in the opposite direction. In the interviews, I perceived and collected information about the presence of a large pool of young job seekers and how they regarded call centres as good places to work in. These workers also used their social links in order to apply for and obtain information about jobs (Granovetter 1973; Castilla 2005). In this way both sides of the labour market use social networks to collect information in the search for a job or to fill vacancies. The 'channels' used in these social networks seem to be very diverse, and include 'close' family connections:

> Q How did you get this job?
> A Thanks to my wife.

Q And how did she get her job?
A She was recommended by a friend who was working in the call centre of Dinamarca Street. She worked in human resources and asked my wife if she would be interested in a vacancy at Wal-Mart's account, where I am now working. My wife accepted and took the job. However, after some time but she was transferred to another account... When she left this job she suggested me to replace her... and I did so.
—Interview with outsourcing worker, Phonemex Wal-Mart.

Sometimes friends of employees are recruited:

A friend who used to work here recommended me this place because I was looking for a job. He told me which documents I would need, so I came and dropped in my CV. I did it in the call centre of Monterrey Street, in that branch... Then they called me for different interviews and I was hired in the end.
—Outsourcing worker, Phonemex Telefónica.

Sometimes members of the 'extended' family of an employee are recruited:

The sister of my sister in law was working here and we frequently talked about her job, her friends here and the environment... She was also my classmate at school and it did not seem to be a problem to find the time to combine school and work... So I decided to apply for this job.
—Outsourcing worker, Phonemex Financia BBVA Bancomer.

Sometimes a combination of friends and internet websites help people to find employment in the call centres:

Q How did you get the job?
A I applied for the job on the website. You can look at it and see the vacancies they offer... When I was checking this I thought that my profile would be good for them, due to my experience and education, you know... Anyway, the thing is that before submitting my application I asked one of my friends for his opinion, he used to work here...
Q What did he say?
A To be honest, he was not very enthusiastic but he said that it was OK. Then I submitted my application and I had some interviews with people about the project, my skills, experience, education and so on... and it was very easy. The first interview was with Phonemex, and the second one with Microsoft.
—Interview with outsourcing worker, Phonemex Microsoft

Sometimes other 'acquaintances' of employees are recruited:

One guy that I met in my Master's course sent me a message one day
saying that this company was looking for engineers, and he wondered if I
could be interested in one of the vacancies. I said yes, I sent my CV and I
came to the interview. Then they called me and said that I was not selected
for the original position but wanted to offer me another job in a different
account. So, I am here since then.
—Outsourcing worker, Datatech Sybase.

These responses show how members of social networks have key
information about jobs, such as skills required, compensation, number of
places, details of the client firm and types of schedule. This information is
beneficial for employers and employees alike because new workers who
are recruited through existing employees tend to start their jobs with a
good idea of the work to be performed; which has a positive effect on their
initial productivity level (Castilla 2005).

However, the dynamics between job applications, existing workers and
social capital is not always smooth, especially for certain types of workers
who are sceptical about the way in which managers of human resources
units interpret the role of social capital in recruitment. Technical support
workers (oriented to markets of higher income or revenue generation) are
more likely to be dissatisfied with the way in which human resources
departments recruit new staff. They believe that human resources
managers do not know where to find the right people to perform technical
work:

All the jobs I have obtained were through the people I know; only my very
first job was the exception. It is normal... this is why people in human
resources always have many problems in getting the right person for this
type of job. But here, inside the account of Microsoft, we know what kind
of guys we really need and the responsibilities they might face. So, it is
easier for us to find these guys... so human resources staff asks us
frequently for the contact details of people we know.
—Supervisor, Phonemex Microsoft.

Once again, it seems that tensions between workers and organisations
tend to increase when higher levels of skills are required and when the job
is oriented to markets of higher income. The previous statement expressed
by a supervisor in a Microsoft account suggests that some technical
workers in support services have a different and distinctive image about
other job categories in call centres. In many cases, technical workers
insisted that they were different from the rest because of their skills and

education. In the previous extract, the respondent implied that even people in the human resources department did not know their field of expertise sufficiently well to pick the right person for the job. So, they had to be consulted about where to find the right person for a vacancy. It is worth noting here that some managers referred to technical support workers as 'Hollywood stars', as mentioned in chapter three.

Overall, the recruitment process in the call centre studied runs as follows: the company either asks employees to 'invite' friends and other acquaintances to apply for vacancies in the company or releases an announcement on the internet or in the press. The basic requirements for staff are as follows: they must be 18-year old minimum, have at least some college education or high school diploma, and must be flexible about schedules. Once the candidates submit their applications, they are shortlisted and scheduled for interviews within a couple of days, or a week at most. During the interview candidates are asked about their professional experience, education and place of residence. After this, the candidates take a brief test using a telephone: the candidate has to make a phone call to another person in a different room to simulate a selling call (the famous 'cold' calls). After this, the person from the other room calls back and the candidate simulates that she or he is a customer representative. In doing this brief test, managers evaluate the tone of voice and temper of the candidate. It is simple and brief, but a very effective means of assessing the candidate's basic abilities on the phone and conversation skills with other people.

The aim behind these details of the recruitment process is very simple: to find a suitable person to carry out the work in social terms. Is it the use of old practices such as social networks consistent with the efficient allocation of labour brought about by specialisation? Is it possible that outsourcing in the new economy is not exempt of the importance of social ties at work?

In other words, despite the narratives of dramatic transformations at work where meritocratic mechanisms supposedly substitute old idiosyncratic methods, social networks and, more importantly, the content of these social ties, seem to represent a set of characteristics that are important for organisations; that is reducing transaction costs in recruitment and disciplining and controlling workers in the workplace. Even in an environment that is highly monitored by IT technologies, that is, where technical control is strong, social bonds between workers appear still to be relevant as a control mechanism. In this regard, the next section explores how these social networks are used to recreate social divisions inside call centres in order to generate additional mechanisms to control and discipline workers.

## 5.3. Control, discipline and labour segregation

The evidence presented in this book confirms that the main problems between subcontractors and client firms are related to the building of trust and cooperation, something that has been identified in other studies of outsourcing (Sako and Helper 1998; Lorenz 1999). However, much of the literature and research has focused on manufacturing while the outsourcing of services has received less attention. This research argues that there are special challenges for the coordination and cooperation of the organisations involved in the outsourcing of front-line services.

In previous chapters I have confirmed how the customer–employee interface of service work generates tensions between the organisations involved: while client firms are more interested in the customisation of the service provided (in order to retain customers) subcontractors seem more interested in standardising processes (in order to reduce costs and compensate for the risks taken as subcontractors). These tensions can be observed at the different stages of the administration of the labour force: recruitment, selection, training, operation and compensation. In order to alleviate these tensions, the organisations studied use different mechanisms: 1) contracts for services (in order to reduce labour costs); 2) narrow job designs (in order to fragment the labour force); and 3) a more intensive use of supervisors to control workers.

These are useful mechanisms for subcontractors when there are multiple client firms (and employers) within the workplace. It is important to bear in mind that these subcontractors have to deal with up to several dozens of client firms at the same time in the same place. In other words, we have plenty of evidence that client firms play a central role in the administration of the workforce in outsourcing and that this involvement is likely to increase in market segments that provide higher revenue for the organisations involved.

Nonetheless, this organisation of work (based on narrow job designs, the use of contracts for services and intensive use of supervisors) also generates additional problems with the workforce. In previous sections we have seen how different workers' experiences and employment conditions (including wages, bonuses and interactions with the client firm, among others) triggered systematic complaints from call centre workers. However, it seems that collective and individual displays of resistance are relatively scarce or at least less vigorous than in other industries (*e.g.*

manufacturing). In this chapter, the basic argument is that social divisions are used as mechanisms to provide stability and control in subcontracted workplaces. Specifically, findings of this research suggest that the social environment created within call centres inhibits workers' collective resistance while providing employees with multiple mechanisms to cope with stress and dissatisfaction at work.

### 5.3.1 An overview of workers' social experiences in call centres

At first glance, the image of a call centre workplace resembles one of a 'school' environment. In many ways, large, subcontracted call centres are similar to school corridors, where students of different ages take classes in separate rooms, always with a teacher [supervisor] sitting in a desk at a higher level, monitoring and supervising the activities of the students [employees]. Clearly, this is a less dramatic depiction than the one created by some writers, who have referred to call centres as modern *panopticons* or 'assembly lines in the head' (Garson 1988; Fernie and Metcalf 1998; Taylor and Bain 1999).

Under this apparently rigorous and direct control, reinforced by strict bureaucratic rules and supported by powerful technical devices, call centre managers might face the same challenges, tensions and strategies of resistance as their equivalents in many other workplaces. Workers speak to each other when supervisors are distracted or looking in a different direction. Employees frequently have fun while working, even flirting and gossiping. As in many schools, the main entrances and surroundings of the call centres that I visited were densely populated with young workers chatting, smoking, drinking and eating before and after work. In summary, my first impression was that the call centre workforce was socially integrated in an effective way. Many of the problems or acts of resistance from employees were tolerated by managers and supervisors, who interpret these reactions as copying strategies that help to maintain a certain harmony in the workplace.

There is a reason for this dynamics and rationale of the workplace environment experienced in call centres in Mexico. As mentioned, the ideal candidates for sales and customer service positions (not technical support) are people with unfinished college education, which belies the assumption that call centres seek to recruit highly skilled staff in developing countries (Taylor and Bain 2005); also, call centres' practice of recruiting college dropouts seems to be at odds with the general assumption that services in the new economy mainly employ highly educated workers. Instead, call centres might ask for 'students' in order to meet their need for part-time employees, also enabling them to use non-standard contracts; at least, this is what I could see on job advertisements and workplace observations. However, it is interesting that workers also 'play' this game and see themselves as 'students' even if they are no longer pursuing any kind of education or degree.

In most of my interviews workers described themselves as college students in part-time jobs. However, as the interviews progressed and the interviewees trusted me more, many of them agreed that, in fact, they were no longer in education and that they had dropped out from college some time ago. Most of these employees interviewed got the job shortly after dropping out from the school or they dropped out of school shortly after getting the job. Importantly, according to some of the people interviewed, having a part-time job seemed to be a reasonable excuse to justify their poor academic performance. Moreover, when I asked them if they needed the job to secure financial resources at home, an overwhelming majority answered: 'No'. It seems that most of these workers simply did not find their way in the school and found call centre work as a way to compensate for their academic failure before their parents. Most of the time, these workers told me that they used the money they made as pocket money, to go on holidays, to go out, to do shopping, because they didn't need money for rent and food as they lived at home with their parents.

Therefore, most of these workers have in common this 'ambiguous' profile: being college students in part-time call centre work, and it would be interesting to know whether call centres make a conscious decision to select workers with this specific profile to fill most of the jobs they offer. Are people from this background the only candidates available? Or does this type of worker offer particular advantages in the operation of front-line service work in call centres?

According to Jenkins (1988), informal social networks as a means for recruitment are a key variable to explain discriminatory selection at the point of entry of internal labour markets. For Jenkins, there are two types of criteria, suitability and acceptability:

> Suitability is functionally specific, inasmuch as it is concerned with the individual's ability to perform the tasks required by the job. Criteria of suitability might include physique, particular experience or formal education, trade or professional qualifications... Acceptability is functionally non-specific, concerned with the general control and management of the organisation: will the recruit 'fit in' to the context in question, is he or she 'dependable', 'reliable', and hardworking, will the worker leave after a short time?
> (Jenkins 1988:319).

For Jenkins: "criteria of acceptability, highly subjective and dependent upon managerial perceptions, include appearance, 'manner and attitude', 'maturity', gender, labour-market history and age and marital status" (Jenkins 1988:320).

However, Jenkins himself recognises that there is no clear distinction between the two. In this case, when call centres recruit and select workers following the clues dictated by social networks and the college dropper profile, the organisation puts some extra pressure on workers, restricting or driving their aspirations to move to other accounts or leave the job. In this way, social bonds among workers help to control and discipline the workforce, something very useful in an environment exposed to different employment conditions (even when undertaking the same type of job) due to the diversity of client firms.

Therefore, it seems that subcontractors seem to pursue labour division and segregation for two main reasons, one external and the other internal. The external justification is that labour segregation seems to reduce transactions costs as a good support for the organisation of work and customer segmentation strategies. A crucial part of a 'convincing' customer–worker relationship is rooted in building up the 'enchantment of customer sovereignty' – control over the service interaction with customers (Hochschild 1983; Ritzer 1993; 1998; Korczynski 2002; 2009). Customers are expected to believe that they control the interaction, that they are always right (Hochschild 1983). In order to make this 'illusion' credible, call centre companies need to reproduce a scheme coherent with the social structure. For instance, perfume or kitchen products sellers must be women and those giving technical support for electronic products or software must be men – at least in Mexico where front-line service presumably would have a strong gender and sexist profile.

Therefore, it would be expected that gender and class stereotypes reinforce the construction of workers' subordination during the service interaction with customers (Hochschild 1983). In this respect, the relation between workers and customers has an important cognitive element that goes beyond the visibility of physical appearances. In the tone, the accent, the vocabulary or even the volume of the voice, the customer might recognise a particular type of social relation that has an effect on the economic transaction (Hochschild 1983; Hochschild and Machung 1990) so it displays the impact of social structures on economic outcomes (Granovetter 2005). In this sense, labour segregation allows the matching of customer–agent partners that make this exchange comfortable for customers; it is a seducing tactic.

This matching strategy between customer and agents in call centre work has been identified previously by Batt (2000) and Batt and Moynihan (2002), but in relation to different types of managerial approaches in the workplace rather than the socio-demographic characteristics of the labour force. However, the division of the labour force by socio-economic characteristics is central to labour market segmentation theory (Piore 1970), and manufacturing experiences have offered much evidence of it.

As mentioned, a very interesting thing is that, despite the values and cultural norms that most of these workers and managers had, I did not find in this research strong evidence of gender discrimination. I only found only limited evidence that women were preferred over men for sales positions and that managers preferred men over women for dealing with irritated or difficult customers, but it does not seem systematic and conscious. These findings do not seem to be line with evidence of gender prejudice in call centre jobs found in other contexts (Belt 2002; Glucksmann 2004). It is also surprising because it might be expected that there would be a strong division of labour in a society that maintains strong gender roles. Therefore, I would need to collect more evidence about the gender experience before making a conclusive statement about gender discrimination in these large subcontracted call centres.

Nevertheless, front-line female workers told me that they did not apply for better jobs, such as supervision positions, because these jobs would involve them spending more time at work and having greater responsibilities, and they had to go back home as quickly as possible after work in order to take care of their children and husbands. So, household responsibilities are important in shaping the experience of work for female workers, at least in Mexico. This demonstrates that, despite my lack of evidence about gender discrimination inside these organisations, other structural factors might limit women's career development in call centres.

The use of informal mechanisms of recruitment for workers reveals the importance of the social context in the workplace (Maguire 1986; 1988). As mentioned, one of the big challenges for managerial control in inter-firm relationships is the blurring boundaries between organisations, the dispersion of authority, and the confusion created by the existence of multiple clients. Therefore, if authority is eroded by its multiple faces and conflicting interests then another mechanism is needed to provide coherence and stability in the employment relationship. Paradoxically, workers themselves might play a fundamental role in building up social control inside the workplace, as happens formally in self-managed teams.

In these call centres, workers recommend friends and acquaintances. Once in the workplace, these informal bonds work as peer pressure mechanisms and barriers among different accounts, in other words, the use of informal mechanisms as social networks provides an external link of social control and discipline. I frequently observed that many workers were confused about who was the 'real' or, at least, the 'most important' client or authority – the customer, the subcontractor or the client firm? But they were always very clear about the differences among them as different *types* of workers. These were reinforced by human resources initiatives such as social events and sport competitions, which were essential means of reinforcing divisions and rivalries between workers. In all these events, workers were likely to be placed in organised teams based on their account affiliation, which in turn was 'populated' using social networks; in doing so subcontractors reduced mobility among the accounts while limiting the chances of collective organisations such as unions being formed. How does this mechanism affect workers? In the following section two experiences are presented.

## 5.3.2 Emotions and autonomy

In most of the sociology of work literature, attempts to control customer–worker interactions are seen as the ultimate phase of human alienation under capitalism (Hochschild 1983; Hochschild and Machung 1990; Ritzer 1993; 1998; Sennett 2009). However, there is also considerable research indicating the limitations of control over front-line service work because of the unpredictability and complexity of customer–worker interaction (Leidner 1993; Batt 2000; Korczynski 2002; Bolton and Boyd 2003; Korczynski 2007; 2009).

One strategy of dealing with this uncertainty and lack of control is the creation of pre-configured interactions embodied by the use of scripts. In doing so, organisations such as call centres might secure a great degree of control over the interaction between customers and workers (Garson 1988; Taylor and Bain 1999). However, workers do not seem to be neutral agents in this process and tend to display different levels of effort and autonomy depending on individual circumstances, especially when multiple employers are present.

This section presents two cases of call centre workers and how they move away from pre-configured scripts when developing intense or special interactions with customers. These cases also illustrate how this situation is a fundamental factor in explaining the importance of social divisions at work, and how workers develop coping strategies and discipline themselves, but they also show how employees might display higher levels of autonomy and discretion in providing customer services.

Gisela Hernández is the first example; she is a customer representative agent. She got the job because her boyfriend and another friend encouraged her to apply for a vacancy (they were already employees in the call centre). After a couple of interviews, she was hired to work for a government campaign of real state credits. In this account, Gisela and her boyfriend were working together. When the contract between the federal government and the call centre expired, they were both moved to an account selling credit cards. According to Gisela, they did not want the new positions but a human resources manager persuaded them to stay there temporarily because a new account, for specialised banking services, was about to be opened, and Gisela and her boyfriend were promised two jobs there. Nowadays, Gisela works for this specialised account known as UEAC, which handles customer complaints from Bancomer.

Gisela lived in the southern area of Mexico City, near to the main campus of the National University of Mexico. The place where she works, and where the interview took place, is also located in the south of Mexico City, close to her house. She is also an accounting and management college student at the National University of Mexico, but she does not study at the main campus, the one in the south and near to her home. Actually, she needs to go in exactly the opposite direction, to the extreme north of the Metropolitan Area, because she was assigned to the Naucalpan campus, in the State of Mexico. Interestingly, Gisela's boyfriend, who I also interviewed (before I knew that they were partners), commented that they were also classmates at the university. Actually, the large amount of time spent together moving across the city, for work and studies, played a crucial role in developing their relationship.

Gisela's boyfriend said that at the beginning they were only friends but "after spending all this time together... things changed". As mentioned in the introduction to this chapter, call centre workers in Mexico City normally travel long distances to commute between work, home and other destinations, so travelling across the city was a fundamental part in reinforcing the work, academic and emotional links between Gisela and her boyfriend.

Gisela's boyfriend is an important influence on her work experience in the call centre; he is the supervisor of the account where she works. As a supervisor, Gisela's boyfriend has to process the files and discuss the content of the scripts with a bank representative. He explained to me that he and his group were expected to deal with all the calls received (thus give a 100 per cent response) and provide effective solutions to queries, and that he was in charge to make sure that this actually happened. In other words, his job was monitoring and supervising the work performed by the other members of his team. In our conversation, he complained that many of his colleagues did not like their jobs, and sometimes did not answer the phone or simply simulated that they were busy. He used phrases such as "It drives me crazy" to describe his feelings when colleagues were not performing their work properly. However, he also emphasised that he had to be calm because his salary depended on the performance of the whole group: "We are all the same here, we are a team and I need their collaboration."

Gisela was frequently caught in the middle of disputes between her boyfriend and her colleagues. She argued that it was unfair that her boyfriend's salary depended on the group's performance, and believed that some people did not deserve the job they had there (thinking in the same way that her boyfriend did). For this reason, perhaps, Gisela insisted that her main commitment was to 'her clients', people dealing with the bank, and that she felt responsible about how they were treated; so her loyalties and commitment were to the customers not her colleagues. To illustrate this point, Gisela shared with me two very interesting experiences in dealing with customers' complaints and revealing the emotional challenges of work and social interaction in call centres and how other agents reacted to the 'personalisation' of these interactions.

Gisela's first story was related to a customer who called because he did not recognise a withdrawal of 5,000 pesos (approx. £250). He was worried because this amount was equal to his monthly pension. Gisela told me that she could not remember very well how she got involved in this issue; the man told her that he was widow, that his daughter was beaten by her husband and suffered a miscarriage:

> He told me many things about his life and he was an old man. He told me that he was trying to get an answer from Bancomer [the bank] but he never got one. So, he said that he only wanted to complain, that's it, that he did not expect the money back anyway, that he only wanted to complain... to be heard I believed.

However, Gisela explained to me that she wanted to help this man. Therefore, she asked him to send her all his bank and pension documents and he did so. Since that day the man called her every day. At first, the calls were only to check whether there was any progress on his complaint but, little by little, these daily conversations triggered a more personal exchange. Gisela said that it was a really nice experience for her because each time this man called he asked for her. Agents are not supposed to personalise calls but the rest of the staff knew the story and every time he called they shouted: "Hey Gisela! This is your grandpa; I will transfer him to you." Eventually, the man asked Gisela questions about her personal life. In the end, this customer got his reimbursement, and he called to say goodbye, but Gisela did not come to work that day: "For me it was fantastic to help this man."

It is understandable that agents feel empathy for customers in such disgraceful situations, and seems normal that they invest extra time and effort in order to help them with their problems, even if this is not considered part of the script or any other pre-configured interaction process. As mentioned, Gisela's experience did not conform to the one of alienation brought about by emotional work detected by Hochschild (1983). She did not feel that her feelings were manipulated or that she was faking her genuine interest in solving a client's problem. Gisela invested time and dedication to her tasks without any expectation of extra-pecuniary compensation. This shows that the interactions between customers and agents cannot all be strictly controlled and predicted by rigid bureaucratic rules or IT devices.

However, interactions with customers are not always happy and satisfactory. Gisela also shared with me another story, which was less rewarding:

> A lady blamed me about her divorce but I did not have any idea about it. She was a lady who got a bill from two different credit cards, one from Wal-Mart and the other from Soriana. She told me that she never asked for those credit cards and wanted to cancel them. As an agent, you know, you always remember the names in these cases... this was Mrs Sánchez de Tagle. So, she called every day to check if there was any progress. However, we could not do anything because the contract was signed by her husband, so he was legally responsible for the card and we sent all the documents to him.

Gisela explained that the customer's husband was called Francisco Gómez and one of the credit cards was signed by a man called Víctor Hernández. For this reason, the husband was furious and thought that the woman had an extra-marital affair. Therefore, the woman was also furious and called Gisela many times every day in order to demand apologies and a clarification.

According to Gisela the information was correct or, at least, corresponding to what she saw registered in the system. Somehow the woman had two different credit cards derived from two contracts signed by two different men (at least on paper). According to Gisela, there was no means to prove that the registers were wrong. The case was sent to the federal financial authorities and eventually the cards were cancelled and the woman divorced:

> Q Did she stop calling?
> A No, she called me crying, blaming me and the bank for her divorce... She called here and the same thing happened all the time... She asked for me, and my colleagues mischievously transferred me the call whispering: 'This is your favourite friend, the crying woman... and she is looking for you again!' She repeated over and over again that everything was our fault. I was trying to fake my voice saying that I was another person but she always recognised my voice. Eventually, she got calm, she apologised and stopped calling.

These two experiences from Gisela illustrate many of the challenges and opportunities involved in front-line service work. On the one hand, there is no question that Gisela's work as a customer representative could have a very intense emotional charge but, contrary to the predictions of some critical authors about the devastating effects of rigid scripts (Hochschild 1983; Garson 1988; Fernie and Metcalf 1998; Ritzer 1998; Taylor and Bain 2007), Gisela was able to manage her emotions with high levels of autonomy. Despite all the pressure, Gisela was able to dedicate extra effort to solve the problems of one of her clients, without receiving compensation for doing so. On the other hand, Gisela always kept her formal position despite the pressures received from the client having problems with her credit cards and her husband. It is true that Gisela tried to avoid her sometimes (violating the number one code of conduct in call centres: "You always answer the phone"), but she also had to deal with the pressure of being the target of her co-workers' jokes. Furthermore, these jokes reflect the crucial importance of human interactions in front-line service (Mulholland 2004).

These interactions reflected not only the type of interactions that workers might develop with customers over the phone but also the kind of environment and relationships created among workers. As pointed out before, in this particular case, Gisela was in a difficult position between showing loyalty to her co-workers and understanding her partner's problems at work.

Interestingly, the challenges of emotional work with customers seem to provoke many tensions among workers as well as between managers and workers. As mentioned, informal means of recruitment and customer segmentation create important barriers and divisions between workers, fragmenting class identity and eroding the possibilities of collective organisation.

An example of the tensions among workers is embodied by the experience and opinions of Jaime González, a customer service agent working for the US Airways account in Phonemex. During the interview, Jaime continually expressed his lack of interest in having a closer relationship with people in other accounts (something that was common among other employees interviewed). Jaime said that people at US Airways prefer to socialise among themselves rather than with staff from different accounts because agents in other accounts did not like them: "They hate us a little bit, because they look at us and think that we are the 'clowns' of the company."

Interestingly, Jaime had the typical posh accent that distinguishes the upper class in Mexico. He also spoke very loudly, displaying self-confidence or attention-seeking. Jaime learnt English because his family sent him every year to summer camps in Canada. When asked about his interpretation of the image of different clients and accounts in the call centre, Jaime said that, despite the fact that Bancomer (a bank) was the most important client for the company (Phonemex), US Airways and Microsoft were very important as well because Phonemex charged these clients in US dollars, so these accounts were the second and third most valuable clients for the company. Interestingly, Jaime said that these accounts were also important because of the 'type' of people working there: "Of course, the skills of workers in these accounts are higher, better."

I chose to write about Jaime's experience because he was very open and shameless about expressing his opinion about the differences between people working at US Airways and other staff in Phonemex:

> The main difference between people here [US Airways] and those over there working for Bancomer is... with all my respect, that people in US Airways look better, smarter, we have better presence, image you know... and we have better education. On the other hand, people at Bancomer well... with all my respect again, it looks like they were picked up from a 'mom and pop' store. That they were just walking around on one of the streets nearby and were simply invited to work here... that way, very simple... not a very selective process... Their training lasts only three days and ours one month, there is no comparison at all. The way they do things at Bancomer is very different from the way we do things at US Airways. At Bancomer they need to call Pedro Perez [a very common name in Mexico] and see if he wants a credit card. In our case, we need to look at the whole process, in English and efficiently, in a few words: quickly, smoothly, and with good humour.

This statement by Jaime is fascinating because it reflects how successful customer segmentation, job designs and social networks are as a means of recruiting staff that allow the creation of a segregated labour force (without a collective consciousness). Jaime's statement shows not only the rivalry among workers from different job categories, but also how his view extends to include the customers of these workers! For Jaime, these customers were also 'inferior' and he used the name 'Pedro Perez' in a pejorative way.

Curiously enough, Jaime also recognised that he was a constant target of 'racist' expressions from customers in the United States, when describing the attitudes that were not tolerated when interacting with customers:

> Q What kind of situation is not tolerated by your supervisors?
> A Well, finishing or interrupting a phone call without a good reason. We need a very good one to do so… And I will tell you something… something that I was told… informally… by some people on the quality program. If somebody is offending you, using very bad expressions or words against you, you might be allowed, at least informally… by your supervisor… to finish the conversation and just hang up the phone… but yes… it varies from supervisor to supervisor… For example, people have said to me things such as 'Fucking wetback'. In these circumstances you are supposed to say something like: 'Thank you for calling US Airways' and finish the call. Personally… I have added something like: 'Yes, I am a fucking wetback but you won't get a flight today!' But just a couple of times… I was also very angry.'

Once again, the information provided by Jaime González shows how difficult it is to predict or control interactions between customers and agents. On one hand, Jaime was proud of how he differed from other workers; he insisted that his job in a different account from most employees gave him higher status. But, on the other hand, he was also the victim of bad treatment from some of his own customers. Only a couple of times according to him, when he was insulted and abruptly concluded the phone call he always added those extra words against his customers, which made him feel a little better, although it contradicted the rules of call handling in call centres. This attitude was presumably tolerated by supervisors despite the use of intense mechanisms of control such as IT systems to prevent these situations.

## 5.4. Are social divisions at work a conscious managerial strategy?

To what extent are these social divisions consciously used and reinforced by managers? In another interview, Roberto Fernández, a supervisor from the same account as Jaime González (US Airways), explained his perception about the social dimension of labour segregation when talking about the entry-level requirements.

Roberto said that there were other important requirements in addition to the skills when selecting staff; he said that it would be rude to recognise the existence of these 'non-written' rules but that he was aware that these differences among workers were crucial in the workplace, even for him. During my interview with Roberto, when I commented on other respondents' answers to the same questions, he immediately recognised who had given them. Roberto referred to Jaime González as *'el fresota'* (the 'super-posh' guy). Roberto was a lower-middle class Mexican educated in a public university, and he lamented the lack of professional opportunities he had in the call centre despite his good performance:

> I have lived through this myself, and could be related to your skin colour but it is mostly about your social class, the place where you live, you can see that... Just go around and look at the [people working in] other accounts. Look at how they speak and what they wear. But this is common in Mexico, even in cultural and intellectual circles... Let me tell you something... Once I went to a cultural event with another friend and suddenly I said to my friend: "Have you noticed that we are the only dark people in the room? They are going to kill us!" [laughs]. Actually, my dark skin colour can be an obstacle to my professional progress but even more important is my social class, my connections.

During the first part of the fieldwork, I was certain that customer segmentation, job designs and labour segregation were connected in a very coherent way. Workers were selected and divided into groups to deal with differentiated customers and this division, following social dimensions, helped to avoid the workers forming bonds according to their class background. In this way the organisation was more efficient in disciplining workers and avoiding unions being formed. It seems to be a very effective strategy for managerial purposes!

However, as the fieldwork stage progressed and I collected more information and made more observations, it became clear to me that managers also tried to prevent workers forming any sort of strong social group within accounts! Perhaps managers wanted to obtain equilibrium between the 'healthy' tensions among workers so they would not form unions or any other form of collective representation, and the emergence of friendship connections that might lead to discipline being relaxed.

In this regard, Roberto Fernández said that strategies to erode group cohesion were sometimes the cause of problems and inefficiencies in the workplace, for example leading to turnover problems. According to him, there was a higher turnover of staff on the evening shift. Staffing levels for the morning shift were much more stable and it was possible to find staff with two or three years of seniority, far higher than elsewhere in the industry and the company itself. He said that at first managers tended to allocate new workers to the evening shift because the learning process was better on this shift.

However, according to Roberto, this policy had a negative impact on supervisors of the evening shift. Roberto explained that he had to invest much time assisting new employees, for example correcting their English pronunciation or attempting to improve their work habits (such as punctuality). He said that, after some weeks, he was always able to build up good teams and better agents, but then the company suddenly started to impose a new policy: every two months managers rotated team members among supervisors. According to Roberto, this rotation created a sense of confusion among workers and supervisors, which affected the quality of the service:

> They left you with only two of the original team members and the other eight or ten guys were new agents once again! After another two months changes again... We were tired about this and start protesting, we argued that we could not work well with all these changes... but we were told that we had to learn to work with everybody here, that it was a 'learning cycle' [making a signal with his hands and fingers], working with everybody... that this was the healthiest thing for the account... I never understood that, but eventually they gave up this method, luckily; now there are only minor changes after six months.

When asked about the reason for these changes, Roberto said that the goal was to create diversity and to avoid friendships developing between workers and supervisors. Specifically, managers wanted to avoid supervisors having 'favourites'.

In the end, the evidence collected indicates that the connection between customer segmentation, job designs and labour segregation is crucial, but not all managers were very aware of this, and it is not clear to what extent managers were truly conscious of this connection and its social implications. The construction of an external social order that was possible thanks to discriminatory practices of social differentiation could be internalised to the point that managers might found it 'natural' rather than socially constructed. Within this construction, social relations at work were the main instrument to discipline workers. However, this social order is fragile, it creates tensions among workers, customers and supervisors all the time but, paradoxically, these tensions are similar to the problems and frictions of the external social order, making the environment of the workplace more 'real'. In this regard, this private construction of an external social order might be a good 'copy' of the original social landscape.

These social bonds also allow workers to develop coping strategies (such as kidding, flirting and faking in the workplace) in order to deal with stress and problems at work. However, the evidence presented here comes from individual workers. To what extent might call centre workers overcome the fragmentation of the work experience in order to build a collective response to managers? In the next section, this research describes the experience of the first (and probably the only truly representative) union in the call centre industry in Mexico.

## 5.5. Workers' collective response: organised labour and the union at Technotronics

The *Sindicato de Telefonistas de la República Mexicana* (Union of Telephone Workers of the Mexican Republic, STRM, www.strm.org.mx) is the most important union in the telecommunications industry in the country. It was created in 1950 by workers of the company *Teléfonos de México* (Mexican Telephones, Telmex) and it is considered the most important union in the private sector. Historically, the STRM has played a significant role in resisting the mainstream corporate unionism in the country and with other big unions (from workers of the National University, Metropolitan University and electricity companies) has formed the *Unión Nacional de Trabajadores* (National Union of Workers, UNT), which is an alternative organisation to the pro-government *Confederación de Trabajadores de México* (Workers' Confederation of Mexico, CTM) (Bensusán and Rendón 2000).

Despite its militant and progressive role, the STRM has been the target of several criticisms, including for having a kind of 'perpetual' leader in the person of Francisco Hernández Juárez and for funding and giving militant support to other organisations such as *Partido de la Revolución Democrática* (Party of the Democratic Revolution, PRD) (Zepeda Patterson 2007).

During the second part of the 1990s, a group of young workers from Technotronics, the most important call centre company in the country at that time, were looking for the support of the STRM in order to form a union. They were looking for this union because it had the collective contract for workers at *Teléfonos de México* (which was also the owner of Technotronics). The task was not easy because there were confronting positions within the union itself:

> There were two different positions inside the union. On the one hand, a group of more, let's say... 'progressive' people, these guys were younger and felt a certain sympathy for those workers at Technotronics. These workers truly believed that unionising call centres would be the right strategy to fight Telmex's outsourcing practices. On the other hand, there was a group of older workers against unionising call centres. In their opinion, the union had to concentrate all its energies into putting more pressure on Telmex to bring outsourced segments such as call centres back into the organisation. Their point was very straightforward: they did not consider call centre workers as 'truly' telephone workers.
> —Union official at the STRM and academic researcher.

Despite all the controversies and internal divisions, Technotronics workers received the support of the STRM in the end, and section 159 inside the union was created (for call centre workers). After a long and difficult process, workers at Technotronics negotiated their first collective contract with the company in 1999.

The relationship of Technotronics workers with other members of the telephone union is ambivalent. On the one hand, call centre workers have an office in the union building and they were members with full rights, but on the other hand I also perceived certain feeling of isolation. In my visit to their offices, I noticed that they were located in a marginal space within the building. Also, in my conversation with unionised workers from the call centre they argued that they were seen with certain distrust because they were younger and had different opinions on some delicate matters:

> There are some important differences between the other telephone workers and us... I do not know... probably it is related to the age difference... We recognise that we live in a different time, that we need to make a bigger effort to be competitive in the market; we know that and we want to bring some collaborative initiatives on the table to discuss with managers and reach solutions, but... I have the impression that other workers in the union are not very sympathetic to this kind of initiative.
> —Union member, Technotronics.

However, call centre workers in the company seem to be optimistic about this sort of initiative. Union officials gave a PowerPoint presentation about the history of the union in Technotronics, and described the reasons for unionisation as follows:

Administrative Services 'Technotronics', as the company was called at the beginning, used the type of schemes that are used by big corporations in manufacturing and services in order to avoid giving collective contracts. These practices are a clear example of labour triangulation [outsourcing] controlled by the CTM [the pro-government Workers' Confederation of Mexico], and are conceived to have a high turnover, no benefits and no long-term employment resulting from precarious conditions. Wanting to follow these practices, Technotronics managers created a scheme that gave them high returns. After only one year in operation, the company started to recruit college students in part-time jobs. In doing so, the company acquired staff with high skills and labour flexibility without making a significant investment in training and without generating any long-term expectations at work because recruits were only offered temporary jobs, so there was a higher return because there was no need to give benefits for seniority, or for employees to work in shifts and rotate their jobs. In addition, there was no significant investment in good infrastructure and no adequate hygiene and safety conditions for workers.
—PowerPoint presentation given by union officials at Technotronics.

According to the union officials, after unionisation the employment conditions at Technotronics improved dramatically: workers got a collective contract that is revised every two years (with revisions to wages each year), and this contract includes paid holidays, end of year bonuses, support for medical expenses and an internal career structure (limited to the agents' category and consisting of four different levels). Therefore, this structure does not include supervisors or any other managerial position (STRM 2000).

However, the emergence of a union inside the company brought an immediate response from the administration. The president of the company at that time described the situation as follows:

I did my job in building up a very good and strong company. I attempted to resist a union being formed, but it was too much for me in the end. After that first negotiation, when we had many problems with each other, I realised that I would not be able to do it again [have another negotiation with the union]. The trust between the parties simply vanished... You cannot have a union in this business because you need flexibility and quick adaptability, but when you need to negotiate almost everything with the union you always lose precious time and resources... I mean, your reaction speed diminishes and this hurts the business. When the union was introduced I recommended reducing the size of the company and keeping the scope of operations limited to internal clients, in other words, cancelling the expansion plans. As a result of this, the owners created Telvista, in Tijuana.

Telvista was created in the Mexico-US border city of Tijuana, thousands of miles away from Mexico City and from the union. Unlike Technotronics, Telvista has clients in the 'open' market, so the company does not have to face the restriction imposed on Technotronics (designed to 'minimise' the effect of the union). More recently, Technotronics opened two new facilities in Mexico City and agreed with the union to stabilise the workforce at about 2,000 workers. Before the unionisation, Technotronics had almost 2,500 workers.

Until 2009, the union at Technotronics was the only militant union in Mexican call centres. There are other unions, but they are designed to openly cooperate with managers (signing 'sweet-heart' contracts). Also, these unions tend to be controlled by the pro-government CTM, which in turn is linked with the long-standing *Partido Revolucionario Institucional* (PRI, Party of the Institutional Revolution).

The union in Technotronics illustrates how outsourcing can be used effectively not only to reduce costs but also to avoid the risks of union militancy. When *Teléfonos de México* was privatised in the early 1990s, the company started an expansion process based on inter-firm arrangements (Chavez Becker 2006). To that purpose, *Grupo Carso*, the holding that includes Telmex, founded other companies in different sectors (such as Inbursa for financial services or Technotronics for call centres). In using these services, Telmex reduced its transaction costs for administering the labour force; however, union militancy eventually reached the subcontracted company as well. As a response, *Grupo Carso* decided to create a completely new company, Telvista, in a different place, far away from Mexico City. Using geographic relocation, this company was clearly attempting to avoid having to deal with a union, something that has been also identified in other industries (Cowie 1999). In summary, Technotronics was condemned to commercial isolation and its expansion restricted.

Finally, the experience of the union in Technotronics also shows how liberalisation and deregulation policies for capital mobility and companies' expansion (allowing the use of outsourcing arrangements), and the lack of enforcement of labour regulation protecting workers' rights, have created an institutional context that might offer attractive returns for creating labour intensive industries in Mexico.

# Conclusion

This chapter analysed to what extent social divisions can be considered an additional mechanism for controlling and disciplining workers. In previous chapters, customer segmentation, narrow job designs, supervision practices and contracts for services were identified as crucial working practices in subcontracted front-line services, especially when multiple clients (and employers) are present in the same subcontracted organisation. However, these practices seem insufficient to explain the relatively low horizontal mobility of workers and the relative absence of a more vigorous collective resistance in the form of more militant unions, despite the differences in work and employment conditions in different accounts within the same organisation.

Thus this chapter looked at social divisions and explored to what extent these divisions are used as mechanisms to provide employers with more control over workers. The central concern of this research is to understand to what extent the reactions of subcontractors to the problems of cooperation and trust with client firms have important effects on workers' experiences and employment conditions. As observed in this chapter, employees' social networks are used to reduce the transaction costs of recruitment and selection. Also, members of these social networks provide information about jobs available, compensation, how to interact with the client firm and characteristics of the job that tend to have positive impacts on the levels of productivity of new workers, at least during the first weeks in the job.

However, the strong divisions among workers in the operation stage are reinforced by these social networks. Workers in different accounts perceived each other as different, even if they come from the same places and schools, but working for particular clients offered them a point of distinction and separation from other workers that reduces the chance of them to establishing stronger collective organisations and resistance. Therefore it seems that social divisions partially explain workers' lack of mobility and the absence of a stronger collective identity in multi-employer sites; it seems that social divisions are a type of glass wall dividing workers horizontally.

In the first section of this chapter there was a description of the geographical and social origins of many workers in subcontracted call centres in Mexico City. Most of them, those who form the ideal pool of candidates for call centre work (that is, people between 18 and 30 years old with unfinished college education), live in the north and east areas of the city, which are commonly identified as low income regions.

Importantly, there is an image that call centre workers are college students in part-time jobs, but in fact most of these workers have already dropped out college. Nonetheless, it seems that workers are prepared to assume this role, partly because it justifies their poor academic performance and enables them to gain partial independence from their families.

Interestingly, these workers also play a primary role in the recruitment of new employees thanks to the use of social networks. In fact, organisations actively encourage workers to invite friends and other acquaintances to apply for the jobs available. But what are the outcomes of this mechanism? Why are firms interested in bringing in existing workers' acquaintances and extending their social bonds? There are two plausible explanations for this, one external and the other internal. On the one hand, customer-oriented organisations such as call centres need to control and manipulate the customer–worker interface (Ritzer 1993; 1998) and, in order to do so, these organisations try to reproduce a type of relationship that imitates the external social structure (Korczynski 2007). In this way, workers are allocated to different job designs and customer segments depending on what is expected in specific services. Also, voice intonation and volume might create the service image expected by customers (for example, a posh accent when trying to sell an exclusive credit card or a more neutral accent to deal with general services or inquiries). On the other hand, the pursuing of social divisions in the workplace seems to provide organisations with an effective means of controlling the workforce in a highly diversified environment. Despite the economic incentives to move around among different accounts and services, workers tend to develop strong social links within their accounts and intense rivalries with other workers.

In this chapter, two cases were presented. One was a worker who had an emotional relationship at work (actually, it was her partner who encouraged her to apply for a job in the company) and whose empathy for her clients erodes her sense of solidarity with other workers. However, it seems that some workers develop a strong sense of social differentiation that significantly limits their interactions with other workers. The second case discussed was a worker who felt that he and his co-workers in the same account were different from other workers; he felt that they had higher skills and education, and that even their customers were better and more exclusive in social terms.

In this way, it seems that social divisions inside work create a kind of glass wall between workers and reduce the possibility of collective organisation. Technical support staff and bilingual workers stand out, however, as they systematically resist and attack the pejorative image of working in call centres. Those interviewed for this research often argued that their technical credentials and abilities were very different from the bulk of sales agents and customer service representatives. They saw themselves as forming a little meritocracy inside call centres, 'an exception to the rule'. Interestingly, these bilingual and technical workers often reported higher levels of stress and dissatisfaction than their counterparts in sales and customer services. These cases also demonstrate that, despite the strong monitoring and controlling mechanisms in front-line services (Hochschild 1983; Ritzer 1998; Taylor and Bain 1999), many of these workers were able to exercise higher levels of autonomy and discretion at work, as has been noted in other investigations of service work (Leidner 1993; Korczynski 2002).

It was not clear to what extent managers truly realised the importance of social divisions and consciously encourage labour segregation. My observations and responses from people in the field does not provide a clear response to this question; it seems that managers have internalised social divisions and distinctions to the point that they are seen as something 'natural' rather than a social construction. A very important piece of evidence to support this argument is how managers might want to rotate workers among different supervisors in order to avoid social bonds to be formed (like friendship), which might affect the levels of discipline in the workplace. Therefore, there is a high degree of variation and firm specific understanding about the meaning of social divisions and their effects on the workplace.

Finally, the chapter concludes with a brief analysis of the only real union in Mexican call centres, the union in Technotronics. In this company, the collaboration and support from the Telephone Workers' Union was essential to unionise the labour force but there were important divisions and conflicts. There were two important outcomes from this unionisation: a) the improvement of employment conditions in the organisation, and b) the commercial isolation and downsizing strategy followed by the owners of the company after the union was established.

In the end, it remains difficult to know to what extent social divisions inside the workplace are consciously recreated in the workplace as a form of domination and control. Perhaps, the most disorienting finding of this chapter is that it was not possible to see any significant gender and skin colour discrimination in the workplace. If social divisions play a fundamental role in disciplining workers it would be expected – in a country with a clear bias against women and dark-skin-coloured people – that gender and skin colour segregation would be part of the working experience. Even more surprising is the fact that workers and managers alike admit that certain types of work (sales) would be more appropriate for women, but there was no particular type of work that was considered more suitable for dark-skinned people.

There are three plausible explanations for this. First, that gender segregation does not occur because the type of skills required does not allow for any significant segregation between genders. Therefore, there is an even distribution of genders across different accounts, customer segments and job designs in call centres in Mexico.

Second, another plausible explanation could be much more straightforward: in this research, I do not have the tools or the scope to observe gender discrimination more broadly. The lack of evidence of gender discrimination within these organisations does not mean that there are fewer difficulties for women than for men in obtaining these jobs. Actually, it is possible to say that the existence of gender discrimination is a good way to explain the even distribution of male and female workers in Mexico City – without gender discrimination in place, there would be a higher proportion of women in these companies. Why was this gender discrimination not detected by this research? Simply, because I did not have direct access to recruitment and selection processes. I only had access to those individuals who finally got the job. I did not know the proportion of female applicants for any job and what proportion of them were accepted or rejected, and the reasons why. However, this research was able to identify certain traces of discrimination (by gender in particular) in managerial circles.

Third, I was expecting that light skinned workers would be more likely than dark skinned workers to occupy more prestigious jobs, but did not find strong evidence of this. In Mexico people tend to believe that all those in better social positions have light skin, but this is not necessarily always the case, as Bank Muñoz has demonstrated in the manufacturing context (2008). In summary, most of the social stereotypes of the Mexican society were present in the minds and conversations of managers and workers in the call centre industry, but their effect on workers' experiences and employment relationships have to be considered in combination with job designs, customer segmentation and supervision approaches. In the end, social class and its effects on the tone of voice, pronunciation and volume were of more importance in segregating the workforce.

# CHAPTER SIX

# THE BOUNDARIES
# OF THE FIRM RE-ESTABLISHED:
# THE EXPERIENCE OF MANAGERS

## 6.1. Managerial jobs in the new service economy: the case of call centre managers

In the literature of work and industrial development, the word 'divide' is often used to express a dramatic or fundamental change in the organisation or work. In 1984, the seminal book of Michael Piore and Charles Sabel, *The Second Industrial Divide: Possibilities for prosperity* (Piore and Sabel 1984), explains how economic development and progress are marked by technological divides. In the capitalist system, the first great divide came when mass production emerged and the second one was possible thanks to flexible production models. Despite the longitudinal and historical profile of these technological divides one of the main conclusions of Piore and Sabel is, in fact, cross-sectional, in the sense that several production systems are possible at a single point in time. Specifically, Piore and Sabel pointed to the example of flexible specialisation when looking at the experience of industrial districts in the north of Italy. This form of capitalism was peculiar as it promotes cooperation rather than competition. Years later, Vicky Smith, used 'divide' in a rather less optimistic way than Piore and Sabel. In her book *Crossing the great divide: workers risk and opportunities in the new economy* (Smith 2001), Smith used the word to express the fears and anxieties provoked by the structural transformations taking place over recent years, from manufacturing to the service-based economy and from internal labour markets to market-mediated employment relationships. In some ways, the results presented in the previous chapters of this book seem to be in line with Smith's considerations in the sense that labour market biases of gender and skills in the new economy do not seem to be as polarised as expected. A complex combination of skills, social attitudes and prejudices explains much of the variance in labour market outcomes, something difficult to predict without a careful examination of individual cases.

In this chapter, I will talk about the same type of divide that Smith analysed but not to workers but to managers. Until now, most studies of call centre work have focused on the experience of front-line workers, those agents who represent the classical image of the employee dealing with customers through telephonic conversations, the type of workers who were analysed in the previous chapters. However, call centres have more than front-line service jobs. In order to operate call centres, these organisations largely depend on a managerial structure divided into different areas. Generally speaking, staff in managerial positions enjoys better employment conditions that clearly belong to a primary labour market segment (Piore 1970; Doeringer and Piore 1971).

According to my interviews, observations and data collected in this research, the typical operational structure of a call centres in Mexico was as follows: normally one supervisor for each 15-20 agents; there is about one coordinator for every five supervisors (and probably up to 100 agents) and one call centre manager normally administers units with at least five coordinators. In the four companies visited in this research, the average for each unit was about 450 to 600 employees. All these positions, from agents to call centre operations managers, are directly related to the operation of the firm and most of these managers have close interactions with front-line workers. At the same time, there was also another group of employees who, despite having little contact with the *operation* of the call centre (handling calls), are essential in running the organisation – managerial and administrative employees distributed in areas such as human resources, sales, finances and planning. These areas also have administrative staff, such as secretaries, assistants, analysts and directors, hierarchically organised. Finally, at the top of the organisational chart, is the president of the company or the CEO (Table 6-1 and Figure 6-1).

## Table 6-1. Job hierarchies in call centres

|  |  |  |
|---|---|---|
| Administrative and managerial jobs | President<br>General directors<br>Unit managers<br>Coordinators<br>Analysts<br>Assistants | *Primary labour market* |
| Non-managerial positions | Supervisors<br>Assistants<br>Integrators<br>Back-room officers<br>Technical support<br>Customer services<br>Sales | *Secondary labour market* |

Source: fieldwork notes.

Figure 6-1. A typical organisational chart of the call centre analysed

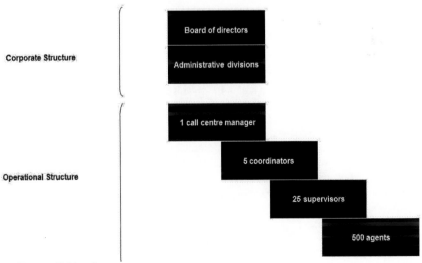

Source: fieldwork notes.

Interestingly, and contrary to what would be expected according to the logic of employees' mobility in the new economy (Sennett 1998; Barley and Kunda 2004), the interviews of this research revealed that many of these managers came from entry-level positions (many times within the same organisation), and that these managers have developed industry and firm specific skills through the years:

> I started working since I was 18 years old. I worked in a call centre as a customer service representative in Inbursa [a Mexican bank]. I was there while I was in college. Later I had the chance to start again in the same type of job but in a company called Technotronics. Then in 2001 I had the opportunity to join Phonemex.
> —Call centre manager, Phonemex

Some of these managers had crossed the whole organisational structure during their careers with only limited or no experience in other sectors, which is, once again, something not expected in the flexible and high mobility environment of the new economy:

> On the 5th of August in 1999 I started as a marketing agent in the company Marcafon. After eight months I was transferred to the quality area. I was there for one year and a half. After this, I received an offer to join Phonemex because they were opening their first centre in the city of Monterrey [north of Mexico]. I started there as a supervisor and worked in different accounts. Eventually, I was promoted to coordinator and I was required to come to Mexico City, and I was here for two years. Then again I was sent back to Monterrey as coordinator in several accounts and then I was promoted as the main person responsible for one of our main clients, BBVA [a foreign bank]. Now I am the manager of the whole unit. I have worked for six years and a half in the organisation but for eight years in the industry. I have climbed the whole structure!
> —Call centre manager, Phonemex.

These experiences seem to contradict much of the evidence provided by front-line workers in previous chapters. On the one hand, workers in lower front-line service jobs (sales, customer services and technical support) repeatedly reported that career opportunities were minimal or completely absent, and that there was almost no way to have a long-term professional career in call centres. These front-line service workers insisted that they had tried many times to reach better positions without any success. On the other hand, the vast majority of managers I interviewed told me that they had started as front-line agents and, after some years of being promoted, had reached managerial level. Which of these versions is the most accurate? Well, my best guess is: both. My argument is that there are no formal internal labour markets at entry level positions that could be associated with career opportunities in the long run. Instead, there is an intricate network of passages and connections that not all the workers get to know about or understand (I will come back to this idea in the next section of this chapter about the importance of loyalty and commitment for managers' careers).

Employees at entry level and in front-line jobs may seem to be in the fragile position associated with secondary labour markets (Piore 1970; Doeringer and Piore 1971), but managerial jobs appeared to provide more stability and protection. As mentioned earlier, managers and administrative staff were likely to have permanent and full-time jobs with good salaries and benefits for the Mexican context. The wages of call centre operations managers could reach up to 50,000 Mexican pesos monthly (equivalent to about £2,500), and they might be given a luxury car, financial support for relocation expenses (when they were moved to or from other cities), private medical insurance and attractive pension plans. Administrative staff working with directors, such as secretaries or entry-level analysts, had lower earnings but still attractive contractual conditions such as a permanent contract, private medical insurance and a pension plan. Many employees in these positions declared that these were excellent jobs because, in addition to some firm-specific skills, they were also acquiring sophisticated financial, managerial or accounting skills that were applicable to other companies in different industries. Compensations, broadly speaking, were good.

Nonetheless, many of these managers often complained, about the high levels of stress and dissatisfaction they experienced with their jobs. As the fieldwork of this research progressed, I became aware that many tensions in call centres were concentrated within the managerial circle rather than between workers and managers.[1] Most of the time, managers were expected to work harder and invest more time in getting things done than any other type of employee, especially agents. Evidently, this higher level of commitment was supposed to be compensated with a higher salary and superior employment conditions (Baron and Kreps 1999).

Therefore, despite the mainstream narratives in the business and some economics literature reporting dramatic changes in employment conditions for managers (Handy 1989; Goffee 1992; Bridges 1995), it seems that there is no strong evidence of major changes over recent years (McGovern

---

[1] In the end, this research identified as much tension within groups of workers and managers as between these two groups.

et al. 2007). Not at least in the case of call centres in Mexico. Here managers are still a privileged group and enjoy excellent employment conditions, which are far superior to those of the workers in call centres.

But how do managerial employees get these jobs? What is the crucial determinant that allows them to cross the great divide between front-line service work and managerial jobs in call centres? The next section will try to address these questions.

## 6.2. The importance of loyalty and commitment in managerial careers

Narratives of work in the new economy generated by mainstream business thinkers and magazines imply that also managerial careers are following the logic of labour flexibility (Handy 1989; Pink 2001). Specifically, in the new economy managers are expected to develop less firm-specific skills, to move across organisations and to be oriented towards working in professional projects in multiple firms rather than aspiring to be the 'organisation man' described by White (1956). For example, long-standing employment trajectories in a single organisation used to be strongly associated with progressive increases in salaries and benefits, as these were seen as compensations rewarding loyalty and commitment to the organisation (Osterman 1996; Cappelli 1999; 2000; Cappelli and Neumark 2004). In some cases, career prospects could also represent a chance for social mobility when workers are able to cross the 'great divide' separating managerial and non-managerial positions within the same organisation. Internal labour markets retain employees with firm-specific skills and protect them from the turbulence of economic downturns and unemployment (Jacoby 1999; Cappelli 2000; Marchington et al. 2005).

In the new economy context, managers tend to be portrayed as individuals with a strong sense of self-sufficiency, goal-orientation and leadership (Handy 1989; Reich 1991; Bridges 1995; Pink 2001; Reed 2009). However, according to the information collected in the interviews, managers were not likely to see themselves as isolated individuals pursuing personal projects and considering different organisations as successive stations in a long-lasting professional career. In fact, the managers interviewed were more likely to see themselves as part of a network of relationships with other individuals. For example, when talking about how they got their jobs, most of the managers interviewed made reference to the use of personal networks (just as workers in lower positions did):

Q How did you get your current job?

A It was when a group of ex-staff from Technotronics moved to Phonemex and they invited me to come. It was good because I started in a better job here, as one of the coordinators of the BBVA Bancomer [a bank] account. Eventually I was promoted to general operations manager in this centre.

Q What do you think has been the crucial aspect of your success?

A Since 2001, I have always been close to important people in this organisation; they have taught me many things and give me useful advice to progress in my career.

—Call centre manager, Phonemex.

This young call centre manager (he was 32 years old at the time of the interview in 2007) was highly motivated and competitive, and had an academic degree from a private university in Mexico City. In many ways, this person could be the prototype of a manager in the new service economy: young, ambitious and with good prospects for promotion. However, this manager also stated the importance of having a good social network to secure his progression and permanence at his job. According to him, the creation and development of these connections was supported by his long-term commitment to a group of people rather than to the entire organisation. He and other managers often referred to the idea of a 'team' or 'group' which shares a certain history (many of them also came from Technotronics), status and social class. They emphasised the importance and merits of working in a team of young executives that has taken advantage of the expansion of the industry.

Another young manager (30 years old) from the same group described how he had got his job:

Q How did you progress so quickly in this industry?

A Look, I think I was lucky because call centres are something relatively new in Mexico... Well, I have already 10 years of experience in the industry and I am only 30 years old! The point is that the industry had an explosive growth over the last five years. I am one of the pioneers... I was lucky because my career has progressed as the industry has grown... However, I need to say that I have also my own merit because of my skills and hard work...

Q And how did you start in Phonemex?

A Again I need to say that I was lucky because I had the chance to start as coordinator in Technotronics and then... when I was invited to come here, I did not have to struggle too much in order to become noticed... You know, if you start as an agent, you need to do much more to become visible because there are so many workers like you around.

All the members of this generation of young managers have much the same background and experience, and had completed their college education and started in entry level positions in call centres. Little by little, these managers were building up a set of networks with other people in the company. As mentioned earlier, at first glance these statements reflect an optimistic vision of career opportunities inside call centres. All these young managers recognised that they were lucky when joining the industry while it was being expanded, which allowed them to have more opportunities, and they made a good use of them. In many ways, these managers felt that their efforts and loyalty were truly compensated by opportunities and promotions.

However, not every manager within the organisations studied believed that providing these opportunities was the most useful strategy for companies in expansion. Another manager, the 'oldest' (only 34 years old) and a foreigner (from El Salvador), believed that it was not a good idea to promote young people from entry-level positions to managerial jobs as the company expanded. According to him, one of the main problems for Phonemex in Mexico was that the subsidiary had grown so rapidly that some processes had not been undertaken correctly. Specifically, this manager was talking about the formation of good and competent managers in Mexico. According to him, executives did not perform to a consistently high level; instead there was much variation in their performance, which had negative effects on the operation. He illustrated this point when talking about his personal experience when working in the Phonemex subsidiary located in El Salvador:

> In El Salvador our performance improved while we developed career plans; sometimes I get calls from guys over there to let me know that they have been promoted and I must confess that I feel very happy for them. Especially since many of them started as agents but also because they have received adequate formation and training... therefore, their promotions are also good for the organisation... In El Salvador, the support areas grew before the expansion of the whole company. In other words, when we were small we made the effort to create a big and strong administrative base for support, and this base was very important and useful in the expansion... In Mexico, well... it was the other way around because the base was always small and never grew at the same pace.

This manager seemed to be a sort of dissident or critical voice about other managers' opinion about the way the organisation was administered. He posed the issue of better planning and having a stronger support base in order to secure a higher level for managers' formation and training.

However, he also recognised that it was not clear to what extent it was only call centres that were responsible for these problems. He thought that a large part of the pressure for expansion comes from client firms, because of their continuous demands for bigger accounts and more staff to cover their services. Therefore, if call centres wanted to keep these accounts they needed to accept this explosive expansion.

According to the information collected, it seems that loyalty and commitment are crucial aspects in maintaining the managerial networks needed to succeed in the industry. In these networks, managers appeared to play the role of nodes that keep and transfer information and resources across the industry. This information is not a trivial issue, especially when it is related to events that shape the evolution of the sector. A very good example of this is the experience of the union in Technotronics. In Phonemex, for instance, a large number of the upper managerial staff came from Technotronics, the first large call centre created in the country and owned by *Teléfonos de México* (as described in the methodology chapter).

In this respect, there is little doubt that Technotronics is a fundamental reference for managers and workers in Mexican call centres. For example, most employees in the managerial structure in Technotronics moved into different organisations within the industry and eventually reunited in Phonemex:

> I worked in Grupo Nacional Provincial for several years, always in the human resources area... after this I was in a company named Technotronics ... a subsidiary of Teléfonos de Mexico. I was there three years and a half. Later, I worked for a consulting company in human resources. After this, I started with my job as the Human Resources Director of Phonemex for Mexico and Central America, three years ago.
> Human Resources Manager, Phonemex

This information confirms, once again, that managers use their social networks to find jobs like any other types of workers do, and that these social networks at professional level are maintained thanks to the loyalty and commitment of their members. The previous respondent never mentioned this during the interview but it is evident that he was part of the core managerial team in Technotronics; he left the company at the time of unionisation, and re-joined their 'previous' team in Phonemex years later.

Another manager was interviewed separately from the one quoted above, but it is evident that they had a strong connection with each other:

My labour history has been always in human resources. I started in Grupo Nacional Provincial, an insurance company. After this, I tried for a short time to work in the consulting sector, also providing specialised services in human resources. After 2001 the sector suffered an important contraction and the market was difficult. Then I was called by Phonemex and since then I am here. I have worked for two and a half years in the organisation and am in charge of the human resources of two different units, Puebla and Plaza Inn.
—Human Resources Manager, Phonemex

These examples illustrate how group loyalty and commitment have been significant in shaping the career trajectories of a group of young managers in call centres. These young managers, despite their academic credentials, skills and experience, did not operate exclusively as the individual agents depicted by many images of white collar workers in the new economy (Handy 1989; Pink 2001; Reed 2009). Somehow, even in different organisations, a sense of community can be perceived; all of them probably had no more than six years in Phonemex (the company started in 2001 in Mexico), but they had known each other for longer than that. It seems that these managers shared a set of common values and beliefs about the industry, had loyalty and commitment to the group to which they belonged and which had promoted their careers in the industry,[2] and, very importantly, shared the same concerns about unionisation.

To what extent are these networks of loyalties and commitments the only requirements for employees to advance in managerial careers? Do people without 'connections' have any chance of making a good and well-paid career? The next section presents the case of those managers who seem to be outside the main networks.

## 6.3. Alternative experiences in managerial careers

Even in this environment where social capital and common background appear to be fundamental for career progress it is possible to find some interesting exceptions, cases that might exemplify the meritocratic aspect of the rhetoric about the new economy employee (Pink 2001; Reed 2009).

One human resources manager had no previous contact at all with the industry. Beatriz Chávez was trained as an industrial engineer and after

---

[2] Also, the reader might remember the case of one of the corporate directors and executives interviewed at KPM. He stated that the company itself was created by a group of colleagues previously employed by the same bank. This would be the classical case of an 'old boy' network.

finishing college she worked in a plastics factory for about ten months. Then she was made redundant and started to teach English, mathematics, technical drawing and industrial maintenance at college level for a year or so. Later, she got a job in Phonemex in the city of Pachuca (a medium-sized city about 60 miles north to Mexico City) in June 2002. She started as a sales agent in a credit card account. In fact, she wanted to work for Bancomer (a bank), so she submitted an application to the bank, but the bank was outsourcing some areas to Phonemex; for this reason they were not recruiting people at that time. After receiving Beatriz's application, the bank asked her if she would be interested in doing exactly the same job she was applying for but in a subcontracted call centre. Beatriz accepted because she considered that it was a good opportunity for her. At that time, she was working in Tizayuca (a small city near to Pachuca), and the daily commuting was very stressful to her.

Beatriz admitted that working in a university environment was nice because she received frequent updates and feedback from colleagues and working with young students was motivating; but she found the effort hard in other respects. However, working in Pachuca would save her money and time, so she liked the idea of staying in Phonemex. The remarkable part of her story is that she was originally hired as an entry-level agent but almost immediately was promoted to a managerial position. Here she explains the situation:

Q How did they notice that you were there?
A I do not know really, I think this was one of these situations where you are in the right place at the right time! My shift was divided into two segments so I used to go home to have my lunch and then come back for the second part of the day. On the third day in the job, the recruitment manager called me home and told me that they wanted to talk to me immediately... I was a little worried because of the 'urgency' of the call [she used her hands and fingers to emphasise the word]. He said that they had an offer for me and wanted to know my answer as soon as possible. These are the sort of things that I am grateful to Phonemex for, that they give opportunities to young people. They gave me the chance to be in charge of human resources, although I did not have any experience other than the subjects that I took at college. We were only 68 employees, and it was growing little by little... I was learning during the process. In this respect, it was not a shock for me.

After this beginning, Beatriz was promoted on several occasions. After a year she moved 'horizontally' and came to Mexico City to work in the corporate headquarters in human resources. Then, when the organisation opened a new centre in *Puebla* Street (also in Mexico City), Beatriz was appointed as the human resources manager for this new facility. She was at the centre of *Puebla* Street until November 2006. During this period, another two centres were opened, *Legaria* and *Dinamarca*, and for a short time Beatriz was also responsible for all the three centres together. Then, the last move was when she was asked to be responsible for the human resources administration of the centre in *Plaza Inn*. Thus Beatriz's case seems to be unusual: she did not use her personal network to get the job; in fact the whole industry and even the area (human resources) were new for her.

Interestingly, nearly all the managers interviewed whose careers seem to have benefitted from social networks were male. In KPM, which is smaller than Phonemex, the director of human resources, Ana Torres, also got her job using more formal and meritocratic means:

> I used to work as an agent in a call centre while I was studying management at the college. Later, I did an internship at the human resources unit of one company, also a call centre. However, I applied for this job through a staff agency. They told me that I was selected because I covered two important fronts for them, marketing and human resources, which are crucial for call centre work.

As mentioned earlier on, it is very interesting that these two examples of people who did not use their personal networks to find a job were female managers. Is it possible to argue that female call centre managers in Mexico are disadvantaged compared with their male counterparts because of the rules and politics of the workplace and managerial circles as stated by many authors writing about other industries and societies (Walby 1990; Edwards and Wajcman 1999; McRae 2003; Wajcman 2004; Walby 2007)? It is hard to generalise with such a small number of observations, but there are certain features to highlight: female managers were concentrated on human resources areas; none of the female managers interviewed was in an affective relationship nor has children; and the female managers interviewed took a longer time to reach their jobs than their male counterparts. However, when I explicitly asked if they felt discriminated against in the workplace for being women their answer was a clear 'No'.

As mentioned, my observations and notes in the field indicate that there is no flagrant discrimination against female workers in the call centre analysed but this does not mean that female workers and managers are not in a disadvantaged position compared with their male counterparts. To the contrary, I observed that, in general, female workers faced more restrictions on their time than male workers, which is a constant finding when exploring labour trajectories of women and men (Edwards and Wajcman 1999; Bensusán and Rendón 2000; Rendón 2003; Wajcman 2004). Some of the managers interviewed admitted that they had postponed becoming mothers in order to advance in their careers, and front-line female workers told me that they did not apply for better jobs, such as supervisions, because these jobs would involve more time and responsibility, and they had to go home as quickly as possible after work in order to take care of their children and husbands. So, there is no question that there is still an important difference in the way women and men experience their progress in managerial careers and the challenges they face.

Not many managers obtain their jobs through networks. Datatech and other companies tend to announce vacancies and get candidates using more formal means such as job market agreements with universities and other institutions. Therefore, the suggestion that workers obtain jobs through merit and their high-mobility profile (Pink 2001; Reed 2009) is not borne out by workers in call centres in Mexico, unless they have above average skills and are located in high-revenue costumer segments. For most managers in highly technical areas, the process of recruiting seems to be more influenced by meritocracy and skills:

> When I finished my bachelor degree I started working in the stock exchange as a system analyst. After this, I began with my own company in systems development and telecommunications equipment. At the same time and with other three partners, I opened a company to sell office furniture. I was doing both things for about five years. Later, I was in an importing company. I was responsible for the central zone, which includes Mexico City. Finally I applied for this job in Datatech, first in the area of business solutions. I was there for three years and then I moved into my current position as a general director of the centre for global services of Datatech. I have been working here for three years.
> —Call centre manager, Datatech.

Most call centre managers recognised the advantage of working in the industry during periods of expansion. In doing so, they had received more opportunities for promotion and better employment conditions than usually given in other industries. This suggests that loyalty and long-term commitment are important to progress in a managerial career in the sector. However, it is also important to consider that other more meritocratic factors were part of the experience of some of the managers in the industry. But, who are these managers? According to the information available and my observations, female and technical managers and workers seem to be more dependent on meritocratic channels and evaluation than any other type of employee. Very importantly, despite the narratives of flexibility and skill orientation, female workers and managers are still facing important informal barriers which prevent them from competing on equal terms with their male counterparts.

## Conclusion

The aim of this chapter was to examine how managers' employment conditions are affected by outsourcing arrangements, and if there is any difference from the experience of front-line service workers. As mentioned, some people would consider this question to lack interest and have an obvious answer. However, popular narratives on the new economy suggest that there have been fundamental changes for managers' careers and opportunities (Pink 2001). Evidence of this chapter suggests that managers are still a privileged group with comparatively good employment conditions, which of course is nothing new. However, the information available also indicates that it is still important for organisations to have loyal and committed managers; this is why firms compensate managers well, especially male managers.

In Mexican call centres, the expansion of the industry has been supported by the creation of internal labour markets for managerial employees. Without this structure, the expansion and sustainability of the sector, its current prosperity, would have been jeopardised.

The use of internal labour markets to reward managers' loyalty and commitment inside subcontracted call centres suggests that the boundaries of the firm are clearly re-established at this point. If the experience of front-line service workers is largely shaped by the tensions and problems between the organisations involved (here, client firms and subcontractors), the impact of client firms on managers' employment conditions seems to be very small. Thus managers seem to be tied to their organisations in a way that is not predicted in mainstream business literature where there is a conceived wisdom (Handy 1989; Bridges 1995) that employees in the new economy are more mobile and individualistic than their counterparts in other industries and at previous times (Cappelli 1999). In this respect, it is frequently suggested that employees in apparently more competitive environments need to be more mobile and have more generic skills so they are not tied to their company and have more opportunities to move around across different organisations. They would also be much more individualistic and have a lower tendency to forge links with other organisations.

However, the evidence collected for this chapter does not support this idea. The information presented in chapter four showed that workers in low-level positions, that is, sales, customer services and technical support, did not enjoy significant opportunities for promotions, with the only exception of some groups working in technical support. It seems that organisations in the sector obtained the loyalty and commitment of workers not by using internal labour markets but through the use of more strict organisational rules. The example of credit card sales representatives illustrated this point when companies decided to introduced tighter monitoring rules in one case, and a third-party evaluation in the other, in order to improve the quality in the task of collecting customers' personal information.

Therefore, this research did not find any substantial evidence contradicting the conventional perception about conditions of work for call centre agents: these are relatively good jobs for people in the Mexican labour market but conditions are still far below of those obtained by managers. The 'status divide' between front-line workers and managers is still alive and still influences the degree of loyalty and commitment employees have towards organisations in the long run.

Despite their relatively privileged position in the labour market, managers still prefer to be tied to organisations that provide secure employment in the long term. However, the influence of social networks and groups is also important in two ways. First, the expansion of call centres in Mexico probably provided a unique opportunity for extensive managerial promotions in the previous years, which might not be possible on the same scale in a mature industry. Second, most managers expressed more loyalty and commitment to the people they worked with than to the organisation, demonstrating the power of personal networks and loyalties. This loyalty can be seen in the movement of managerial groups across organisations rather than multiple individual movements. In conversations with people in the industry, people used to refer to "Mr A's Group" or "Mrs B's Group" as a way to identify different interests and commitments inside the organisation and the industry.

It is evident that more research is needed in this area in order to know to what extent loyalty to specific groups of people is more important than organisational attachments to determine managers' mobility. However, there is no doubt that most managers in call centres still prefer stability and permanence to endless moves.

Men make more use of social networks than women. The overwhelming majority of the managers interviewed whose career advancements were considerably shaped by social capital are male; most female managers use more meritocratic procedures to obtain work and tend to be confined to traditional 'female' areas inside management such as human resources. These findings seem to be in line with many similar observations about the disadvantages of women in the labour market (Walby 1990; Edwards and Wajcman 1999; Wajcman 2004; Walby 2007). However, technical workers seem to be less likely to use social networks as a way to shape recruitment and advancement in their managerial careers. According to the information collected, technical managers and workers prefer to rely on a meritocratic system to evaluate and promote people inside the organisation rather than the 'people you might know' practice.

In summary, the information presented and discussed in this chapter does not support the idea that there has been a fundamental change in the distribution of rewards among employees in emergent industries of the new service economy; there is no convergence between managers and workers. On the contrary, the divide between workers and managers is still important and the higher levels of loyalty and commitment expected from managers are encouraged through the use of internal labour markets, especially for male managers. In conclusion there are many old practices in the new service economy.

# CONCLUSIONS

This book examined the outsourcing of service work in the new economy using the call centre industry in Mexico as a case of study. Its aim was to look at how the relationship between subcontractors and client firms shapes workers' experiences and employment conditions.

The findings of this research confirm that the main problems between subcontractors and client firms are related to the building up of the cooperation and coordination mechanisms needed to undertake the services involved. These problems have also been identified and analysed extensively in the case of manufacturing (Sako and Helper 1998; Lorenz 1999). However, there has been relatively less attention paid to the experience of service work in outsourcing arrangements (Walsh and Deery 2006).

A central argument of this book is that the customer–worker interface adds substantial complexity to the tensions and problems between subcontractors and client firms in the administration of the subcontracted workforce. In this respect, more attention is needed to understand the effects of multi-employer relationships over workers' experiences and employment conditions in the service sector. In addition, the exploration of the Mexican case might allow for a better understanding of the effects of inter-firm relationships on service work in the context of a developing country with significant capital deregulation and weak labour protection.

The evidence collected in this research suggests that, for the Mexican case, the emergence and expansion of labour-intensive industries (such as call centres) and the use of outsourcing arrangements have been motivated by four factors, mainly: a) low restrictions to capital mobility; b) the lack of enforcement of workers' rights; c) an attractive labour supply; and d) a growing local market for new services. This combination seems to create attractive returns for investments in new service industries in Mexico.

Overall, the findings presented by this investigation indicate that conflicts between subcontractors and client firms exist at all the stages of the administration of the labour force in subcontracted workplaces: recruitment, selection, training, operation and compensation. The costs associated with these problems of coordination, and the real 'damage' that they might represent, seems to vary from company to company and from account to account. However, it seems that the level of tension between organisations increases in customer segments reporting higher revenues. In other words, it seems that client firms have more incentives for intervention as the return reported by the services undertaken by subcontractors also increases.

The findings of this research identify those practices that can be more affected by – or associated with – the difficulties of negotiation and coordination between subcontractors and client firms: narrow job designs; customer segmentation; the use of contracts for services; supervision approach; union avoidance; the use of internal labour markets to secure manager's loyalty; and the reinforcement of social divisions in the workplace.

What are the effects of these practices on workers' experiences and employment conditions? To what extent have these mechanisms been effective in dealing with the problems generated by the outsourcing of call centre work? The aim of this concluding chapter is to revisit the analysis of these seven elements making a critical evaluation of the findings presented. Finally, this chapter closes with some reflections about future research.

## Narrow job designs

In order to organise work in a context that has a large diversity of tasks and several client firms, it seems that subcontractors employ narrow job designs in order to divide the labour force and deal more effectively with the demands and problems arising from multiple sources.

In this research, three major technical divisions were identified: sales, customer services and technical support. There were clear differences between them and in the impact they have on workers' experiences and employment conditions. It is evident that younger and less qualified workers tend to be allocated to sales work, which is considered the low-end job category in call centres, with less attractive wages, and bonuses, and only few opportunities for training and promotion. At the other extreme, technical support workers have more prestigious jobs, hold attractive wages, good bonuses, have more opportunities for training and, in some cases, good prospects for developing careers inside the organisation or in the sector as a whole. Despite this diversity, many authors argued that autonomy and discretion in call centres are largely limited by the restrictions imposed by scripts and the close monitoring of information technologies means (Fernie and Metcalf 1998; Taylor and Bain 1999; Taylor et al. 2002; Taylor and Bain 2007). These findings seem to be borne out in the many routine jobs in call centres: the largest concentration of jobs in the industry is on sales and customer services. There are usually fewer technical support jobs.

However, the findings of this research also suggest that workers' satisfaction levels do not necessarily increase with higher levels of autonomy and discretion. This seems to contradict many other observations about the experience of work in call centres but in a different national context (Baldry et al. 2007; Taylor and Bain 2007). According to the evidence provided in this research, other factors shape the experience of work and individuals' assessment of employment conditions. Younger workers immersed in the demanding routines of sales work appear to experience less frustration, because they have lower expectations in the labour market as a result of their young age. Also, it seems that young workers frequently find multiple coping strategies in the workplaces, such as taking unjustified breaks, playing games, flirting and making jokes. However, older workers in technical support services seem to have few reasons to feel satisfied with their jobs. They have higher aspirations in the labour market and do not appear to be comfortable with the sometimes degrading image of a person working in a call centre.

It is clear that the organisation of work following narrow job designs (in which workers are not even allowed to cross the 'spaces' of other workers) is useful in dealing with multiple demands from different client firms in a context of a great diversity of services. Instead of dealing with a large group of clients demanding exactly the same type of service, subcontractors might fragment the demands of clients supported by the technical divisions provided by these narrow job designs. In other words, it seems that job designs might help subcontractors to prevent client firms of cooperating or coordinating among them.

However, this research found that workers' experiences and employment conditions are not exclusively dependent on job designs. If this were true, there would be no variation in the work of different accounts performing the same job. Instead, what this research found is that workers performing the same activity but for different client firms were likely to have different experiences and employment conditions. Although useful, job designs seem to be insufficient to explain the diversity of work experiences and employment conditions when multiple clients and services are present in the same subcontracted workplace.

## Customer segmentation

As mentioned, subcontractors with multiple clients, like the ones studied here, have to deal with different demands for the customisation of the services provided. However, in order to reduce costs, subcontractors might prefer to standardise processes (Korczynski 2002). These opposite ways of providing a service are probably the main challenge when front-line service work is subcontracted.

However, not all client firms demand the same level of customisation or seem interested in being directly involved in the administration of the labour force. A recurrent strategy to deal with the demands from client firms for specific levels of service is to manage the workforce following customer segmentation strategies, something that has been reported by other authors but not in connection with client firms in outsourcing (Batt 2000). This approach assigns different types of managerial strategies depending on the revenue reported by each customer segment (Batt 2000; Batt and Moynihan 2002; Batt et al. 2006).

In other words, subcontractors do not respond in the same way to the demands from all the client firms they have. Instead, they have different responses depending on the revenue obtained from each client and the market served. For workers in call centres, these different responses might have important implications. For example, those employees working in services for residential and mass consumption markets are likely to enjoy the least privileged employment conditions and have less satisfying work experiences while workers servicing high income markets are more likely to be highly involved in their work. Importantly, these differences between workers' experiences and employment conditions seem to take place among workers performing the same activity, with the same job design.

Thus customer segmentation seems to be an important factor in explaining the role of client firms in the administration of the labour force in subcontracted workplaces. However, as this research progressed, additional factors were detected as relevant in explaining workers' experiences and employment conditions. This research suggests that the idiosyncratic monitoring style of individual supervisors also plays an important role in shaping workers' experiences and employment conditions in outsourcing.

## Supervision approach

In this research, I found that many idiosyncratic factors, such as the personal behaviour of client firm representatives and supervisors, can play an essential role in explaining differences among workers' experiences and employment conditions in subcontracted workplaces with multiple clients.

In the end, supervisors and client firm representatives act as a communication and negotiation bridge between all the actors participating in the production of front-line services in call centres: client firms, subcontractors, workers and customers. The interviews in this research made it clear that supervisors and client firm representatives are key players in the negotiation of employment conditions for workers; for example, in adjusting schedules, payments, bonuses or special permissions.

In addition to using IT systems to monitor workers' performance, supervisors make decisions about how and when to discipline and control workers. For example, during my period of observation, I noticed that supervisors detected that some agents were talking to each other, making jokes or having extra breaks without authorisation. Supervisors tolerated these behaviours when there was not too much demand for the service.

The key role of supervisors in shaping employees' experiences in highly monitored work of the new economy (such as call centres) has attracted research attention recently (Deery et al. 2010). However, most of the analyses of service work have been focused on the experience of front-line workers paying less attention to the role of managers as negotiators in supervision practices with client firms. Findings of this research suggest that managerial positions also play an important role in the administration of the problems or tensions between subcontractors and client firms.

## Managers and organisational boundaries re-established

All the previous sections emphasise the problems generated by blurring organisational boundaries in the administration of the subcontracted workforce. If the authority and power of the organisations over the administration of the subcontracted workforce is contested at every point there would be no sustainability for this organisational arrangement; transaction costs would be very high. However, we have seen that these problems can be handled using different strategies such as narrow job designs, customer segmentation or adjustments in the supervision approach. In addition, the boundaries of the firm appear to be re-established into managerial circles.

What is the reason behind the re-establishment of the boundaries of the firm at managerial circles? Perhaps, the most important reason is the need to support the expansion and sustainability of the organisation (Ospina 1996; Podolny and Baron 1997). Contrary to the arguments of the mainstream business literature about the characteristics and expectations of managers in the new economy, where they are supposed to have fewer firm-specific skills and more mobility (Handy 1989; Osterman 1996; Pink

2001; Reed 2009), most managers in the call centres analysed were strongly loyal and committed to particular groups inside the industry and their organisations. These managers recognised the importance of loyalty and commitment for the progress of their professional careers.

Two views were expressed. First, most of the managers agreed about the importance of loyalty and commitment for their professional success, but this was essentially oriented towards groups of people rather than the entire brand or organisation. A good example of this is the managerial circle formed in Technotronics. Second, the importance of social capital and networks to advance in managerial careers seems to be more important for male than female managers. Women use more meritocratic channels to achieve promotion. This is hardly a surprise, as with the exception of human resources departments, managerial positions are still dominated by men. In this respect this industry of the new economy largely resembles that of the old economy.

Importantly, my findings suggest that the experience of managers in Mexican call centres is important in explaining the anti-union behaviour encouraged within the organisations studied.

## Union avoidance

Like in any other industry, one of the main challenges for the operation of cost-cutting outsourcing practices is to avoid the presence of unions. At first, recently created subcontracted call centres were not very concerned about the existence of unions inside the workplace because the classic Mexican corporatist system offered enough protection from them. However, a group of young workers from Technotronics looked for support and advice from the National Union of Telephonists, but received, initially, an unclear response. This is a good example of how unions have divergent opinions about how to combat flexible organisational strategies such as outsourcing. On the one hand, there was a group of people inside the union who did not support the idea of unionising young workers in call centres. This group of unionised workers believed that they should concentrate their energies into putting pressure on the company to re-internalise outsourced activities. On the other hand, other group of workers in the union believed that they needed to find a way to unionise workers in subcontracted companies. Eventually the union supported workers in call centres and Technotronics was truly unionised.

Overall, the presence of the union in Technotronics has had mixed results for workers. There is no question that employment conditions have improved inside the company, and presumably within the industry as a whole. However, it is also true that the union has been isolated and its effects over the industry have been reduced as much as possible. *Grupo Carso* has 'sacrificed' Technotronics in order to control the union; the organisation has been downsized and closed to external clients, limiting the expansion of the firm and the impact of the union in the sector.

Is it possible for unions to organise workers in other call centres? There is no clear response to this question but it is difficult to expect (and not desirable, in my opinion) that call centre workers remain without authentic collective representation for much longer. On the one hand, it is true that the difficult economic conditions in Mexico have forced workers to avoid practices that might trigger layoffs; so for example it has been very difficult for workers to resist the erosion of legal protection mechanisms and the use of non-standard forms of employment (such as contract for services). On the other hand, the presence of workers with relatively good education for the local context (usually unfinished college education) could encourage the formation of organisations with a relatively high level of skills to demand an improvement in employment conditions, as it was the case in Technotronics. I believe that, in many respects, the success of union formation largely depends on how workers might understand the context in which call centres and their clients operate, and how this is connected with the social structure of the Mexican society.

## Social divisions and control

Perhaps, the most ambitious part of this research was the attempt to show that there is a strong connection between the external social structure and the organisation of work inside the companies studied; in other words, to understand work as a social activity that is embedded in and shaped by a particular institutional context.

I thought that this would explain the relative passivity and lack of resistance of workers in the call centres analysed. I believed that, somehow, subcontractors have created a type of internal social order that provides certain 'harmony' within the workplace, disciplining and controlling workers, despite the considerable differences in workers' experiences and employment conditions in different accounts. As discussed in detail in chapter five, this idea was conceived while observing call centre workers and comparing their social behaviour with that of youngsters in school who are also divided into different groups, take different courses, and are supervised by different teachers.

The findings collected in this research suggest that the glass walls between workers in call centres are social divisions that are established after employees are recruited using their own social networks (Granovetter 1973; Maguire 1988; Podolny and Baron 1997; Fernandez et al. 2000; Castilla 2005). With the exception of the specialised technical support company Datatech, all human resources managers used their own employees as their main source for recruitment. As a result of this practice, social bonds among workers seem to be reinforced and used as a control and discipline mechanism.

In this respect, it was interesting to examine the extent to which call centre managers are truly conscious about the implications of using informal means of recruitment such as social networks. The results derived from the interviews of this research indicate that managers are rarely conscious of the implications of these decisions; they seem to assume that these social divisions are natural in the workplace rather than socially constructed. Nonetheless, many of the activities developed by human resources managers in these organisations, such as sport competitions, are undertaken to reinforce the rivalry among employees from different sections in the organisation.

Despite all the means of controlling workers in service-oriented organisations such as call centres, employees tend to have and exploit considerable levels of autonomy and discretion at work. Cases where employees devoted extra time and effort in dealing with their customers, and experience many of the pressures of front-line service work were presented. However, recent literature has shown that the benefits of using social networks for recruitment and selection are not as great as expected and this sort of recruitment has limited effects on productivity levels (Fernandez et al. 2000; Castilla 2005). Thus it seems that social networks reduce the transaction costs associated with recruitment and selection (especially in customer services and sales) but productivity levels only improve during the first months at work; afterwards there is the same level of productivity from employees who were recruited through social networks ('referred workers') as from those recruited through merit (Fernandez et al. 2000; Castilla 2005). This might happen because referred workers know more about the work than non-referred workers when they start, and the former might enjoy some extra support and information from the people they know inside the workplace so they learn more quickly (Podolny and Baron 1997; Fernandez et al. 2000; Castilla 2005).

However, this part of the research was unfortunately also the most confusing. The amount of information was massive, and pointed in many different directions. The social connections of workers suggest that employees can respond differently to the same type of stimuli. During my period of observation, workers displayed commitment and loyalty to different actors: subcontractors, client firms, customers and other workers. I had expected gender and skin colour to influence social divisions, and yet it was difficult to evaluate their real influence in workers' experiences and employment conditions. As mentioned in chapter five, the aim of organisations to reproduce a credible service interaction based on Mexican cultural stereotypes suggested to me that I should expect female and dark skin colour workers to be overrepresented at the low end of the job categories in call centres (sales and customer services). However, I did not find any strong evidence for this. I argue that there are, at least, three possible reasons for this. First, that I did not have access to detailed information about the recruitment process so did not know the proportion of female applicants compared with the number finally hired. Second, I did not have detailed information about the trajectories of female workers inside these workplaces. In any event, how could one analyse gender discrimination in career opportunities if there is no job ladder? Third, I was expecting that light skin colour workers would be more likely than dark skin colour workers to occupy better jobs (with good employment conditions), but did not find any strong evidence for this in my observations. As Bank Muñoz has demonstrated in the manufacturing context (2008), in Mexican culture individuals tend to associate better positions with light skin colour regardless of the actual colour of the person in question. In summary, even though most of the Mexican social stereotypes were present in the minds and conversations of managers and workers in the call centre industry, their real effect on workers' experiences and employment relationships has to be considered in combination with job designs, customer segmentation and supervision approach. Therefore, this area needs further research.

In any event, the research showed that employees who perform front-line activities in workplaces with multiple employers have a weak sense of identity as do not feel that they belong to any particular group.

## The use of contracts for services

The use of contracts for services has been left as the last subject in this concluding section because of its controversial profile. With the exception of technical workers in the company Datatech, all the workers interviewed in this research held a contract for services, which is not a standard labour contract but a commercial arrangement. In practice, this type of contract allows subcontractors and client firms to terminate their relationship with employees if the contract between organisations expires. There are no legal obligations at all for any of the employers after this. Because this is a commercial contract between employers and employees, both parties are seen as equal, and workers do not deserve any special attention.

In Mexico, the current labour law (created in 1971) was conceived on the assumption that workers are the weakest participant in the employment relationship, so this relationship must be balanced with the participation of the state in the form of a 'paternalistic' law in 'favour' of workers. In practice, it seems that this type of labour regulation has been used by corrupt unions to tolerate precarious working conditions in exchange for special arrangements with companies and the government. However, non-standard forms of employment have emerged unofficially as it is the case of the contract for services.

From a legal point of view, one of the most important advantages of outsourcing, at least in the Mexican case, is that this type of arrangement excuses client firms of any legal responsibility to workers employed by subcontracted organisations. Subcontractors in turn use the commercial profile of these contracts for services in order to avoid any labour protection regulation. Nonetheless, there is an important debate among Mexican lawyers. Some lawyers argue that the subordination of workers to the orders of subcontractors and client firms is undisputable evidence of an employment relation that must be regulated by the labour law, even if there is no contract at all. In this respect, contracts for services should be considered illegal according to the Mexican Constitution because any labour activity paid by a salary has to be regulated by the labour law, but not by the commercial law. Other lawyers argue that the interpretation of the law is not the most important issue (if the contract for services is appropriate, fair or even illegal). For this group of lawyers the main problem is the lack of enforceability of the law in Mexico. In Mexico, the lack of a strong institutional context for workers and companies leads to unions and workers to be in the most vulnerable position. Very importantly, most of the managers, academics, consultants and unions officials interviewed agreed that employing workers with this type of contract gives labour-intensive industries in Mexico a big competitive and comparative advantage.

## Final thoughts

As mentioned, it would be misleading to argue that the practices analysed in this research (job designs, customer segmentation, supervision approach, union avoidance, internal labour markets for managers, social divisions and contracts for services) are undertaken or designed by subcontractors only as a reaction or response to their problems of negotiation and coordination with client firms. All these practices have additional benefits or were in place before the widespread use of outsourcing and the emergence of the call centre industry. However, they all stand out when looking at the challenges of trust, cooperation and negotiation between the organisations involved in the outsourcing of front-line service work and shape the experience of employees in one way or another.

What are the main lessons and contributions derived from this book? Perhaps, the most relevant finding is that even in the new economy, where IT systems are designed to monitor and coordinate work closely, where employment relations seem to be fragmented and split among different employers, the social profile of work is still an important determinant of workers' experiences and employment conditions. Work in post-industrial societies seems to continue to be strongly embedded in the social dimension of these interactions, as showed by the personal experiences of workers, supervisors and managers analysed in this book. It does not matter that client firms are not legally responsible for subcontracted workers or that subcontractors use commercial contracts with workers: the complex nature of work and the particularities of front-line service work have 'forced' organisations to develop employment relations *de facto* with workers under outsourcing arrangements.

In this respect, if the experience of work is shaped by a complex combination of individual and contextual circumstances then it might be almost impossible to make any prediction about workers' experiences at all. However, the findings of this research confirm that workers in customer segments of higher value are more likely to have better employment conditions. Also, the level of intervention from client firms seems to increase with higher levels of revenue reported by particular accounts. Subcontractors and client firms seem to set the rules and agreements (formally and informally) for managing the subcontracted workforce, and these rules and agreements seem to depend on economic incentives. Therefore, it seems that a transaction cost approach is useful to predict the involvement of client firms and subcontractors in the administration of the workforce but would be insufficient to explain workers' reactions to the intervention of multiple employers.

Therefore, the intervention of multiple employers is also shaped by the institutional context where this process takes place, the type of worker hired, the supervision approach and social bonds among workers. In summary, this is a two-way process and we can see important and unexpected evidence that reinforces the relevance of the social dimension. For example, findings of this research suggest that workers in higher customer segments and enjoying more autonomy and discretion at work are not necessarily more satisfied with their jobs, so individual and social expectations seem to be important in shaping workers experiences as well.

Finally, what I found most attractive of this research is that it confirms that the relationship between organisational change and employment relations and work is a fruitful and relevant terrain for future research; more investigation in this field will allow a better understanding not just of the dynamics of the labour process in contemporary societies but also of the connections between different organisations, forms of work and industries.

# BIBLIOGRAPHY

Alcalde Justiniani, A. 2005. "Limitaciones jurídicas en la protección de los trabajadores", in *Relaciones triangulares de trabajo subcontratación y/o tercerización ¿fin de la estabilidad laboral?* edited by M. López Martínez, 55-60. México: Fundación Friedrich Ebert.

Álvarez-Galván, J.L. and C. Tilly. 2006. "Trabajo marginal: trabajadores en el comercio y los servicios en México", in *La Situación del Trabajo en México 2005*, edited by E. De la Garza Toledo and C. Salas Páez, 355-373. México: Plaza y Valdés.

Álvarez-Galván, J.L. and C. Tilly. 2006. "Participación extranjera en el autoservicio mexicano: el efecto Wal-Mart." *Comercio Exterior* **56**-11: 945-958.

Álvarez-Galván, J.-L. 2008. "Desarrollo paralelo en México y en el Reino Unido: algunos datos de una relación de 80 años de comunicación telefónica." *Contact Forum* **12**-24: 30-31.

—. 2010. *Liberalisation and Retail: The Effects of Foreign Capital on Mexican Retail*. Germany: LAP Lambert Academic Publishing.

—. 2011. "Trabajo y empleo en la nueva economía: el caso de los centros de atención telefónica de la Ciudad de México", *Comercio Exterior* **61**-3: 945-958.

Aspe, P. 1993. *El camino mexicano de la transformación económica*. México: Fondo de Cultura Económica.

Atkinson, J. 1984. "Manpower Strategies for Flexible Organisations." *Personnel Management* **16**-8: 28-31.

Baldry, C., P. Bain, P. Taylor, J, Hyman, D. Scholarios, A. Marks, A. Watson, K. Gilbert, G. Gall and D. Bunzel. 2007. *The Meaning of Work in the New Economy*. Basingstoke: Palgrave Macmillan.

Bank Muñoz, C. 2008. *Transnational Tortillas: Race, Gender, and Shop-floor Politics in Mexico and the United States*. Ithaca: ILR Press.

Barajas Montes de Oca, S. 1995. *Conceptos básicos del derecho del trabajo*. México: Fondo de Cultura Económica.

Barley, S. R. and G. Kunda. 2004. *Gurus, Hired Guns, and Warm Bodies: Itinerant Experts in a Knowledge Economy*. Princeton: Princeton University Press.

Baron, J. N. and D. M. Kreps. 1999. *Strategic Human Resources: Frameworks for General Managers*. New York: John Wiley.

Batt, R. 2000. "Strategic Segmentation in Front-line Services: Matching Customers, Employees and Human Resource Systems." *International Journal of Human Resource Management* **11**-3: 540.

Batt, R., V. Doellgast and K. Hyunji. 2004. *U.S. Call Centre Industry Report 2004: National Benchmarking Report Strategy, HR Practices & Performance.* Ithaca: Cornell University, School of Industrial and Labor Relations, Centre for Advanced Human Resource Studies: 50.

Batt, R., V. Doellgast, and K. Hyunji. 2006. "Service Management and Employment Systems in US and Indian Call Centres", in *Brookings Trade Forum 2005: Offshoring White-collar work -The Issues and Implications,* edited by S. Collins and L. Brainard. Washington D.C.: The Brookings Institution.

Batt, R., D. Holman and U. Holtgrewe. 2007. *The Global Call Centre Report: International Perspectives on Management and Employment.* Ithaca: ILR Press.

Batt, R. and L. Moynihan. 2002. "The Viability of Alternative Call Centre Production Models." *Human Resource Management Journal* **12**-4: 14-34.

BBC 2009. Profile: Carlos Slim. London, British Broadcast Corporation. **2009**.

Bell, D. 1973. "The Coming of Post-Industrial Society." In *Social Stratification: Class, Race, and Gender in Sociological Perspective* edited by D. Grusky, 750-775. Boulder: Westview Press.

Belt, V. 2002. "A Female Ghetto? Women's Careers in Call Centres." *Human Resource Management Journal* **12**-4: 51-66.

Bensusán, G. and T. Rendón (Eds.). 2000. *Trabajo y trabajadores en el México contemporáneo.* Mexico: Porrúa.

Bolton, S. and C. Boyd. 2003. "Trolley Dolly or Skilled Emotion Manager? Moving on from Hochschild's Managed Heart." *Work, Employment and Society* **17**-2: 289-308.

Bouzas, J. A. 2005. "Globalización y subcontratación", in *Relaciones triangulares de trabajo subcontratación y/o tercerización ¿fin de la estabilidad laboral?* Edited by M. López Martínez, 61-64. México: Fundación Friedrich Ebert.

Braverman, H. 1974. *Labor and Monopoly Capital: The Degradation of Work in the Twentieth Century.* New York: Monthly Review Press.

Bridges, W. 1995. *Jobshift: How to Prosper in a Workplace without Jobs.* London: Nicholas Brealey.

Brown, R.K. 1988 "The Employment Relationship in Sociological Theory", in D. Gallie ed. *Employment in Britain,* Oxford: Blackwell.

Browning, H. C. and J. Singelmann. 1978. "The Transformation of the US Labour Force: The Interaction of Industry and Occupation." *Politics and Society* **87**-4: 481-509.

Bryman, A. 2004. *Social Research Methods.* Oxford: Oxford University Press.

Burnett, A. 2009. Mexico in Depth. London, BBC. **2009:** website.

Cappelli, P. 1999. "Careers Jobs are Dead." *California Management Review* **42**-1: 146-167.

—. 2000. "Market-Mediated Employment: The Historical Context", in *The New Relationship: Human Capital in the American Corporation* edited by M. Blair and T. Kochan, 66-101. Washington D.C.: The Brookings Institution Press.

Cappelli, P. and P. Neumark. 2004. "External Churning and Internal Flexibility: Evidence on the Functional Flexibility and Core-Periphery Hypotheses." *Industrial Relations Journal* **43**-1: 148-182.

Castells, M. 1996. *The Rise of the Network Society.* Cambridge, MA: Blackwell Publishers.

Castilla, E. 2005. "Social Networks and Employee Performance in a Call Centre." *American Journal of Sociology* **110**-5: 1243–1283.

Chandler, A. D. 1977. *The Visible Hand: The Managerial Revolution in American Business.* Cambridge, Mass: Belknap Press.

Chávez Becker, C. 2006. *Estudio preliminar sobre la industria del call centre en América Latina.* México: Centro de Solidaridad, AFL-CIO - CWA - UNI - STRM.

Child, J. 2005. *Organisation: Contemporary Principles and Practice.* Oxford: Blackwell Pub.

Coase, R. H. 1937. "The Nature of the Firm." *Economica, New Series* **4**-16: 386-405.

Collin-Jacques, C. and C. Smith. 2005. "Nursing on the Line: Experiences from England and Quebec Canada." *Human Relations* **58**-1: 5-32.

Connell, J. and J. Burgess. 2004. *International Perspectives on Temporary Agency Work.* London: Routledge.

Cowie, J. R. 1999. *Capital Moves: RCA's Seventy-year Quest for Cheap Labour.* Ithaca: Cornell University Press.

Daniels, P. W. 1993. *Service Industries in the World Economy.* Oxford: Blackwell.

Davis, D. E. 1994. *Urban Leviathan: Mexico City in the Twentieth Century.* Philadelphia: Temple University Press.

de Buen Lozano, N. 2005. "Contexto histórico de las relaciones triangulares del trabajo", in *Relaciones triangulares de trabajo subcontratación y/o tercerización ¿fin de la estabilidad laboral?* edited by M. López Martínez, 49-54. México: Fundación Friedrich Ebert.

De la Garza, E. 2005. "Antiguas y nuevas formas de subcontratación." *Relaciones triangulares de trabajo subcontratación y/o tercerización ¿fin de la estabilidad laboral?* Edited by M. López Martínez, 27-40. Mexico: Fundación Friedrich Ebert.

—. 2006. "Los proyectos de reforma laboral de la UNT y del CCE-CT", in *La situación del trabajo en México, 2006,* edited by E. De la Garza Toledo and C. Salas Páez, 497-528. México: Plaza y Valdés.

De la Garza, E. and C. Salas Páez (Eds). 2006. *La situación del trabajo en México, 2006.* México: Plaza y Valdés.

Deery, S., R. Iverson and J. Walsh. 2010. "Coping Strategies in Call Centres: Work Intensity and the Role of Co-workers and Supervisors." *British Journal of Industrial Relations* **48**-1: 181-200.

Deery, S. and N. Kinnie. 2002. "Call Centre and Beyond: A Thematic Evaluation." *Human Resource Management Journal* **12**-4: 3-13.

Deery, S. and N. Kinnie. 2004. *Call Centres and Human Resource Management: A Cross-national Perspective.* New York: Palgrave Macmillan.

DiMaggio, P. 2001. *The Twenty-first-century Firm: Changing Economic Organisation in International Perspective.* Princeton: Princeton University Press.

Doellgast, V. 2007b. "Collective Bargain and High Involvement Management in Comparative Perspective: Evidence from US and German Call Centres." *Revised submission to Industrial Relations.*

—. 2008. "National Industrial Relations and Local Bargaining Power in the US and German Telecommunications Industries." *European Journal of Industrial Relations* **14**-3: 265–287.

Doellgast, V. and I. Greer. 2007. "Vertical Disintegration and the Disorganisation of German Industrial Relations." *British Journal of Industrial Relations* **45**-1: 55-76.

Doeringer, P. B. and M. J. Piore. 1971. *Internal Labour Markets and Manpower Analysis.* N.Y: M.E. Sharpe.

Donnelly, R. 2009. "The Knowledge Economy and the Restructuring of Employment: The Case of Consultants." *Work, Employment and Society* **23**-2: 323-341.

Doogan, K. 2009. *New Capitalism? The Transformation of Work.* Cambridge, Polity.

Dussel Peters, E. 2000. *Polarizing Mexico: The Impact of Liberalization Strategy.* Boulder: L. Rienner Publishers.

—. 2008. "GCCs and Development: A Conceptual and Empirical Review." *Competition and Change* **12-1**: 11-27.

Dussel Peters, E., L. M. Galindo and Eduardo Loria. 2003. *Condiciones y efectos de la inversión extranjera directa y del proceso de integración regional en México durante los noventa. Una perspectiva macro, meso y micro.* México: Facultad de Economía/UNAM-BID/Intal.

Economic Commission for Latin America and the Caribbean (ECLAC). 2007. *Foreign Investment in Latin America and the Caribbean.* Santiago de Chile: United Nations.

Edwards, P. K. and J. Wajcman. 1999. *The Politics of Working Life.* Oxford: Oxford University Press.

Expansión. 2009. *Las 500 Empresas más Importantes de México 1993-2008.* México: Expansión.

Felstead, A. and N. Jewson (Eds.). 1999. *Global Trends in Flexible Labour.* London: Basingstoke Macmillan Business.

Fernandez, R., E. Castilla and P. Moore. 2000. "Social Capital at Work: Networks and Employment at a Phone Centre." *American Journal of Sociology* **10-55**: 1288–1356.

Fernie, S. and D. Metcalf. 1998. "Not hanging on the telephone: payment systems in the new sweatshops." *Centre for Economic Performance, Discussion Paper No. 390:* London: London School of Economics.

Fluss, D. 2005. *The Real-time Contact Centre.* New York: AMACOM Books.

Frenkel, S. 1999. *On the Front Line: Organisation of Work in the Information Economy.* Ithaca: ILR Press.

Frenkel, S., M. Tam, M. Korczynski and K. Shire. 1998. "Beyond Bureaucracy? Work Organisation in Call Centres." *The International Journal of Human Resource Management* **9-6**: 954-979.

Fujii, G. 2006. "México: dinamismo exportador con bajo crecimiento económico" in *La situación del trabajo en México, 2006* edited by E. De la Garza Toledo and C. Salas Páez, 17-38. México: Plaza y Valdés.

Gambetta, D. 1988. *Trust: Making and Breaking Cooperative Relations.* Oxford: Basil Blackwell.

García, B. 2009. "Los mercados de trabajo urbanos de México a principios del siglo XXI." *Revista Mexicana de Sociología* **71-1**: 5-46.

Garson, B. 1988. *The Electronic Sweatshop: How Computers are Transforming the Office of the Future into the Factory of the Past.* New York: Simon & Schuster.

Gartrell, D. 1982. "On the Visibility of Wage References." *Canadian Journal of Sociology* **72**: 117-143.

Garza, G. 2006. *La organización espacial del sector servicios en México.* México: El Colegio de México.

Geary, J. 1992. "Employment Flexibility and Human Resource Management: The Case of Three American Electronics Plants." *Work, Employment and Society* **62**: 251-270.

Gereffi, G. 1999. "International trade and industrial upgrading in the apparel commodity chain." *Journal of International Economics* **48**: 37-70.

Gereffi, G. and M. Korzeniewicz. 1994. *Commodity Chains and Global Capitalism.* Westport: Praeger.

Gershuny, J. I. and I. D. Miles. 1983. *New Service Economy: The Transformation of Employment in Industrial Societies.* London: Frances Pinter.

Giddens, A. and K. Birdsall. 2001. *Sociology.* Cambridge, England: Polity Press.

Glucksmann, M. 2004. "Call configurations: varieties of call centre and divisions of labour." *Work, Employment and Society* **18**-4: 795-811.

—. 2009. "Formations, Connections and Divisions of Labor." *Work, Employment and Society* **43**-5: 878–895.

Goffee, R. and R. Scase. 1992. "Organisational Change and the Corporate Career: The Restructuring of Managers' Job Aspirations." *Human Relations* **45**-4: 363-85.

Granovetter, M. 1973. "The importance of weak ties." *The American Journal of Sociology* **78**-6: 1360-1380.

—. 1992. "Economic Action and Social Structure: The Problem of Embeddedness." In *The Sociology of Economic Life,* edited by M. S. Granovetter and R. Swedberg, vi-xix. Boulder: Westview Press.

—. 1992. "The Sociological and Economic Approaches to Labour Market Analysis: A Social Structural View." In *The Sociology of Economic Life,* edited by M. Granovetter and R. Swedberg, 233-263. Boulder: Westview Press.

—. 2005. "The Impact of Social Structure on Economic Outcomes." *Journal of Economic Perspectives* **19**-1: 33-50.

Granovetter, M. and R. Swedberg. 1992. *The Sociology of Economic Life.* Boulder: Westview Press.

Grint, K. 1998. *The Sociology of Work: An Introduction.* Malden: Polity Press.

—. 2005. *Sociology of Work.* Cambridge: Polity.

Hakim, C. 2000. *Research Design: Successful Designs for Social and Economic Research.* London: Routledge.

Halford, S. and T. Strangleman. 2009. "In Search of the Sociology of Work: Past, Present and Future." *Sociology* **43-5**: 811–828.

Handy, C. 1989. *The Age of Unreason*. London: Business Books.

Hannif, Z. and F. Lamm 2005. "When Non-Standard Work Becomes Precarious." *Management Revue* **16**-3: 324-350.

Harrison, B. 1994. *Lean and Mean: The Changing Landscape of Corporate Power in the Age of Flexibility*. New York: Basic Books.

Harrison, B. and M. Kelley. 1993. "Outsourcing and the search for 'flexibility'." *Work, Employment and Society* **72**: 213-235.

Herzenberg, S., J. Alic and H. Wial. 1998. *New Rules for a New Economy: Employment and Opportunity in Post-industrial America*. Ithaca: ILR Press.

Hochschild, A. 1983. *The Managed Heart: Commercialization of Human Feeling*. Berkeley: University of California Press.

Hochschild, A. and A. Machung. 1990. *Second Shift: Working Parents and the Revolution at Home*. London: Piatkus.

Hodgson, G. 1998. *Economics and Utopia: Why the Learning Economy is not the End of History*. New York: Routledge.

Holmes, J. 1986. "The Organisation and Locational Structure of Production Subcontracting." In *Production, Work, Territory: The Geographical Anatomy of Industrial Capitalism*, edited by A. J. Scott and M. Storper. Boston, 254-269. London, Allen & Unwin.

Houlihan, M. 2002. "Tensions and Variations in Call Centre Management Strategies." *Human Resource Management Journal* **12**-4: 67-85.

Hyman, R. 1987. "Strategy or Structure? Capital, Labour and Control", *Work, Employment and Society*, **1**, 1: 25-55.

ILO. 2007. *Global Employment Trends Brief*. Geneva: International Labor Organisation.

IMT. 2006. Dinámico desarrollo de la industria de Call Centres Outsourcing en México. *Contact Forum* **11**.

—. 2007. "La industria del call centre hoy." In *11o. Congreso Internacional IP & Contact Forum*. México: IMT.

INEGI. 2005. *Conteo de Población y Vivienda. México, Instituto Nacional de Estadística, Geografía e Informática*. México: INEGI.

—. 2007. *Encuesta Nacional de Ocupación y Empleo, Instituto Nacional de Estadística, Geografía e Informática*. México: INEGI.

Jacoby, S. 1999. "Are Career Jobs Headed for Extinction?" *California Management Review* **42**-1: 123-145.

Jenkins, R. 1988. "Discrimination and Equal Opportunity in Employment: Ethnicity and 'Race' in the United Kingdom." In *Employment in Britain*, edited by D. Gallie, 310-343. Oxford: Basil Blackwell.

Kalleberg, A. 2001. "Organizing Flexibility: The Flexible Firm in a New Century." *British Journal of Industrial Relations* **39**-4: 479-504.

Kay, J. 1995. *Foundations of Corporate Success: How Business Strategies add Value.* Oxford: Oxford University Press.

King, G., R. Keohane and S. Verba. 1994. *Designing Social Inquiry: Scientific Inference in Qualitative Research.* Princeton: Princeton University Press.

Kinnie, N., S. Hutchinson and J. Purcell 2000. "'Fun and Surveillance': The Paradox of High Commitment Management in Call Centres." *International Journal of Human Resource Management* **11**-5: 967-985.

Kinnie, N., J. Purcell and M. Adams 2008. "Explaining Employees' Experience of Work in Outsourced Call Centres: The Influence of Clients, Owners and Temporary Work Agencies." *Journal of Industrial Relations* **50**-2: 209-227.

Korczynski, M. 2002. *Human Resource Management in Service Work.* Basingstoke: Palgrave.

—. 2007. "Service Work, Social Theory, and Collectivism: A Reply to Brook." *Work, Employment and Society* **21**-3: 577-588.

—. 2009. "The Mystery Customer: Continuing Absences in the Sociology of Service Work." *Sociology* **43**-5: 952–967.

Krugman, P. and M. Obstfeld. 1997. *International Economics: Theory and Policy.* Reading, Mass: Addison-Wesley.

Lacity, M. and R. Hirschheim. 1993. *Information Systems Outsourcing: Myths, Metaphors, and Realities.* Chichester: J. Wiley.

Lazonick, W. 1991. *Business Organisation and the Myth of the Market Economy.* Cambridge: Cambridge University Press.

—. 2002. *American Corporate Economy: Critical Perspectives on Business and Management.* London: Routledge.

Leidner, R. 1993. *Fast Food, Fast Talk: Service Work and the Routinisation of Everyday Life.* Berkeley: University of California Press.

Levitt, T. 1972. "Production-line Approach to Service." *Harvard Business Review* September-October: 41-52.

Lichtenstein, N. 2006. "A Template for Twenty-first Century Capitalism." In *Wal-Mart: The Face of Twenty-first Century Capitalism*, edited by N. Lichtenstein, 3-30. New York: The New Press.

—. (Ed.). 2006. *Wal-Mart: The Face of Twenty-First-Century Capitalism.* New York: The New Press.

López, J. 1998. *La macroeconomía de México: el pasado reciente y el futuro posible.* México: UACPYP-Porrúa.

Lorenz, E. 1988. "Neither Friends nor Strangers: Informal Networks of Subcontracting in French Industry." In *Trust: making and breaking cooperative relations,* edited by D. Gambetta. 123-145. Oxford: Basil Blackwell.

—. 1992. "Trust, Community, and Cooperation: Toward a Theory of Industrial Districts." In *Pathways to Industrialization and Regional Development,* edited by M. Storper and A. J. Scott, 185-201. New York: Routledge.

—. 1999. "Trust, Contract and Economic Cooperation." *Cambridge Journal of Economics* **23**-3: 301-315.

Maguire, M. 1986. "Recruitment as a Means of Control." In *The Changing Experience of Employment: Restructuring and Recession,* edited by K. Purcell, S. Wood, A. Waton and S. Allen, 88-112. Basingstoke: Macmillan in association with British Sociological Association.

—. 1988. "Work, Locality and Social Control." *Work, Employment and Society* **21**: 71-87.

Marchington, M., D. Grimshaw, J. Rubery and H. Willmott. 2005. *Fragmenting Work: Blurring Organisational Boundaries and Disordering Hierarchies.* Oxford: Oxford University Press.

Marx, K. and F. Engels. 1948. *Manifesto of the Communist Party.* New York: International Publishers.

Marx, K. and F. Engels. 1978. *Wage Labour and Capital.* Peking: Foreign Languages Press.

McGovern, P. 1998. *HRM, Technical Workers and the Multinational Corporation.* London: Routledge.

McGovern, P., S. Hill, C. Mills and M. White. 2007. *Market, Class, and Employment.* Oxford: Oxford University Press.

McGovern, P., V. Hope-Hailey and P. Stiles. 1998. "The Managerial Career After Downsizing: Case Studies from the 'Leading Edge'." *Work, Employment and Society* **12**-3: 457-477.

McKinsey. 2003. *Retail in Mexico and Brazil.* New York: McKinsey & Company.

McMichael, P. 2004. *Development and Social Change: A Global Perspective.* Pine: Forge Press.

McRae, S. 2003. "Constraints and Choices in Mothers' Employment Careers: A Consideration of Hakim's Preference Theory." *British Journal of Sociology* **54**-3: 317-338.

Merton, R. K. 1959. "Notes on Problem-Finding in Sociology." In *Sociology Today: Problems and Prospects,* edited by Robert K. Merton, 5-15. New York: Basic Books.

Micheli, J. 2002. "Digitofactura: flexibilización, internet y trabajadores del conocimiento." *Comercio Exterior* **52**-4: 522-536.

—. 2005. "Trabajadores de Telemarketing." In *Relaciones triangulares de trabajo subcontratación y/o tercerización ¿fin de la estabilidad laboral?* edited by M. López Martínez, 97-104. México: Fundación Friedrich Ebert.

—. 2007. "Centros de atención telefónica y telemercadeo: paradigma de la economía de masas." *Comercio Exterior* **57**-3: 218-231.

—. 2007. "Los call centres y los nuevos trabajos del siglo XXI." *Confines* **35**: 49-58.

Moss, P., H. Salzman and C. Tilly. 2008. "Under Construction: The Continuing Evolution of Job Structures in Call Centres." *Industrial Relations* **47**-2: 173-208.

Mulholland, K. 2004. "Workplace Resistance in an Irish Call Centre: Slammin', Scammin', Smokin' an' Leavin'." *Work, Employment and Society* **18**-4: 709-724.

Noon, M. and P. Blyton. 2007. *The Realities of Work: Experiencing Work and Employment in Contemporary Society.* New York: Palgrave.

Noyelle, T. 1990. *Skills, Wages, and Productivity in the Service Sector.* Boulder: Westview Press.

O'Connell Davidson, J. 1993. *Privatisation and Employment Relations: The Case of the Water Industry.* New York: Mansell.

Ospina, S. 1996. *Illusions of Opportunity: Employee Expectations and Workplace Inequality.* Ithaca: Cornell University Press.

Osterman, P. (Ed.). 1996. *Broken Ladders: Managerial Careers in the New Economy.* Oxford: Oxford University Press.

Paulet, R. 2009. "The Impact of Place on Call Centres." *Journal of Industrial Relations* **50**-2: 305-318.

Perrow, C. 1986. *Complex Organisations: A Critical Essay.* New York: McGraw-Hill.

Pink, D. 2001. *Free Agent Nation: How America's New Independent Workers are Transforming the Way We Live.* New York: Warner Books.

Piore, M. 1970. "The Dual Labor Market: Theory and Implications." In *The State and the Poor*, edited by S. H. Beer and R. E. Barringer, 210-222. Cambridge, Mass: Winthrop Publishers.

Piore, M. and C. Sabel. 1984. *The Second Industrial Divide: Possibilities for Prosperity.* New York: Basic Books.

Podolny, J. and J. Baron. 1997. "Resources and Relationships: Social Networks and Mobility in the Workplace." *American Sociological Review* **62**-4: 673-693.

Pollert, A. 1988. "Dismantling Flexibility." *Capital and Class* 34: 42-75.

—. 1988. "The 'Flexible Firm': Fixation or Fact?" *Work, Employment and Society* **23**: 281-316.

—. (Ed.). 1991. *Farewell to Flexibility?* Oxford: Basil Blackwell.

Porter, M. 1998. *The Competitive Advantage of Nations.* Basingstoke: Macmillan Business.

Ramírez, Z. 1999. Escenas de un matrimonio: Cifra-Wal-Mart._Expansión. **Ed. 762.**

—. 2002. El vendedor más grande del mundo. *Expansión.* **Ed. 835.**

Reed, M. 2009. "Expert Power and Control in Late Modernity." *Organisations Studies* **17**-4: 573-597.

Reich, R. 1991. *The Work of Nations: Preparing Ourselves for 21st-Century Capitalism.* New York: A.A. Knopf.

Rendón, T. 2003. *La información estadística disponible sobre el empleo y los ingresos derivados del trabajo.* México: Facultad de Economía, UNAM.

Reynoso, C. 2005. "Modalidades triangulares: retos y perspectivas." In *Relaciones triangulares del trabajo subcontratación y/o tercerización ¿fin de la estabilidad laboral?*, edited by M. López Martínez, 15-26. México: Fundación Friedrich Ebert.

Riding, A. 1985. *Distant Neighbors: A Portrait of the Mexicans.* New York: Knopf.

Ritzer, G. 1993. *The McDonaldization of Society: The Changing Character of Contemporary Social Life.* Newbury Park: Pine Forge Press.

—. 1998. *The McDonaldization Thesis: Explorations and Extensions.* London: Sage Publications.

Ruiz Duran, C. 2005a. "El reto del empleo en Mexico." *Comercio Exterior* **55**-1: 6-15.

Ruiz Duran, C. 2005b. *Elementos para reflexionar sobre la reforma laboral en un contexto de debilidad institucional.* México: UNAM.

Russell, B. and M. Thite 2008. "The Next Division of Labour: Work Skills in Australian and Indian Call Centres." *Work, Employment and Society* **22**-4: 615-634.

Sako, M. and S. Helper. 1998. "Determinants of Trust in Supplier Relations: Evidence from the Automotive Industry in Japan and the United States." *Journal of Economic Behavior and Organisation* **34**-3: 387-417.

Samuelson, P. and W. Nordhaus. 2001. *Economics.* Boston: McGraw-Hill.

Secretaría del Trabajo y Previsión Social (STPS). 2010. *Dirección General de Investigación y Estadísticas del Trabajo con información de la Junta Federal de Conciliación y Arbitraje* (www.stps.gob.mx).

Scott, A. and M. Storper. 1986. *Production, Work, Territory: The Geographical Anatomy of Industrial Capitalism.* London: Allen & Unwin.

Sennett, R. 1998. *The Corrosion of Character: The Personal Consequences of Work in the New Capitalism.* New York: W. W. Norton.

—. 2009. *The Craftsman.* London: Penguin.

Silver, B. 2003. *Forces of Labour: Workers' Movements and Globalization since 1870.* Cambridge: Cambridge University Press.

Silverman, D. 2001. *Interpreting Qualitative Data: Methods for Analysing Talk, Text and Interaction.* London: Sage.

—. 2004. *Doing Qualitative Research: A Practical Handbook.* London, Sage.

Simon, H. 1991. "Organisations and Markets." *The Journal of Economic Perspectives* **5**2: 25-44.

Smith, A. 1985. *An Inquiry into the Nature and Causes of the Wealth of Nations.* New York: Random House.

Smith, C., R. Valsecchi, F. Mueller and J. Gabe. 2008. "Knowledge and the Discourse of Labour Process Transformation: Nurses and the Case of the NHS Direct for England." *Work, Employment and Society* **22**-4: 581-599.

Smith, V. 2001. *Crossing the Great Divide: Worker Risk and Opportunity in the New Economy.* Ithaca: ILR Press.

Noyelle. T. 1990. *Skills, Wages, and Productivity in the Service Sector.* Boulder: Westview Press.

Stiglitz, J. 1991. "Symposium on Organisations and Economics." *The Journal of Economic Perspectives* **5**2: 15-24.

—. 2003. *Globalization and its Discontents.* New York: W.W. Norton.

Stinchcombe, A. 1990. *Information and Organisations.* Berkeley: California University Press.

Storper, M. and A. Scott. 1992. *Pathways to Industrialization and Regional Development.* New York: Routledge.

Strangleman, T. 2006. "Book Review: Dignity, Respect and the Cultures of Work." *Work, employment and society* **20**-1: 181-188.

—. 2007. "The Nostalgia for Permanence at Work? The End of Work and its Commentators." *The Sociological Review* **55**-1: 81-103.

STRM, 2000. *Sección 159 Tecmarketing.* México: Sindicato de telefonistas de la República Mexicana.

Taylor, P. and P. Bain. 1999. "An 'Assembly Line in the Head': The Call Centre Labour Process'." *Industrial Relations Journal* **30**-2: 101-117.

Taylor, P. and P. Bain. 2005. "India Calling to the Far Away Towns: The Call Centre Labour Process and Globalization." *Work, Employment and Society* **19**-2: 261-282.

Taylor, P. and P. Bain. 2007. "Reflections on the Call Centre - A Reply to Glucksmann." *Work, Employment and Society* **21**-2: 349-362.

Taylor, P., J. Hyman, G. Mulvey and P. Bain. 2002. "Work Organisation, Control and the Experience of Work in Call Centres." *Work, Employment and Society* **16**-1: 133-150.

Thelen, K. and P. Hall. 2009. "Institutional Change in Varieties of Capitalism." *Socio-Economic Review* **71**: 7-34.

Tilly, C. 1996. *Half a Job: Bad and Good Part-time Jobs in a Changing Labour Market.* Philadelphia: Temple University Press.

Tilly, C. and C. Tilly. 1994. "Capitalist Work and Labour Markets." In *The Handbook of Economic Sociology*, edited by N. Smelser and R. Swedberg, 283-312. New York: Russell Sage Foundation.

Tilly, C. and C. Tilly. 1997. *Work Under Capitalism.* Boulder: Westview Press.

Tonkiss, F. 2006. *Contemporary Economic Sociology: Globalisation, Production, Inequality.* London: Routledge.

van den Broek, D. 2008. "Doing Things Right, or Doing the Right Things? Call Centre Migrations and Dimensions of Knowledge." *Work, Employment and Society* **22**-4: 601-613.

Villarreal, R. 1997. *Industrialización, deuda y desequilibrio externo en México: un enfoque neo estructuralista 1929-1997.* México: Fondo de Cultura Económica.

Wajcman, J. 2004. *TechnoFeminism.* Cambridge: Polity Press.

Walby, S. 1990. *Theorizing Patriarchy.* Oxford: Blackwell.

—. 2007. *Gendering the Knowledge Economy: Comparative Perspectives.* Basingstoke: Palgrave Macmillan.

Wallace, J. and M. O'Sullivan 2006. "Contemporary Strike Trends Since 1980: Peering Through the Wrong End of a Telescope." In *Global Industrial Relations,* edited by M. Morley, P. Gunnigle, and D.G. Collings. London: Routledge.

Walsh, J. and S. Deery. 2006. "Refashioning Organisational Boundaries: Outsourcing Customer Service Work." *Journal of Management Studies* **43**-3: 557-582.

Watanabe, S. 1971. "Subcontracting, Industrialisation and Employment Creation." *International Labour Review* **104**-1/2: 51-76.

Whyte, W. 1956. *The Organisation Man.* Harmondsworth: Penguin.

Williamson, O. 1979. "Transaction Costs Economics: The Governance of
    Contractual Relations." *Journal of Law and Economics* **22**-2: 233-261.
—. 1981. "The Economics of Organisation: The Transaction Cost
    Approach." *The American Journal of Sociology* **87**-3: 548-577.
Yin, R. 1994. *Case Study Research: Design and Methods*. Thousand Oaks:
    Sage Publications.
Zepeda Patterson, E. 2007. *Los amos de México*. México: Planeta.

# DATE DUE

BRODART, CO.

Cat. No. 23-221